MW00749240

THE CHOICE

A Daily Devotional

Written by
Fountainview Academy Students

Fountainview Academy
Box 500, Lillooet, BC, V0K-1V0
Canada

Fountainview Academy
P.O. Box 500
Lillooet, British Columbia V0K-1V0
CANADA

Web Address: www.fountainview.ca
Email: info@fountainviewacademy.ca
Copyright © 2012 by
Fountainview Academy
All rights reserved

Scripture quotations marked KJV are from the King James Version
Scripture quotations marked (NLT) are taken from the Holy Bible, New Living Translation, copyright © 1996, 2004, 2007 by Tyndale House Foundation. Used by permission of Tyndale House Publishers, Inc., Carol Stream, Illinois 60188. All rights reserved.
Scripture quotations marked ASV are taken from the American Standard Version
Scripture quotations marked RV are taken from the English Revised Version
Scripture quotations marked HCSB are taken from the Holman Christian Standard Bible ® Copyright © 2003, 2002, 2000, 1999 by Holman Bible Publishers. All rights reserved.
Scripture quotations marked (ESV) are from The Holy Bible, English Standard Version® (ESV®), copyright © 2001 by Crossway, a publishing ministry of Good News Publishers. Used by permission. All rights reserved.
Scripture quotations marked (NASB) are taken from the NEW AMERICAN STANDARD BIBLE®, Copyright © 1960,1 962,1963,1968,1971,1972,1973, 1975,1977,1995 by The Lockman Foundation. Used by permission.
Scripture quotations marked (NIV) are taken from THE HOLY BIBLE, NEW INTERNATIONAL VERSION®, NIV® Copyright © 1973, 1978, 1984, 2011 by Biblica, Inc.™ Used by permission. All rights reserved worldwide.
Scripture quotations marked (NKJV) are taken from the New King James Version. Copyright © 1982 by Thomas Nelson, Inc. Used by permission. All rights reserved.
Scripture quotations marked (MSG or Message) are taken from The Message. Copyright © 1993, 1994, 1995, 1996, 2000, 2001, 2002. Used by permission of NavPress Publishing Group.
Scripture quotations marked "NCV™" are taken from the New Century Version®. Copyright © 2005 by Thomas Nelson, Inc. Used by permission. All rights reserved.

This book was
Edited by Mike Lemon, Matthew West, Morgan Barrow, Michael Jensen, Saraiah Turnbull, and Mason Neil
Dedication written by Michael Jensen and Morgan Barrow
Cover Design by Jerick Arceo
Cover Photo by Jerick Arceo
Authors' Pages by WayAnne Watson
Electronic Layout by WayAnne Watson
Typeset: 7/9/10/12/32 Liberation Sans, 11 Liberation Serif

PRINTED IN U.S.A.

ISBN 10: 0985658908
ISBN 13: 978-0-9856589-0-8

THE CHOICE

A Daily Devotional

Written by
Fountainview Academy Students

Fountainview Academy
Box 500, Lillooet, BC, V0K-1V0
Canada

Fountainview Academy
P.O. Box 500
Lillooet, British Columbia V0K-1V0
CANADA

Web Address: www.fountainview.ca
Email: info@fountainviewacademy.ca
Copyright © 2012 by
Fountainview Academy
All rights reserved

Scripture quotations marked KJV are from the King James Version
Scripture quotations marked (NLT) are taken from the Holy Bible, New Living Translation, copyright © 1996, 2004, 2007 by Tyndale House Foundation. Used by permission of Tyndale House Publishers, Inc., Carol Stream, Illinois 60188. All rights reserved.
Scripture quotations marked ASV are taken from the American Standard Version
Scripture quotations marked RV are taken from the English Revised Version
Scripture quotations marked HCSB are taken from the Holman Christian Standard Bible ® Copyright © 2003, 2002, 2000, 1999 by Holman Bible Publishers. All rights reserved.
Scripture quotations marked (ESV) are from The Holy Bible, English Standard Version® (ESV®), copyright © 2001 by Crossway, a publishing ministry of Good News Publishers. Used by permission. All rights reserved.
Scripture quotations marked (NASB) are taken from the NEW AMERICAN STANDARD BIBLE®, Copyright © 1960,1 962,1963,1968,1971,1972,1973, 1975,1977,1995 by The Lockman Foundation. Used by permission.
Scripture quotations marked (NIV) are taken from THE HOLY BIBLE, NEW INTERNATIONAL VERSION®, NIV® Copyright © 1973, 1978, 1984, 2011 by Biblica, Inc.™ Used by permission. All rights reserved worldwide.
Scripture quotations marked (NKJV) are taken from the New King James Version. Copyright © 1982 by Thomas Nelson, Inc. Used by permission. All rights reserved.
Scripture quotations marked (MSG or Message) are taken from The Message. Copyright © 1993, 1994, 1995, 1996, 2000, 2001, 2002. Used by permission of NavPress Publishing Group.
Scripture quotations marked "NCV™" are taken from the New Century Version®. Copyright © 2005 by Thomas Nelson, Inc. Used by permission. All rights reserved.

This book was
Edited by Mike Lemon, Matthew West, Morgan Barrow, Michael Jensen, Saraiah Turnbull, and Mason Neil
Dedication written by Michael Jensen and Morgan Barrow
Cover Design by Jerick Arceo
Cover Photo by Jerick Arceo
Authors' Pages by WayAnne Watson
Electronic Layout by WayAnne Watson
Typeset: 7/9/10/12/32 Liberation Sans, 11 Liberation Serif

PRINTED IN U.S.A.

ISBN 10: 0985658908
ISBN 13: 978-0-9856589-0-8

Introduction

The choice: should I get out of bed or should I sleep in for a few more minutes; should I wear the red top or the black one; should I call or send an email? It is often bewildering to think about how many choices we are confronted with daily. From what to say to what to eat; from who to hang out with to who to marry; from how to spend money to how to make it—many desire the best option, but far too frequently wind up experiencing emptiness and endless misery. This is because behind every choice we make stands the ultimate choice. "God sets before man life and death. He can have his choice. Many desire life, but still continue to walk in the broad road" (*Story of Redemption*, pg. 391). From the genesis of humankind, everything hinged on the freedom and the power embraced in a choice.

Although He knows the inherent risk, why does God gives us such a dangerous power and freedom to exercise? Why does He give us the choice? The answer can be found in who God is: "God is love" (1 John 4:8). "The law of love being the foundation of the government of God, the happiness of all intelligent beings depends upon their perfect accord with its great principles of righteousness. God desires from all His creatures the service of love—service that springs from an appreciation of His character. He takes no pleasure in a forced obedience; and to all He grants freedom of will, that they may render Him voluntary service" (*Patriarchs and Prophets*, pg. 34).

Consequently, His love for you has moved God to place good and evil before you; you have to decide between these two options, because your eternal destiny depends upon THE CHOICE you make.

THE CHOICE is a collection of inspirational thoughts and experiences written by Fountainview Academy's Grade 11 English class (Graduating Class of 2013). Their assignment was to study selected chapters from the writings of Ellen White and the Bible, and then to write nineteen devotional readings each, using verses from the Bible. After marking and editing their work, I had the assistance of six students: Matthew West, Morgan Barrow, Saraiah Turnbull, Mason Neil, Michael Jensen, and WayAnne Watson. They helped format the book; organize the order of the devotional readings; do the electronic layout; and make corrections to the book prior to publication. It is our hope that, as you read daily from these pages, you will more fully value THE CHOICE our Savior extends to you.

Mike Lemon
English Teacher
Fountainview Academy
British Columbia, CANADA

As a class, we dedicate The Choice to a man whose life personifies the message of this book—a man whose every action is defined by his unwavering commitment to serve the Lord. Even in the face of an illness that threatened not only his spirits but his very existence, his faith in God remained steadfast, his witness unquenched.

To this selfless example of resolute determination, tireless service, and silent inspiration, we devote this book in the hope that every reader will be drawn to make the same resolution—to choose, every moment of every day, Who to serve.

Thank you, Markku Toijanen, for living a life that clearly demonstrates Who you chose to serve.

Night Sky

*For now we see through a glass, darkly; but then face to face: now I
know in part; but then shall I know even as also I am known.*
- 1 Corinthians 13:12 KJV

A canopy of dense darkness stretched over my head, filling the
void between the mountaintops surrounding me. This covering was
perforated by hundreds of little specks: some stars, others planets,
and still others pieces of the Milky Way galaxy. It was an impressive
sight even to my naked eyes. But with the aid of a telescope, I was
able to see so much more. Jupiter suddenly had moons! What
appeared to be a bare patch of sky was now studded with numerous
dots that had been invisible just seconds before. Through the lens of
the telescope, a whole new universe came into view.

As humans, we often find it difficult to trust someone, because
we think that we know. We know where to get food, we know how to
build houses, we know how to drive cars, and we know that $E=mc^2$.
Consequently, we think that we know how to run our lives. But each
and every one of us has lived with only a dim perception of reality:
our naked eyes see the bare patch of sky. Just as a quick glimpse
through the lens of a telescope reveals that there are thousands of
moons, galaxies, and nebulae that we never saw before, to God,
whose voice created the universe, even our clearest vision is fogged.
As 1 Corinthians 13:12 says, "… we see through a glass, darkly; but
then face to face: now I know in part, but then shall I know even as
also I am known" (KJV). We view life through a dim mirror, perceiving
a distorted picture. So why are we so willing to trust ourselves? Why
not trust God, the creator of the universe; the one who designed us
so we could build houses, drive cars, and buy food? The one who
engineered physics so that E does equal mc^2. Putting it simply, would
you rather drive an obstacle course with a blind person at the wheel,
or with the courses's engineer? The choice is yours.

~ Michael Jensen

Are You a Backpacker?

… Whoever wants to be my disciple must deny themselves and take up their cross daily and follow me. - Luke 9:23 NIV

As we rounded another bend, my dad and I came face to face with more hikers coming down the trail toward us, and a couple minutes later we passed two elderly couples stopping to look at the bright red, yellow, and orange leaves in the valley below. When we turned off onto a side trail, we met fewer hikers; and the hikers we did see were a different kind. Earlier, most of the hikers had been dressed casually, perhaps carrying a water bottle or a small day-pack. They looked as if they were just on a short hike to say that they had hiked part of the Appalachian Trail. Now, the hikers were dressed in synthetic clothing and carried big backpacks adorned with sleeping mats and cooking pots. These weren't just hikers, they were backpackers.

Unfortunately, my dad and I had to turn around and head back to the main trail before we reached our goal. We were just day-hikers, and, unlike the backpackers, we didn't reach anywhere in particular.

Way too often I'm just a day-hiker in my Christian walk. I don't really commit myself, and when things get difficult, I drag my feet and wonder whether it is worth it, whether I should keep going. The backpackers were the ones actually reaching their goal, and similarly, it's when I really surrender to God and ask Him for help to be fully committed, that I actually reach my goal of being Christ-like. Those who are Christians only when it's easy, won't make it to Heaven; but those who are committed to Christ, who follow Him up the rough trail no matter what; they are the ones who will end up in Heaven. I want to be committed—I want to be a backpacker for Christ.

~ Katie Sloop

Safe in His Searching Eyes

Thou knowest my downsitting and mine uprising, thou understandest my thought afar off. - Psalms 139:2 KJV

One morning, my family noticed a young bear sitting by our compost pile munching on some scraps he had found. When we went out to get a closer look, he didn't want to leave because he was enjoying himself so much. Instead, he decided to hide. It was hilarious to see him stand behind the tree he chose, because even though he was a small bear, he stuck out on both sides. The only thing we couldn't see were his eyes. I suppose he thought we couldn't see him because he couldn't see us. He kept peeking out to see if we were still there, and when we didn't leave, he finally gave up and ran over the bank.

Over and over, I have seen children do the same thing. When they are afraid of someone or something, they just cover their eyes and the scary things "disappear." Their reasoning is this: *if I can't see them, they can't see me*. This makes for a very convenient game of hide-n-seek.

Adults play the same game. Our reasoning is this: *if I deny that there is a God, then I can live my life like I want to*. If I don't think about God, He won't know what I am doing, and then I won't have to be afraid of the judgement. The truth is, God can see us wherever we are, and there is nothing we can do to hide ourselves or our thoughts from Him.

Are you running away from God because you are afraid to be in His presence? Instead of hiding from Him, why not go to Him; tell Him now that you are afraid because you don't feel good enough; and ask Him to take away your sins and make you clean. Then rest in His arms and trust Him to make you ready to meet His searching eyes in the end.

~ Bethany Corrigan

Puppy Love

… He would gather together in one the children of God who were scattered abroad. - John 11:52 NKJV

When I was a small child, my Dad loved raising and training dogs. We'd had Aspen, our golden retriever, since she was eight weeks old. Because Dad bought Aspen to train her as a Search and Rescue dog, he had her "fixed" so she couldn't have puppies. Aspen, however, really wanted to be a mom.

One day, I noticed that my stuffed animals were disappearing. One by one, they vanished. I asked my siblings about them, but each denied even seeing my missing toys. One day, as Mom was cleaning out a storage closet, she found Aspen curled up in the dark depths, with all my stuffed animals safely tucked in around her. I wanted my toys back, so we took them away from her and cleaned off all the slobber. In a couple of days, however, they were all gone again and this time under the bed, with—of course—Aspen. Several times, we went through the process of taking back my stuffed animals and hiding them, but Aspen would search until she found them all again and brought them back to her "nest." If she couldn't find my stuffed animals, she would substitute our kittens. We'd find Aspen with the kittens cuddled up around her, just as if they were her puppies. She wanted to be a mother so badly that she nurtured whatever toy or animal she could find, even though they were not anything close to puppies.

Just as a mother loves to embrace her children, our Father longs to gather us close to Him, and take us to live with Him forever. Satan tries to separate us from God by pointing out that our sins are so deep it looks as if we aren't actually children of our Saviour. But Jesus will never give up searching for us until He finds us and brings us home.

~ Sarah Wahlman

Let it Snow!

Come now, and let us reason together, saith the Lord: though your sins be as scarlet, they shall be as white as snow; though they be red like crimson, they shall be as wool. - Isaiah 1:18 KJV

As I look out my window on a cold, winter morning, I am greeted with a world that has been transformed with a heavy blanket of pure, white snow. The once bare trees are now laden with small, white mounds, and the black, broken surfaces of the marred fields have been smoothed over with thick icing. This snow covers everything: the hay-filled barns, the sleeping houses, and even the empty roads. Everything is peaceful and silent.

When I see freshly fallen snow, I am always amazed at how it conceals all the unsightly blemishes of the scarred earth and makes everything look brand new. This covering reminds me of Christ's righteousness. In the same way that the snow covers and transforms everything to make it new, Christ's righteousness completely covers and washes away my sinful stains of selfishness. Sometimes I wonder if my sin is too big to cover; but, just like the snow conceals even the jagged mountain tops, Christ's righteousness covers even the dirtiest, most obvious evidences of my sin.

Do you want to be forgiven? Do you feel like your sins are too big, too dirty, too habitual, or too deep for Christ to cover up? They aren't. Jesus promises that even if they are blood-red, He is able to cover them with the blood that He shed on Calvary for this very purpose. Jesus wants to cover your sins with His righteousness just as thoroughly as a fresh layer of pure, white snow fully blankets a sleeping world. Won't you ask Him to "snow" on you today?

~ Sarah Miller

To Gain Success

Imprint these words of mine on your hearts and minds...
- Deuteronomy 11:15 HCSB

A long time ago, a young man wanted to find the secret to living successfully. So, he went to the king and begged him to teach him how to be successful. The king took a moment to think before silently handing the young man a full cup of wine. Then the king commanded his soldiers in front of the young man: "While this young man walks around the city, watch over him, and if he spills a single drop of wine, kill him immediately!" The young man was so confused and terrified. He didn't know why the king had ordered such a thing, but to keep his life, he left, carefully carrying the full cup of wine. He walked around the city without spilling a drop. By the time he came back to where the king was waiting, he was soaked with his sweat.

The king started to speak to him, asking, "What have you seen while you were walking around the city?"

"Your majesty, I couldn't see anything."

"Haven't you seen the people in the streets, all the merchants, and didn't you hear the music from the bars?"

Frightened, the young man stuttered, "No, I didn't see or hear anything because I was so focused on the task you gave me."

To his surprise, a smile crept on the king's face. "You have found the secret to being successful! Just as you put your whole heart into not spilling the wine, you must put your whole heart into every aspect of your life. Then you will have strength to overcome trials and avoid all temptations."

Just like the man kept the wine from spilling by focusing on it only, if I keep Jesus as my main focus, I too will gain victories in the challenges that come my way.

~ Hannah Lee

Just a Little Won't Hurt

*For God shall bring every work into judgement, with every secret
thing, whether it is good, or whether it be evil.*
- Ecclesiastes 12:14 KJV

I was babysitting my brother and nephew; and, if they did their
chores, they could play their PlayStation® afterwards. I was washing
the dishes and Ethan asked if I wanted to play with him. I told him no,
that I didn't think video games were very good for me; and he said,
"But Sarah, just a little bit won't hurt." It startled me when he said that,
because I realized that he was repeating exactly what people say all
the time about the little things that are not good for us.

I asked him, "If you have just one speck of poison, not even enough
to make you sick, will that hurt you?"

He answered, "Of course not."

"What if you take another small speck, of the same amount, and
then another? You might think it won't hurt you, but it starts adding up
inside your body. Eventually, it would kill you and then you would see
(if you were still alive) that the very first speck really did hurt you more
than you would have thought. By then, though, it would be too late."

We say and think all the time that one little sin, one little lie, one
little misdeed won't really hurt us. But one sin will lead to another, and
they start to add up. These sins will kill us. The one little sin that you
thought was of no account will lead to your destruction. Only Jesus
can remove the sins from our hearts and keep the poison from killing
us. He died on the cross; He took the death that the poison would
have caused us to suffer, so that we might live. Today, accept the
sacrifice He made for you and don't let sin poison your life.

~ Sarah Wahlman

Deaf to the World

Seek the Lord and His strength, seek His face continually.
- 1 Chronicles 16:11 KJV

There once was a large community of frogs that lived in the woods, far from any human civilization. These frogs liked to hold competitions; they would swim, hop, and run—at least as well as a frog can run. In the middle of the frog community was a large rock—about ten feet tall. None of the frogs had ever been to the top of this rock, but none of them had ever tried. So the frogs decided to hold a race to get to the top of the rock.

The day of the race dawned and all the animals came to watch. Each frog got ready and stood at the starting line. One of the bears snapped a large stick, signaling the start of the race. The frogs tore off and started scaling the rock. The crowd started jeering, "It's impossible! Don't try! Give up now; it's just a waste of your time!" One by one the frogs began to give up. They would drop to the ground and hop away in defeat. Finally, almost all of the frogs had dropped out. The deer and bears and moose looked up to the top. There stood one frog, looking around him and off into the distance at all the forest he had never seen before.

"How did you do it?" The moose asked.

"What's the trick?" The deer questioned.

The frog just stared off into the horizon. Finally, the animals got in front of him and asked again. The frog blinked, then slowly hopped down off the rock. He was deaf.

In our lives, God is calling us to a higher standard. However, there are some people in our lives telling us to turn back. "It's too hard!" they may say, but we know that God will give us the power to press on. We can choose to listen to God's voice calling us on, or we can listen to those behind us, telling us to give up. Won't you choose to only listen to God's voice today?

~ Mason Neil

Only God Knows

And those who know Your name will put their trust in You; For you, Lord, have not forsaken those who seek you. - Psalm 9:10 NKJV

Travis and I were not only cousins, we were great friends, too. He and I were similar in age, so we got along really well. We lived about four hours away from each other, so we didn't get to visit that often; but when we did, we would get up to all sorts of mischief. We would ride motor bikes, wrestle goats, go swimming in the lake, go possum hunting, ride horses, and play in the mud and sand. You name it, we did it. One time we even tried pulling a trolley behind his pet calf; which, I might add, didn't end so well. We had great fun together, but the fun ended when I found myself burying Travis on my 11th birthday.

Ten months earlier, Travis had begun experiencing severe headaches. After a few tests, it was discovered that he had a cancerous brain tumor. The tumor was removed, and he started radiation therapy; but the cancer spread to other parts of his body, and more tumors grew back. Over time, Travis got weaker and weaker until he was no more. Despite our earnest prayers and begging God to heal Travis, God did not heal him.

Sometimes God doesn't answer our prayers the way we would like to have them answered. This is the real test of our faith. It's easy to trust God when we get what we ask for, but it's hard when we don't. We would have really liked God to heal Travis, but that was not what God saw fit to do. We have to trust that God has everybody's best interest in mind. This is hard, and at times I struggle to trust God in all aspects of my life; but He helps me to know that He is there, planning what is best for us. I wish that Travis could have lived and I could still spend time with him, but I know that God allowed what was best. I look forward to when Travis and I will be in heaven together, and he and I will be able to spend time with each other knowing that it will never end. Then we will both be able to understand God's purposes.

~ Kyle Smith

Teach Me, Lord

… God … knoweth all things. - 1 John 3:20b KJV

It was a Friday night with howling wind and pouring rain. Only a few hours earlier, our power had gone out, throwing our campus into temporary blackness. As I sat in the darkened chapel during vespers, I somehow could not focus on the service. My mind was on other, more important things. I was overwhelmed and devastated because, in two short days, I would be saying goodbye to my friends, "my second family" as I like to call them. They were moving away, and there was absolutely nothing I could do about it. It seemed to me that as my year progressed, more and more had gone wrong. Whether it was a bad grade on a math test or a fight with a friend, it felt like rocks were being thrown at me from all sides, and there was no escaping these dangerous flying objects.

How could you let this happen? Why is everything going wrong, Lord?

I felt like I had been yelling at God for so long, yet despite my protests, nothing appeared to have changed. Life seemed so complicated, and I was stuck with this dead-end view.

When the vespers service ended, we gathered into a circle to sing our Friday night song: *I Want to Go to Heaven*. This tradition had always been my favorite time of the week, but I was not looking forward to it tonight. As I stood, grasping the hand of the woman I felt I was losing, I didn't even try to hold back the tears. I did not understand how God could let this happen.

Now as I look back, I still have a hard time truly understanding why this had to happen; but I have realized that even though I may not know the reason for things, God does. He sees each one of us, each struggle, each hard time. "… Thou God seest me…" (Genesis 16:13 KJV). He has a specific reason for everything that He does, and my job is to trust that He will see me through.

~ Elizabeth King

10

Don't Hide, Seek

And they entered into a covenant to seek the Lord God of their fathers with all their heart and with all their soul - 2 Chronicles 15:12 KJV

Concealed behind the horse saddle, snickering, I was greatly enjoying my game of hide and seek. One problem with this particular game was that I was the only one aware that the game was going on. You see, I had asked my entire family if they would play with me, and the answer I got from all of them was, "I'm too busy" or "maybe later." So, taking matters into my own hands, I hid behind a horse saddle and waited for someone to notice. My parents were so busy at the time that it took quite a while for them to realize. However, once they did, there was a mad rushing around, and I could distinctly hear my name being called. In about half an hour, my neighbors also discovered I was missing, and soon the entire street was frantically searching for me. During the time of this game, I would occasionally sneak to the door and watch all the people desperately seeking for me, and all I would do was laugh.

My harmless game of hide and seek became frightfully real. I had hid from my parents for most of the day only to be found by my great-aunt. Even though I didn't realize it, they were worried out of their minds. Exactly like my parents were worried, sometimes God worries about us too. He sees that we are lost, and He yearns for us to be found again. God will do what He can, but we must have the will to be found as well. I never got in trouble; and when Jesus finds us, He doesn't punish us either. He is just so relieved when we are found that He wants to celebrate. In Luke 15:10, Jesus says, "… there is joy in the presence of the angels of God over one sinner who repents" (NKJV). So I encourage you, don't hide from our Father in Heaven— seek Him instead.

~ Chris Unfrau

Faith

*So the Lord said, "If you have faith as a mustard seed, you can say
to this mulberry tree, 'Be pulled up by the roots and be planted in the
sea,' and it would obey you." - Luke 17:6 NKJV*

The pastor was up front preaching about the faith of a woman in
the Bible. This woman had a health condition that had lasted for twelve
years. The story is told in Mark 5:27-29. "When she heard about
Jesus, she came behind Him in the crowd and touched His garment.
For she said, 'If only I may touch His clothes, I shall be made well.'
Immediately the fountain of her blood was dried up, and she felt in her
body that she was healed of the affliction" (NKJV).

The pain was tormenting me. For about five months now I had
been experiencing severe stomach pain. Today was Sabbath, and I
was sitting in church trying to listen to the sermon instead of focusing
on my aching stomach. As I heard the pastor tell of this woman and
her faith, I became angry. I thought that it wasn't fair that this woman
was healed while I wasn't.

After the sermon was over, my friend, Laura, who was sitting next
to me, leaned over and asked me if we could pray together for the
healing of my stomach. I reluctantly agreed, but as we were praying,
my faith was strengthened. By the end of the prayer, I had complete
faith that God could give me relief from the pain. As soon as Laura
said amen, I felt the pain go away, and I had relief for the rest of the
day!

God has promised that if we ask in faith, according to His will, He
will always answer us (1 John 5:14).

~ Raina Walker

Logicless Love

*Let this mind be in you which was also in Christ Jesus, who, being in
the form of God, did not consider it robbery to be equal with God, but
made Himself of no reputation, taking the form of a bondservant, and
coming in the likeness of men. - Philippians 2:5–7 NKJV*

I was finally back in my beloved home state of North Carolina,
and I was pretty sure there wasn't a more perfect place in existence.
My family and I had just returned from spending nine months in a
poverty-stricken, remote, and unwelcoming community thousands of
miles from home. This was the place we felt called to go share the
gospel. Personally, I hated it there and made it almost as miserable
an experience to those around me as I made it for myself. My family,
however, fell in love with the people, the language, and the culture.
They wanted to do something to ease the misery that I only saw and
despised. And so, after returning home for a while, they decided to
go back. Every time my parents discussed their plans with me, my
stubborn resolve to never return strengthened. I fought viciously
against my conscience and vainly tried to convince myself that it
couldn't be God's will for me to go to such a dismal place. It took
months and months of the Holy Spirit's coaxing for me to reluctantly
submit my will to God's.

Thousands of years ago, Christ was faced with a similar decision.
He could either choose to stay in His beautiful, perfect home in
Heaven; or He could come down to our filthy, wretched, and sinful
earth to die for ungrateful sinners. But unlike me, He didn't think of
Himself. He made a decision that defies all reason and logic. He
gave up His blissful home, because He has something that I don't:
incredible, unmerited love for each and every human being.

Christ gave up everything because of His love for you and me. Why
are we so unwilling to give Him anything in return?

~ Saraiah Turnbull

Joy That Can't Be Stolen

You will show me the path of life; in Your presence is fullness of joy; at Your right hand are pleasures forevermore. - Psalm 16:11 NKJV

I am sitting in the front passenger seat of our van as content as a singing robin. My energetic nine-year-old sister, Karissa, is happily relaxed in the third row seat. In the middle row, Mom is busily pulling lunch out of the ice chest beside her. Jonathan, my caring brother, is taking those lunch fixings onto his lap. All the while, my dad is calmly behind the wheel as we speed down the interstate toward Washington. With lunch in the making, we are enjoying just talking together. Karissa excitedly reminds us that she wants to play a car game after lunch.

Mom announces that lunch is ready, and I volunteer to thank God for the homemade sandwich spread and other nourishing treats. With "mmmms" and "yums" we savor the first bite of Mom's sandwiches while gazing out the windows at God's rolling prairies. I am enjoying the trip very much. It is so reassuring to be simply riding along with my family. When Mom, Dad, Jonathan, and Karissa are keeping me company, I find it much easier to be secure and optimistic.

God is our Heavenly Father. When He designed families, I believe that He longed to show us the security and comfort that He wants us to have through Him. Similarly to how riding with my family encourages a sense of security and joy, being in God's presence will bring perfectly confident joy. We can't always be around earthly comforters, like family members. Yet we can continually have God's company. We can know that when we are with Him, He is giving us more assurance and joy than even the most caring family can give.

I want to have fullness of joy and peace continually. Do you? If we tell Jesus that we want to spend the day in His presence, He will gladly be with us all day long. He will come into our hearts and be with us as soon as we ask Him. Through the Holy Spirit, God's presence will be in us. He will be our Shepherd today. With the Good Shepherd as our companion, we can know that we have fullness of joy.

~ Andrew Sharley

Wakeboard Grace, Part 1

… But they, measuring themselves by themselves, and comparing
themselves among themselves, are not wise.
- 2 Corinthians 10:12 NKJV

I felt fearless and confident! I knew that I would flip when it was my turn. Watching a fellow wake-boarder at summer camp, I marked his movements as he flew through the air, effortlessly rotating and landing on the other side of the boat's wake.

My turn came and the boat driver challenged me to "Try it!" He "knew" that I could pick it up quickly from what he had seen of my previous wakeboarding. This really excited me.

As I was pulled out of the water, a chill started up my spine and my stomach dropped—the type of feeling you experience from a roller coaster ride. Just simply standing up on my wakeboard and staring ahead towards the boat made me think twice. I didn't want to try any more. Fear was creating a war within me. I kept telling myself that I would try this flip! I mean, everyone else thought I could, but my movements felt clumsy. My jumping was off and falling was imminent. If a flip was going to happen, it needed to happen soon. The pressure inside of me was intense, especially as fellow campers watched expectantly and shouted, "Just do it! You've got this, Ashley!"

No, I could not make myself attempt a flip. Two painful face-plants were my only accomplishments. Instead of enjoying my favorite sport, I felt dreadful feelings: fear, inadequacy, wounded pride, and failure. The joy was completely gone.

My selfish pride wanted to have the respect and admiration of others. I wanted the "feel-good," "on top of the world" feelings. But should that be a Christian's goal? No way! God accepts me as I am, and, by realizing this, I will grow in Him. Others don't need to accept me for me to feel happy. He accepts me, and because of that, I should accept myself as a child of God, knowing that by being an ever-changing beholder of Christ, I will grow to become more like Him.

~ Ashley Wilkens

Wakeboard Grace, Part 2

… God resists the proud, but gives grace to the humble.
- James 4:6 NKJV

The next morning, peaceful waters lay still, and that peace enveloped my heart. My lack of guts the day before had made me feel miserable because I could not bring myself to attempt a simple wakeboard flip. But what a blessing it turned out to be! Instead of tossing my burdens upon human shoulders, I brought my heavy load of feelings to the Lord. I talked to Him as I would talk to my dad. I asked Him to take away my awful feelings. I didn't want to do a flip just to feed my pride. I wanted to see my worth in His eyes instead of finding value in the praise of others. I begged Him to take away my burden, bless my talents, and make me content.

Early that morning, Breck (our boat driver), his sister, and I woke up before our fellow campers and staff. It was exciting to start the day before everyone else and have extra time out on the water without waiting on others to finish their turns. With a lighthearted attitude, I decided to relish every moment of my favorite sport. My goal was to enjoy the day and have fun.

When it was my turn to wakeboard, I wasn't worried about flipping. But suddenly a strong urge hit me, and I went for it. I flipped! God gave me the strength to try! The way I felt was indescribable—the beauty of nature, the exhilaration of wakeboarding, and, most of all, the love from my Creator!

I learned that there is mighty power in prayer. Taking my burdens to Christ, instead of complaining to someone else, gave me peace. But it didn't end there; on top of the peace, God poured out His grace. In James 4:6, the word "grace" means, "that which affords joy, pleasure, delight, and sweetness." I had prayed with a humble spirit, and the Lord held true to His promise: He gave me this grace!

~ Ashley Wilkens

Press On

But they that wait upon the Lord shall renew their strength; they shall mount up with wings as eagles; they shall run, and not be weary; and they shall walk, and not faint. - Isaiah 40:31 KJV

The silence only revved my heart. I crouched on top of the block, surrounded by five other swimmers with the same intention of beating me to the finish. "Take your marks!" barked the referee, breaking the silence. The horn sounded and we hit the water, streamlined and at top speed. Immediately, pandemonium broke loose. Shouts of, "Go, go, go!" emanated from the stands as we battled our way forward to the finish, 500 meters away. I swam length after length of the pool, aided by my sheer strength and the technique drilled into me each day by my swim coach. My heart rate skyrocketed as I increased my pace after each gruelling length. The swimmers in the lanes around me attempted to match my pace so they could beat me in the final sprint to the wall. As I struggled on, the hypoxic pain grew until I felt like giving up and climbing out of the pool. I focused on the finish and pressed on, encouraged by my teammates (who could tell I was tired) yelling, "Go, Christian, go! Pick up the pace! Don't give up!" I came into the last lap at maximum sprint, only breathing twice in the last 50 meters. I was the first to hit the wall. Finally, I could rest.

Today, we are approaching that last 50-meter sprint to the wall in the great controversy between truth and falsehood. Satan is matching our pace and trying to slow us down so he can beat us in our race to overcome evil. Jesus has given us a book, the Bible, full of the "technique" of life that He wants us to follow. When we step out into the world, He encourages us to practice this "technique" and gives us the strength and courage to endure the temptations and snares that Satan sets for us. Don't give up, but press on until the end. Only then can we declare, "I have fought the good fight, I have finished the race, I have kept the faith" (2 Timothy 4:7 NKJV).

~ Christian Welch

The Faith of a Child

Truly, I say to you, whoever does not receive the kingdom of God like a child shall not enter it. - Mark 10:15 ESV

In the summertime, bees always swarmed around the front porch of my house. I loved to watch these bees, and since I had never been stung before, I wasn't the least bit scared of them. I fed them honey from a spoon and picked flowers for them to draw nectar from.

However, one day when I looked out the door, I saw that one bee had been hurt. My heart ached. I wanted to do all I could to help this bee get better. So while having faith that I could save the bee, I made a home for it to rest in. It was made from an empty box stuffed with flowers and plants from my garden. When the little home was ready, I picked up the bee and carefully placed him in the box. As the days went by, I fell more and more in love with the bee. Though he was little, he was like my pet, and I was excited to see that he was getting better. After about a week of doing my best to nurture the bee, he was ready to be set free.

Jesus told us to have the faith of a child. But what exactly does that mean? If you have been around a small child, you'll notice that she always thinks that the impossible is possible. How many adults do you know who would make a home for a bee, hoping to save it? Not many. On the other hand, how many children do you know who would? Probably a lot more. As we grow older, we learn more about the laws of nature, what can happen, and what can't. However, we also tend to forget what we learned as children: that we have a God who can operate beyond the laws of nature; a God who can make anything happen. Just think about how many more miracles would happen if we had more faith when we prayed. Will you humble yourself and learn how to have the faith of a child?

~ Agnes Grétarsdóttir

18

The Big Picture

Thou wilt keep him in perfect peace, whose mind is stayed on thee: because he trusteth in thee. - Isaiah 26:3 KJV

I sat on the cold black and white tiles of our bathroom floor, hugging my knees and sobbing. Our family had been talking about this for a while, but I never really believed it would happen. How could I leave my Swiss country home? How could I leave my mountains, the creek in which I had spent countless hours, or the sunsets that turned the sky outside my window to fire? Then my heart almost stopped: how could I leave my precious Toby behind? This golden retriever-border collie mix was the dog I had frolicked through the woods and fields with, who had dragged me on his leash through cow pies. He was also the friend I played catch with until my fingers froze, and on whose furry tummy I would almost fall asleep. The thought of having to leave him behind broke my little ten-year-old heart; the tears flowed faster and hotter as I wrestled with this thought.

My dear mother soon came to see what was wrong, and between sobs I told her what was on my heart. She explained that to take Toby with us would mean that he'd have to be locked in a cage on the plane for twelve hours. Toby was claustrophobic. And our Michigan home would not have a fence, posing quite a problem for our energetic dog. We'd had this conversation before, but in my mind, there just had to be a way to take him with us. Many tears later, and with much patience on mother's part, I understood that there was no other option, and that my parents had made the best decision they could: we would give him to someone who we knew would take good care of him.

Looking back, I'm glad I trusted my parents. Toby would have been miserable had he come along. My parents could see the big picture, even when I couldn't. Likewise, God sees the big picture of my life, and when I trust Him with it, I can have perfect peace, knowing that He is in charge.

~ Esther Ferraz

Fully Connected

Thy word have I hid in mine heart, that I might not sin against thee.
- Psalm 119:11 KJV

I admit that I have not always been faithful in my daily Bible readings. It is a very real temptation to shorten them or even put them off entirely. I tell myself that I will study a little longer tomorrow when I have more time, but it often happens that I don't have time the next day either. Day after day, I find myself spending less and less time in the Word, and more time on non-spiritual things. This goes on and on until I have lost a habit that is very hard to regain. I have found that, once I have submitted to the initial temptation, Satan has free rein in my life, and I am much more susceptible to his impressions and temptations. It is then that I am weakest and often fall. While it may seem like a simple task to complete, in the moment of decision, I often choose to postpone this vital time of connection with my heavenly Father.

Once Satan has driven the initial wedge of separation between God and me, he can slowly but steadily split us apart, just as a lumberjack splits a log one wedge at a time. Once I have surrendered one thing to Satan, I have then opened the door to other more serious sins, which form habits that are very hard to break.

I remember a day last year when I hurt my family with harsh, unkind words. Afterward I apologized, but I realized that no matter what I did, I could not take back the spiteful words that had come out of my mouth. If I would have asked Christ to be with me that morning, I would have been able to stop myself before it was too late.

It is still a daily battle for me. Every morning I have to push aside the many distractions assailing my mind and focus solely on what the Lord is telling me that day. Only once I have done this can I truthfully say that "I have fought a good fight, I have finished my course, I have kept the faith" (2 Timothy 4:7 KJV).

~ Derek Glatts

Soldiers, Where Are Your Swords?

… and [take] the sword of the Spirit, which is the word of God…
- Ephesians 6:17 KJV

"Soldiers, where are your Swords?" The exclamation reverberated within the confines of my weary mind. I was sitting in boys' dorm worship, and the leader had asked us to open our Bibles to a specific passage. The young man who expressed the exclamation could see our empty hands. He knew we were unarmed. I knew that carrying God's Word with me was important, but I didn't previously think about the magnitude of it.

When I fight the battles of life, I often forget my Bible, the most important weapon in the face of hardship, persecution and the stresses of human existence in general. Looking back at the Reformation, a time of trial for Protestants, the Catholic Church frowned upon those who tried to read the Bible for themselves. They only allowed the church clergy to read and interpret God's Holy Word. The Reformers relied heavily on their Bibles to differentiate truth from the many falsehoods of the corrupted Catholic Church. As I look back at this troubling time in the history of the Christian church, it reminds me of how important it is to study and memorize God's Word so we can stand for Jesus, even when we face persecution.

That night at worship, I pondered these thoughts. I saw again how the great controversy between God and Satan was a battle for truth. In this controversy, Satan uses deception, subtlety and innuendo as his weapons. He wields them like a sword in the hands of a fearful warrior. Our Sword is the Word of God. Whether it's kept in our hearts or in our backpacks, this important book must be our everyday companion to aid us in facing life's difficulties and questions. If we expect to win this epic battle against one who has had more than 6,000 years of experience, we need to follow our Commander's instructions to carry our Swords onto the front lines of everyday life.

~ Christian Welch

No Misunderstandings

… hath not God made foolish the wisdom of this world?
- 1 Corinthians 1:20 KJV

My mom was away for the afternoon. To our delight, Daddy was going to be at home taking care of us. We set up a play store and were having a great time. Suddenly my dad, who was on an important phone call, told us to go to our rooms because we were being too loud. We were shocked. We didn't understand why he hadn't asked us to be quiet before he punished us for being noisy. We sadly tramped down the hall and sat on our beds.

As the minutes dragged on, I started to wonder how long he would make us stay there. I started to cry. Had he forgotten us? After a long time, Mom walked in the door and called for us. We took this opportunity to flee our prisons and rushed out crying, "Daddy made us stay on our beds the whole time you were gone, and we hardly got to play at all!" She looked very surprised and glanced over at Dad who had just finished his call.

Dad explained, "I told them to go to their rooms because they were making too much noise, but I didn't tell them to sit on their beds. I thought they could play in there." Mom understood. Dad had asked us to go to our rooms, not realizing that when she sends us to our rooms, we are to stay on our beds until she calls. Dad assured us that he was very sorry. He had not intended to punish us.

Sometimes we misunderstand our Heavenly Father, because we are used to how this world reasons. When we choose to let God take control of our lives, He doesn't always do things the way we expect Him to. We may sometimes feel that He is unjustly punishing us because we don't understand His guidance. If we spend time with God learning about Him through the Bible, our misunderstandings will disappear, and we will be glad to let Him take control.

~ Bethany Corrigan

Little is Much

… truly, I say to you, if you have faith like a grain of mustard seed, you will say to this mountain, 'Move from here to there,' and it will move, and nothing will be impossible for you. - Matthew 17:20 ESV

There were about five thousand people in the wilderness listening to Jesus' word. Because His word was so full of life, they forgot about their hunger. Jesus knew they were hungry, and He showed compassion toward them. He said to His disciples: "Give ye them to eat."

This confused those disciples. "Lord, where can we buy that much food for these people? There is a boy who only has two fish and five loaves of bread, but that's all we have."

"Make the men sit down," Jesus said, and He fed the crowd with two fish and five loaves of bread. Everyone had enough food to eat, and there were even twelve baskets of fragments left over. What a miracle!

My home is in China, where there are over a billion people (and there is a huge difference between a billion and a million). With more than a billion people in China, *how do we spread the gospel to them? With which person should we start?*

"Give ye them to eat."

"But Lord, I am just a little one of the billion. How is that possible?"

"If you have faith as small as a mustard seed…"

~ Bryan Chen

Move Over

Humble yourselves therefore under the mighty hand of God, that He may exalt you in due time. - 1 Peter 5:6 KJV

Martin Luther told a story about two billy goats. There was a very narrow suspension bridge strung between two tall mountains. In between was a very large valley that eventually dropped off into a canyon that cradled a roaring river. The two billy goats attempted to cross at the same time. They became aware of this fact when they both met in the middle where the bridge was too narrow for them to pass each other without falling. They couldn't back up because billies don't have a reverse gear; and to fight would mean certain death for both of them as the bridge was already swaying in the wind because of the altitude. After a while, they decided there was only one option: to have one billy lay down on the bridge while the other billy climbed over top of him. Miraculously they made it to their respective sides safely.

How often have I been willing to humble myself and lay down my pride before my brother for the sake of the greater good? How many times have I hardened my heart and been willing to go down with the ship rather than to ask forgiveness for a wrong that I have done, even as simple as a thoughtless word or action? Have I, a professed follower of Christ, treated the people who have done me wrong with the same humble, forgiving, loving attitude that Christ did? We could take the quality of all our relationships to a whole new level if we would but carry a towel and washbasin into our every interaction.

~ Nolan Knuppel

God's Gifts

Rejoice in the Lord always: and again I say, Rejoice.
- Philippians 4:4 KJV

My mom, my brother and I were moving from a small farm to a larger farm where my mom was setting up an orphanage. Everyone was in a bad mood because we had just found out that some thieves had stolen the shower heads and kitchen faucet from our new house. We didn't have a fence around our new home in Brazil yet, and this was especially dangerous because drug dealers lived on some of the nearby farms. Later that day, to our surprise, a happy dog showed up on our small farm (where we were moving from) to cheer us up and take away our negative mindset. We kept going back and forth; since the van we were using wasn't really big, we had to repeat the drive a couple of times. Every time we went back to get more stuff, this dog was still there, always so happy and friendly. On our last trip in the evening, he was still there; and when we were leaving, he jumped in the car ready to go with us—just as if we were his owners. It was exactly what we needed; now we could have a good night's sleep, knowing that if someone came, the dog would alert us.

God showed me how He is always there, giving us everything we need, when we need it. In your life, bad things may happen, but we shouldn't gather together all the unpleasant recollections of a past life—its iniquities and disappointments—talk over them and mourn over them until we are overwhelmed with discouragement. We know that God has something better; so why not thank Him for all the gifts that He gives us every day. "Thank God for the bright pictures which He has presented to us" (*Steps to Christ*, pg. 117).

~ Diane Carvalho

Impossible?

… With men this is impossible, but with God all things are possible.
- Matthew 19:26 NKJV

God had a distinct and major plan for my life: a plan that I thought would never come about because it was absolutely impossible. God wanted me to attend Fountainview Academy, and it is only through His leading that I am here.

I was stunned and speechless when I was told by my dad that I had been accepted into Fountainview. This came at a time when I didn't expect it. My friend and I were walking outside, enjoying the sun's warmth and our friendship together. Glancing behind me, I saw Dad coming in his truck. He flashed his lights at me and stopped to talk to Mum, who was farther behind us. Not knowing what he wanted, I continued to walk on ahead. Out of curiosity, I looked again. This time I knew by the flash of the headlights that Dad wanted me as soon as possible. I turned back to talk to him, not ready for what he was about to say. In fact, when he told me that I was accepted to go to school at Fountainview, I really thought that he was joking.

From that time onwards, every other door that had appeared shut, opened. The day after I found out, some friends donated a thousand dollars towards my expenses. Again, not too many days later, one of my aunties donated the same amount. Multiple relatives and others started to give money to help with my school bill.

Through this, I saw very distinctly that God had a major plan for me in the coming year. When God wanted me in a particular place, He made it possible. God's timing is always perfect; He's never ever late, even if it seems so in our eyes. God has plans for you too—plans that you may think are above what you are capable of achieving. But God wants to reveal His strength to you in ways you've never dreamed of. Will you let Him?

~ Nateesha Dorrington

Showers of Blessings

*I will make them and the places all around My hill a blessing; and
I will cause showers to come down in their season; there shall be
showers of blessing. - Ezekiel 34:26 NKJV*

This summer, one of my church's outreach leaders planned a
Saturday afternoon for our church to pass out GLOW tracts in our
town. When this certain Saturday arrived, the weather was not very
pleasant. The rain's sporadic drizzling caused it to be cold and wet.
When we got to the church, the outreach leader called everyone
together to pray before we left. I bowed my head in prayer, but in my
heart I had a resentful spirit. I wasn't too happy to be going out in the
rain just to pass out a few little tracts.

We loaded the vehicles and paired up with our partners. Then
we drove to the street where we were to pass out our pamphlets,
and my group started down one side of the street. I still wasn't very
enthusiastic about what we were doing. No one was home at any
of the houses we went to, and it was starting to rain more. At that
moment, it hit me that the reason I wasn't having fun was because I
had a bad attitude.

Because I was focusing on the things that I wasn't enjoying, I was
missing all the blessings that God had for me to enjoy. When I realized
this, I started to think about all the blessings God was sending my way.
I had the opportunity to be a part of an outreach program, and I got to
be a part of blessing my town by leaving tracts at each house. Once
my attitude changed, I even started to enjoy the rain.

God has so many blessings for us that we are not able to enjoy
because we have the wrong attitude. I want to always have a cheerful
attitude so I can fully enjoy all the blessings He has promised me.
Don't you?

~ Kami Rose

Saying a Prayer—or Praying?

My voice shalt Thou hear in the morning, O Lord; in the morning will I direct my prayer unto Thee, and will look up. - Psalms 5:3 KJV

The day started out just like any other. I woke up, exercised, and went to my room for devotions. In the book *Thoughts from the Mount of Blessing*, I read about Jesus' meekness and how He never did anything that was selfish or for His own glory. "Wow," I thought, "I need to be like that. Almost everything I do is actuated by a selfish motive, and I definitely am not meek either!" Then I looked at the clock, "Oh, it's time for family worship." I quickly knelt down, said a prayer, and hurried out.

After worship and breakfast, I carried on with the rest of my morning, but things were not going well. When I got upset with my sister for the third time, and then spoke disrespectfully to my mom, I knew I needed help with my attitude. I slipped into my room and prayed, "Dear Jesus, forgive me for getting upset with my family. Forgive me for not really connecting with You this morning. Help me not to be grouchy, but to be cheerful, meekly putting others above myself. Thank You. Amen." It's amazing what Jesus did for me in answer to that heartfelt prayer! I went back to my family and apologized for acting selfishly. The rest of the day went so much better it was hard to believe that it was not a new day.

God always hears and answers a sincere prayer—prayer that we really mean. But when we simply go through the motions of "saying a prayer," we have no assurance that He will hear. If we want to have strength for our Christian walk, we must take time for earnest, heartfelt prayer. We must open our hearts to God as to a friend, knowing that He will never let us down.

~ Aileen Corrigan

Where I Stand

*Not that I speak in regard to need, for I have learned in whatever state
I am, to be content - Philippians 4:11 NKJV*

From the first moment I joined the Fountainview Academy choir,
the only thing I wanted was to be a soprano. Since I knew I could
sing high enough and on tune, I figured those were the only things I
needed. But, when it came time for me to sing for Mr. Cleveland, the
music director, I was informed that my voice had a poorly developed
lower register, and I was promptly assigned to the "host of altos." I felt
a little disappointed, but I resigned quietly to my new place. I knew that
wherever I was standing, I would still be learning.

For a while, it was challenging to find the alto notes in the music,
but a few older girls helped me learn. Eventually, I got bored, and I
started to complain with fellow "wanna-be-sopranos." Every time I saw
a soprano, I felt a little jealous and started thinking things like, "What's
so great about her voice?" The way I was thinking made me start to
dislike certain people. At that point, I knew I needed to change my
attitude.

Before I had realized just how far my thoughts had taken me, I
started to think that jealousy was normal. Surely everybody is jealous
of someone?

I didn't consciously want to feel jealous, but I never tried to stop.
I let my feelings overrule common sense and good judgment. Since
the people I disliked never knew what I felt, I thought it didn't affect
them; but sin originated in Lucifer's heart, and it did affect everyone. I
thought I was the only person being hurt, but as long as I continued to
let my mind run rampant, I was becoming more and more un-Christlike
towards everyone. In order to change, I had to lay aside my own
feelings and leave my life in God's hands. Once I could see past my
feelings and get a clear view of my place in the choir, I found that I had
learned so much, and I had developed my voice far beyond anything
I could have done alone. I now appreciate and enjoy where I stand in
choir because I am an alto.

~ Morgan Metcalf

Amazing Burrs

Yes, the Lord has done amazing things for us! What joy!
- Psalm 126:3 NLT

Not again, I thought as I stood there staring at my horse. Once more she had gotten burrs in her mane. It seemed that no matter what I did, burrs would still get stuck on her mane, and I would have to take my precious riding time to remove them.

I started taking them out one at a time. Pulling this way and that, I did all I could to remove as little of the hair from her mane as possible. I tried putting oil in her mane, which helped some, but I still would get little pieces of the burrs stuck in my hands. By the time I was done, my hands were sore and full of little prickles that I would have to soak and try to pull out later. I did not mind too much though, because I had been able to help my horse. As I took the burrs out, my horse just stood there patiently while I yanked hard on her mane. It was almost as if she knew that she needed help because she was not capable of getting the burrs out herself.

This makes me think of the amazing things God has done and still does for us. I may have been willing to help my horse a little, but He has helped us a lot. I may have been willing to let my hands get hurt a little for my horse, but He was willing to hurt His hands on the cross for us. Through all His pain and suffering on the cross, He did not complain. Even though He may be sad about the burrs of life we get stuck on ourselves, He is very happy to have us ask for help. If you give yourself to God and ask Him to help you take the burrs out of your life, He will carefully and lovingly help pull them out one at a time.

~ Rebecca Hall

She Said Yes

For to me to live is Christ, and to die is gain. - Philippians 1:21 KJV

Wham! The man's hand slammed down on the top of the desk. Bending over, he shoved the barrel of a loaded gun in the face of a girl who was huddled beneath.

"Do you believe in God?" He hissed, daring her to respond, his finger poised over the trigger.

"Yes." She responded, her voice ringing out fearlessly.

He pulled the trigger.

On April 22, 1999, 17-year-old Cassie Bernall was shot to death by one of two teenaged gunmen who stormed the Columbine High School in Jefferson County, Colorado. Eleven people lost their lives that day, but the death of Cassie still brings people to their knees—questioning their own faith in God. She was a girl known for her solid walk with Christ and a desire to serve others. The bracelet on her wrist that said, "What Would Jesus Do?" was more than just mere ornamentation; it was her way of life. She once told her family that her ultimate goal was to truly live out her faith. Cassie did achieve her goal in a way that none of us can truly comprehend.

There are many others who, with Cassie, have made that final declaration. The pages of history are stained with the blood of courageous thousands who have boldly professed their faith in God in the face of death. Cassie knew what would happen if she said yes. Yet she wasn't afraid to die for her Jesus. To her, Jesus was real and worth taking a bullet for. Is Jesus that real to you? If you had been staring down the barrel of the shotgun instead of Cassie, would you have said yes?

~ Sierra Buhler

Chill Pill

Which of you by taking thought can add one cubit unto his stature?
- Matthew 6:27 KJV

I hate homework, I said to myself as I sat, trying to arrange in my mind the countless things I had to do. It was just one of those aggravating weeks at boarding school. Lots of homework, not enough sleep, a lack of social life, and other random activities were taking their toll on me. I felt drained to the core and wanted to lie down and sleep all my problems away.

Maybe Cyrus can help, I thought. I went over to his room to solicit his assistance. I found him goofing off with one of his friends, talking about things far from the curses of homework.

How do they do it? I mused, watching them laugh.

Finally, Cyrus stopped laughing and asked me, "What's up?" I told him I had way too much homework, and concentrating seemed next to impossible in my small room. Instead of his regular answers, he wore a serious expression on his face and said, "Have you given it up to God?"

I thought, *What can God do about my homework?*

"Uh, no." I said.

We ended up praying together and surrendering it into His hands. I must say that that experience was an amazing one. No, the homework didn't go away, but the stress that was usually tied to it did. It was now in God's hands.

God doesn't want us to live a hectic life of stress and busyness. He offers a way of escape: give Him all of your fears and anxieties. When everything is in His hands, there is nothing to worry about. My life is in His hands. Is yours?

~ Chris Donatelli

The Missing Ingredient

You are the salt of the earth; but if the salt loses its flavor, how shall it be seasoned? It is then good for nothing but to be thrown out and trampled underfoot by men. - Matthew 5:13 NKJV

The sun peeked through the classroom window. School was almost over, and I couldn't wait to go home to make a delicious chocolate cake. Once the bell finally rang, I ran out to my bike and headed home. A few minutes after I arrived, I pulled out a recipe book and proceeded to find all the necessary ingredients: cocoa, baking soda, baking powder, flour, milk, eggs, and so on. I dumped them all in a bowl, mixed them together, and shoved the mixture into the oven for half an hour.

"Ding!" my body was filled with excitement as I jumped up from the couch to enjoy my cake. The smell of warm chocolate wafted through the air as I came closer to the kitchen. I sliced a piece of cake, set it on my plate, and filled a cup with milk to drink with my treat. With my fork I cut the first bite and put it in my mouth. "Yuck! That's disgusting!" I exclaimed while spitting out the piece of cake. Something was missing; it didn't taste like the typical chocolate cake. So I went to study the recipe and soon realized that I had forgotten the salt. To some, salt may not seem very important; but those are the ones who don't know how much flavor it adds. Almost any food without salt is boring and unpalatable.

A chocolate cake without salt is like a Christian without love. You cannot be a true follower of Christ without having love in your heart. Christ says in John 15:17, "These things I command you, that ye love one another" (KJV). But how can we obtain this love that makes us different from the world? We can receive it by asking God to manifest a love towards Himself in our hearts. And by loving God, we will begin to love the people around us as well. This dying world needs love. It needs the followers of Christ to remember Jesus' message that "You are the salt of the earth..." (Matthew 5:13 NKJV). When we manifest a pure selflessness towards all, by loving our neighbor as ourselves, we will add the flavor of heaven to this sin-filled planet.

~ Agnes Grétarsdóttir

Act on It

But you are a chosen generation, a royal priesthood, a holy nation,
His own special people, that you may proclaim the praises of Him who
called you out of darkness into His marvelous light…
- 1 Peter 2:9 NKJV

I sat in the room, dumbfounded. It had never occurred to me that this was how people thought. I always had the idea that everyone who knew about healthy living, at least lived it in some way. But after watching a documentary called *Fat, Sick, and Nearly Dead*, my whole perspective was changed. In the documentary, a guy was doing a juice fast for 60 days. While he was doing this, he would go around and meet different people and talk to them about what they thought about health. They answered as if all of them had had a meeting before being interviewed. They all knew that eating healthy and exercising was very important, but none of them really did anything about it. One guy even said that it was his own fault that he had health problems; but he thought it was too late for him, and he didn't want to even try to change his ways. Others simply said, "I don't really care for eating right because I'm going to die anyways; so I might as well enjoy my time." I just couldn't believe my ears when I heard this. Here were people who knew the truth about health, but were too stubborn to do anything about it. When the interviewer asked them how long they thought they were going to live, they estimated that they would not live long (49–60 years). But those people weren't bothered about it at all, and it was as if they were blind.

As Adventists, we have the knowledge of many different truths. We have our Health Message, Sanctuary Message, Sabbath Message, Commandment Message, Three Angels' Messages, and the list goes on. But how many of us fully live up to these truths? Unfortunately, not many. I believe that many of us are beginning to think of these truths as facts, and not ones we are to live by. Or some live by them, but it has become a routine and they don't really know why they do what they do. I believe that now is the time we need to start living up to the truth and be firmly grounded in why we do it. We have truth; what are we going to do with it?

~ Shenel Cruz

God, Help Me!

… My yoke is easy, and My burden is light. - Matthew 11:30 KJV

The reformer Martin Luther struggled greatly with the feeling of being inadequate for heaven. He tried all the different things that the church proposed for salvation, but he never found peace. Then he read the Bible, and found that "… a man is not justified by the works of the law but by faith in Jesus Christ…" (Galatians 2:16 NKJV).

Is it easier to be saved than to be lost? Christians today often think that living a Christian life is too difficult, but Jesus says that His yoke is easy and His burden light. How can this be? A yoke is used in farming to help two oxen pull a load. To teach a young ox, he is teamed up with an experienced ox. At first, he does not pull anything at all; but as time passes, he learns how to walk and work with a yoke. Jesus promises the same to us. We are weak and inexperienced, but He will pull the load for us.

So how do we become yoked with Christ? It is a free gift: we just need to come to Him. Even before we do that, He is drawing us to Himself with His love. "The sinner may resist this love, may refuse to be drawn to Christ; but if he does not resist he will be drawn to Jesus; a knowledge of the plan of salvation will lead him to the foot of the cross in repentance for his sins, which have caused the sufferings of God's dear Son" (*Steps to Christ*, pg. 27). It is much harder to go on fighting against love like that, rejecting the council of the Holy Spirit rather than being yoked with Christ and experiencing peace. Don't you want that peace?

~ Esra Eliasson

Undeserved Kindness

Whoever pursues righteousness and kindness will find life, righteousness, and honor. - Proverbs 21:21 ESV

"Why do you have to be so nice?" I said to my best friend one evening as we were doing our homework. We were studying completely different subjects, but when she saw that I was struggling with my studies, she immediately stopped what she was doing to help me.

You care too much, I thought. *Why can't you just be mean to me for once in your life!*

I was irritated because she was being so encouraging and helpful. What bothered me even more was when she wanted to know if I had asked God for help. I hadn't, and her question caused me to feel extremely guilty.

"If God promises that all things are possible, then what are you worried about? Beth, it's going to be O.K.," she reassured me.

I believe that many times God places people in our lives so that we may be able to catch a bigger, greater glimpse of His perfect character. God knew that I would need my best friend to be there that night to help point me to Jesus and remind me of His changeless love. Even though I didn't feel like listening to her encouragement at the time, now I see the love and kindness that she was trying to show me.

Small gestures from a generous heart can make all the difference in the world. To my friend, it was a small thing to help me instead of doing her own thing; but when she did, I saw Jesus in her. Through this experience, I have learned that it is often the small things that really matter. Why not try doing a small act of kindness? It may change someone's life.

~ Elizabeth King

His Strength

… my strength is made perfect in weakness. - 2 Corinthians 12:9a KJV

My family has always pursued many outdoor activities. The beautiful mountains around our home offer wonderful opportunities for hiking; the many logging roads are perfect for biking; and there are endless places for an adventurous family to go camping. Unfortunately, I used to despise such wilderness trips. After all, who wants to wear out their legs climbing up a steep trail or exhaust their energy on a lengthy bike ride? Of course, I didn't always voice these thoughts to my family, but when I did, it led to hurt feelings, upset plans and frustrated siblings. "Why can't she just learn to enjoy the outdoors?" they wondered.

But to me it wasn't that simple. I didn't like to push myself. It just wasn't in my nature to appreciate such things! After a couple of years, I decided that I needed to change; I didn't want to continue being lazy. At first I thought I could just choose cheerfulness when my family wanted to do something active. However, I soon realized that I couldn't do it on my own. No matter how hard I tried, I usually ended up ruining things with my complaining. Finally I decided that the only way for me to change was to ask God for His help. God began to help me as soon as I asked Him. Each time I had to give up what I wanted, He helped me to jump into the activity my family had planned and enjoy it. Although I don't always want to spend time outside, and I don't always respond appropriately, in the end I really take pleasure in the time spent with my family whatever we do.

God is always ready to help us! He says, "A new heart also will I give you, and a new spirit will I put within you" (Ezekiel 36:26a KJV). Is there something in your life that you know you need to change? Maybe you have already tried changing on your own and it hasn't worked. God has offered His strength in place of your weakness— won't you take Him at His word?

~ Aileen Corrigan

Perfect Peace

*Thou wilt keep him in perfect peace, whose mind is stayed on thee:
because he trusteth in thee. - Isaiah 26:3 KJV*

"Hurry up, you old bus! Can't you go faster, please?" I pushed against the seat in front of me, somehow hoping that I could make it get to the airport sooner. My sister and I were finally on our way home for summer break. Our bus had been delayed at the border, and now it looked like we would miss our flight. When we arrived at the airport, my sister and I jumped off the bus and sprinted to the check in counter with just 45 minutes to spare. The lady behind the counter looked tired and frazzled. After listening to our predicament, she informed us that if we would have arrived only five minutes earlier, we could have made it. We were going to miss our flight.

All throughout that experience, God kept me at peace. "How did He do that?" you may ask. Well, every time I felt a twinge of worry, I heard His voice asking me if I trusted Him. Every time, I would surrender my worries to Him; and in turn, He kept me at peace. Jesus wants us to have this peace every day. Even though your life may be so chaotic that you don't know what to do, there is Someone who sees and is in control of what you are going through. God desires to keep you at rest in His perfect peace regardless of your circumstances.

Do you want this peace? Are you tired of plans that have fallen through, of people or events that don't measure up to your expectations? Jesus is asking you to surrender all this to Him. In return for your worries and stresses, He will sustain you by this perfect peace. Won't you trust Him?

~ Sarah Miller

Nothing Brings More Enjoyment

What then? Only that in every way, whether in pretense or in truth,
Christ is preached; and in this I rejoice, yes, and will rejoice.
- Philippians 1:18 NKJV

I was on Fountainview Academy's California music tour. Not knowing what to expect for our travel meals, we were astounded when they brought out fresh bread with sandwich spread, fried potatoes, and homemade muffins. As we continued, we were treated to delectable dishes ranging from taco salad to hummus and crackers. The fact is that we ate like royalty. In addition to gourmet food, we were privileged to go to a water park and a mall. Yet the highlight of my California tour was not the extravagant food or fun activities. The real highlight for me was sharing my very best friend, Jesus, with two of His children.

This is how it happened. I was greeting guests after our concert, when a humble looking couple came toward me. I thanked them for coming and explained that I only wanted to share my best friend, Jesus. After conversing for a couple of minutes, I asked if we could pray together. The man prayed for me and then I prayed, asking God to hold them in His hands. Upon opening my eyes, I noticed that this man's face had turned a shade happier and he told me, "It's been a long time since someone's prayed a nice prayer like that for us." Wow! Praise the Lord! What intense joy filled my heart at those words. As these precious children of God walked away, those words would not leave my mind.

The gourmet treats, shopping mall, and water park have now faded in brilliance. But still ringing in my ears is the phrase: "It's been a long time since someone's prayed a nice prayer like that for us." Words can't express the satisfaction of being used by God to draw this couple toward Him. Of all my tour experiences, this one still excites me the most. I am convinced that when Jesus commanded us to share Him with others, He gave us the most joyful activity in the universe. I choose to accept this joyful task by asking Jesus to shine through me today. Do you want to share your Redeemer, too?

~ Andrew Sharley

Tuna

But I will hope continually, and will yet praise Thee more and more.
- Psalm 71:14 KJV

When you feel like your spiritual walk has stopped, do you ever think of going faster? Have you ever thought, *My relationship with God is frozen, I need to get moving*? At least for me, I've often felt like this; but I can say that I have been encouraged when I think of tuna.

Tuna can grow from two to eight feet long and weigh from three to six thousand pounds! They can dive up to 750 feet in less than a minute, despite the gigantic changes in water pressure. If a tuna is attacked and it doesn't remember to dive, the startled fish can swim away at a speed of 45 miles an hour. However, above these interesting facts, one trait of the tuna is worth noting: it will never stop swimming. Why? Most fish use muscles to pump water over their gills to supply adequate oxygen to their bodies. But, tuna lack the muscles needed to do this. As a result, tuna must swim continually to avoid suffocation.

We, in our spiritual lives, must be like tuna fish. As the tuna must continuously swim, so we must have unbroken communion with God. The tuna constantly swims without giving the slightest thought to why it's swimming. It simply knows that swimming is fundamental to survival. The same goes for us. We must constantly advance along the sacred journey of our relationship with God or else we too will die.

Now, when you think about this unique fish, think about how it can be a model for your life. Just like tuna, without going forward, you are suffocating your spiritual life and ultimately killing your relationship with God.

~ Chris Donatelli

Comforting Love

*… I will turn their mourning into joy, and will comfort them, and make
them rejoice from their sorrow. - Jeremiah 31:13 KJV*

Heather and I had been pen pals for several years. We had a
genuine love for each other, and she had been a wonderful inspiration
to me. Her letters were full of love and devotion to God, which
encouraged me in my spiritual walk. When we spent time together, I
discovered that I appreciated her quiet, reserved personality.

When I got the news that she had been in a fatal car accident, I
was heartbroken.

It seemed that no one else knew how much I cared for her, and
so they took it like they would any other death. "That is too bad," was
their response. It was too bad, but it was more than that for me. It was
tragic. My friend had died and left behind a little sister, mom, and dad
(if he survived). When I was alone, Mom came up to me and told me
how sorry she was, and that she cared. That was too much for me,
and I burst into tears. She hugged me and cried with me, and I knew
her heart felt the pain too. Mom's understanding showed me a little
about how Jesus relates to our hurt.

Jesus received a message that Lazarus was sick, but Jesus was
delayed on His way to heal him. As He drew near to the house, He
heard wailing and mourning. Lazarus was dead. As soon as Mary and
Martha saw Jesus coming, they came to Him with the heart-rending
cry, "If you would have come sooner our brother wouldn't have died!"
The Bible records that in response, "Jesus wept" (John 11:35 KJV).

God knows our deepest feelings and He understands our grief.
Just like my mom, He knows us better than anyone else, and He cares
for every little hurt. His infinite love yearns to comfort us.

~ Bethany Corrigan

How to Spank a Grizzly Bear

Behold, happy is the man whom God corrects; Therefore do not despise the chastening of the Almighty. - Job 5:17 NKJV

In Montana, hungry grizzly bears often wander into town looking for an easy meal: table scraps, dog food, and even little yappy dogs. When a bear is spotted in town, the wildlife rangers are called to trap the bear; then they must teach the bear that it is not to return. Therefore they must 'spank' the Grizzly bear. There are two ways to spank a grizzly bear, and the first is a 'soft spank.' After the rangers trap the bear, they relocate it to the next county. This usually works, but if the bear finds his way back, the rangers must perform a 'hard spank.' Once again, the bear is trapped, but this time it is released on site. The unsuspecting bear slowly walks out of the cage and starts smelling for more food to eat. At that point, the rangers pull out shotguns loaded with tiny bean bags and aim at the south end of the northbound bear. At the shock of the sound and the pain, the grizzly immediately rears up and starts to run away as fast as his legs can carry him. Next, the rangers set down their shotguns and pull out their rifles loaded with long range rubber bullets. These will not puncture the skin, but will definitely hurt. To reinforce the 'don't-ever-return' message, the rangers shoot cracker shells that explode like fireworks around the terrified bear. Finally, hunting dogs are released for a certain distance in pursuit of the bear.

"The poor bear!" you might say; however, while the rangers' actions may seem cruel, they are really trying to save the bear's life. You see, if the bear comes back a third time, they must kill it in order to protect people. How often we complain about the hardships that we think God brings upon us. Yet we are just like the disobedient bear—returning to places that we should never be in the first place. We must always remember that God is only trying to protect us, trying to keep us away from things that will hurt us.

~ Derek Glatts

Be Still

For thus saith the Lord God … In returning and rest shall ye be saved;
in quietness and in confidence shall be your strength: and ye would
not. - Isaiah 30:15 KJV

"Meow! Meow!" I cringed as I heard the plea to be let inside
repeated for the tenth time. Finally, I marched down the dorm staircase
in my PJs to do something about it. "Rosa, I'm tired of hearing that cat
outside my window! I can't sleep with it out there. Can I take it to my
room?" Surprised, my dean quickly said yes, and without further ado, I
opened the door, scooped up the cat, and marched back up the stairs
to my room. Contrary to my fears, the small black cat slept peacefully
snuggled up against me throughout the cold, dark night.

When it came time for my devotions the next morning, my
newfound friend stood up, stretched, yawned, and plunked himself
down in my lap again. As I bowed my head to pray, a door was
slammed shut in the hallway. Jumping to his feet, the cat's hair stood
on end. I reached out my hand to pet him, and he calmed down for the
moment. A few seconds later, the sound of a squeaky shower faucet
started in the nearby bathroom, setting him off again. As soon as he
was coerced back onto my lap, the process began again. "Calm down,
Cat!" I said, "All that I want you to do is settle down enough to just sit
in my lap! Is that so hard?" Suddenly I saw my relationship with God
being reflected in this strange cycle. As I am walk with God, I become
easily distracted. Fears like meeting deadlines, letting people down,
and not reaching Christ's standard plague my thoughts and life. Then,
quietly through my self-made frantics, I hear a calm Voice saying, "Be
still. Stop and know that I am your God."

Just like I wanted my cat to calm down and rest in my lap, God is
speaking to your heart and asking you to trustingly rest in His arms.
Won't you be still?

~ Sarah Miller

Best Friends Forever

… He is not far from each one of us… - Acts 17:27 NKJV

Becca was my best friend throughout most of my childhood. As little girls, our dollies had most of our conversations for us. When we grew older, our chats turned into hours of suppressed giggles late at night during our beloved slumber parties. We were convinced that nothing could ever separate us; we would be best friends forever.

When I was ten, my family moved across the country. Our parents expected us to make new friends and move on, but Becca and I resolved that we wouldn't let something as trivial as a couple thousand miles make any difference in our friendship. Several times each day we would call each other, talking and laughing until someone else needed the phone. Besides our marathon phone conversations, we constantly emailed and even sent the occasional letter. Now, I can't even remember what we discussed—just that we kept up with the little things that made up our everyday lives, and it paid off. When I saw her nine months later, it was as if we had never been separated.

Eventually, though, the inevitable happened. Slowly and imperceptibly, our calls got less frequent. Our letters stopped. We no longer spent time together, and our close bond dissolved. Becca and I haven't talked in years now, and I don't really know her anymore.

It's the same way with God, my Best Friend. I can talk to Him in prayer anytime I want to, without racking up a long-distance phone bill. I can read His letters to me in the Bible. The more I spend time with Him, the closer we become. But if I neglect our relationship, it will finally dissolve, like my friendship with Becca. It's important to stay close to God now, so that when He takes me home, it will simply be a continuation of the friendship we already have.

~ Saraiah Turnbull

Love that Never Fails

I will never leave you nor forsake you. - Hebrews 13:5 NKJV

"You're the princess and I'm the superhero, and I will rescue you!"

"Why do I have to be the princess?" I whined, "If I have to be the princess, I wanna be a ninja warrior princess!"

"No way! You're a girl! You have to go sit by that tree and sing to the mice."

This conversation pretty much sums up my childhood experience. I wanted to be the hero, but society demanded that I "be the princess and sing to the mice." I hated all of it. I didn't want to be the weak one, in need of a rescuer. Where I live, men view women as decorations, on display for their personal enjoyment, with no rights of their own. It's a very male-based society. I remember one time in particular when I saw a little gypsy girl being beaten by an older boy on the street. I ripped the child from his grip and told him to go away. But to my dismay, he didn't back down. Instead, he stepped closer, threatening me. In my anger and fear I pulled out my pepper spray, attempting to intimidate him while giving him a verbal beating until he finally slunk away. I was always the tough one—I hated feeling helpless. But soon pepper spray was traded for knives, and words substituted for fists. I began fighting gangs in alleyways. All my time was spent in training myself in kick-boxing, martial arts, and sword fighting.

When I arrived at Fountainview Academy a few years later, I was surprised by the joy everyone had. Happiness wasn't something I was used to. I had been expecting to be judged and condemned by these "perfect" Christians. But it was just the opposite. They accepted me into the family as a sister in Christ. What impacted me the most was hearing their prayers. They spoke as if God was right there with them, not for a distant, uncaring God. I slowly realized that He was there, He's always there, and He's not going anywhere. I am a princess! I'm God's daughter and He will always love me. No matter how far I run, I can never run away from His unconditional love. Now I have stopped fighting the way I used to, and instead "fight the good fight of faith" (1 Timothy 6:12 KJV).

~ Moriah Mays

Forgiveness

If we confess our sins, he is faithful and just to forgive us our sins, and to cleanse us from all unrighteousness. - 1 John 1:9 KJV

Holly was fourteen years old when she spent part of her summer in Saskatchewan with her aunt and uncle. She desperately wanted to learn how to drive standard, so her uncle George decided he would take her out around the farm to teach her. Holly was having fun learning to drive, and her uncle George was very proud of her. After a little while she started feeling more comfortable with her new ability. One particular day, as Holly was trying to shift into another gear, she wasn't paying attention to steering or her uncle, and she crashed right into the side of the barn. She was horrified, felt awful, and couldn't think of what to say. Uncle George started laughing, turned his head towards Holly, and said, "OK, you can park here." She couldn't believe it: even though she had just put a hole in the side of his barn and dented the front of his truck, he forgave her and wasn't angry at all.

We go through life asking God to teach us and help us through our experiences. We feel like everything is going well until we suddenly mess up big time. I always expect God to look down from Heaven and tell me how stupid my mistake was. Instead, if I ask for His forgiveness, He comforts me and helps me grow from the experience. He wants us to truly repent; then He forgives us for our sins and forgets all about them.

~ Raina Walker

Willing or Stubborn?

*… know thou the God of thy father, and serve him with a perfect heart
and with a willing mind: for … if thou seek him, he will be found of
thee, but if thou forsake him, he will cast thee off…*
- 1 Chronicles 28:9 KJV

My mom loves horses. Once, while looking for another horse
to buy, she came across an ad in the newspaper for an untrained
broodmare. Thinking that she could train it herself, my mom bought
her. Soon it became apparent that Marcy needed more than a little
fine-tuning. Whenever a bit was placed in her mouth, she would fight
it with kicking, bucking, and cantering. Putting the saddle on her was
even worse. She was unsafe to ride, and eventually we sold her; she
was untrained, uncompromising, and stubborn. On the other hand, my
absolute favorite horse to ride was our pony Flicka. If I got a running
start, I could jump up onto her back without her even flinching. We
would gallop around the rolling hills and fields of my farm as one unit.
I adored her because of her willingness to go where I wanted to go
and do whatever I wanted to do. I had same measure of love for Flicka
as I had disgust towards Marcy, whom I hated to ride. She stubbornly
followed her own way, made her own trails, and did her own thing.
Unfortunately, I often find myself acting like Marcy. As soon as I feel
the Holy Spirit tightening the reins of my conscience, I begin to do all
sorts of irrational things to buck Him off my back. My heart is filled with
rebellion. But if I instead allow Christ to be the rider, He and I are able
to work together as one person. He knows the trails better than I do,
and He knows what beautiful things we can do together if I am only
willing to be taught by Him.

God knows that the only way you will be truly happy is by
submitting to Him; that is how He made you. Right now He is asking
for you to let Him come into your heart and take the reins. He allows
you to decide whether your heart will be willing or stubborn.

~ Sarah Miller

Sweet Pea

And the great dragon was cast out, that old serpent, called the Devil, and Satan, which deceiveth the whole world. - Revelation 12:9a KJV

Lucifer was a favorite in heaven—dearly loved of God. Unfortunately, he became discontented with his position and started hurting other angels with his lies. The only way God could keep the angels safe and happy was to cast Lucifer from his home to Earth. This tragedy was vividly portrayed to me when I was raising my own chickens.

Sweet Pea was my favorite chick. He was the one that would sit on my lap and eat from my hand, and I could always count on him to come to the fence and greet me. After about four months, I began to notice that three of my chicks were growing larger combs and wattles than the others. I guessed that they were probably roosters, and sure enough, three months later they started crowing. The first rooster to crow was my special Sweet Pea. Unfortunately, Sweet Pea started to loose his sweetness. As soon as he saw another rooster, his feathers went up and he charged. One day, Mom went to my chicken house and found one of the roosters dead. Apparently, my little "sweet" rooster had kept another rooster out of the barn where the shade and water were. I decided to give the third rooster away, so that Sweet Pea wouldn't kill him too. With the other roosters gone, I thought Sweet Pea would return to his old sweet self, but instead he turned his wrath on the hens. After seeing him pull out their feathers and make them miserable, I was forced to put him in a cage.

Because Lucifer, now called Satan, let self-centeredness take the place of God in his heart, he destroys everything and everyone else under his control. We have all fallen under his power; but if we choose to let God put His others-centered love in our hearts, we will be free from Satan's grasp.

~ Bethany Corrigan

Give Thanks

In every thing give thanks: for this is the will of God in Christ Jesus concerning you. - 1 Thessalonians 5:18 KJV

In this verse, Paul tells us to give thanks in everything. This means not only when things are going well but also when nothing seems to be turning out right.

My family lives on a farm, and the water in our house comes from a well at the bottom of our field. This means that the water is pumped up the hill to our water buildings, and then another pump sends it two hundred feet up to our house. A few days ago, the pump nearest our house failed, leaving us without running water. Because of this, we had to drive five minutes to fill water bottles several times a day for cooking, dishes, and drinking. The creek next to our home had not frozen yet, and so we hauled buckets of water from there to use to flush the toilets. Although this took a lot of extra time and energy, we were thankful for the fact that we usually have running water.

When I found out this morning, however, that it would be at least a week before the pump was fixed, I was tempted to be frustrated and upset. It took a little bit of creativity to think of something to be thankful for. After thinking a few seconds, I thought, "We have electricity, which means we can still do some cleaning and cooking." After I thanked God for our electricity, I was no longer upset about our water situation. I was content, realizing that I was blessed beyond so many others on this earth. I also saw that I could be thankful for the lack of water itself because it gave me an opportunity to learn to trust God's wisdom no matter what!

Cultivate the habit of thankfulness. No matter how bad things are going, or how discouraged we are, being thankful for the blessings God gives us will never fail to lift our spirits.

~ Aileen Corrigan

Stop the Bleeding!

O Lord, heal me... - Psalm 6:2 NKJV

Suddenly a stream of blood poured out of my nose as I walked down the hallway. Adrenaline rushed through my body as I leaped for the bathroom door. I hunched over the sink, shaking, as I cried out for help. This was no normal nosebleed. I would stand over the sink for at least an hour before having to return to the ER. This was not the first time, and unfortunately this wouldn't be the last time I would get such a nosebleed.

The doctors tried their best to solve the external problem, yet with no success. I returned nine times to the ER before I was referred to a specialist. How that finally happened was only by God's grace. The last time I returned to the hospital with another nosebleed, the doctor who was on call had to leave. Another certified doctor, who was on break, came in for just ten minutes to check on me. Thankfully, I had come just in time to have this knowledgeable doctor look at me. She looked me over and within a minute she said, "I think there is a deeper problem. This is not just some normal nosebleed; you need to see a specialist at once." When I saw the specialist, he informed me that I had a tumor that was growing rapidly, and that if it was not surgically removed, it could be life-threatening. He said that I was lucky I had repeated nosebleeds, because most people are diagnosed after it is too late to perform surgery.

I hated having nosebleeds; I could not understand why God didn't stop the bleeding. But He knows my body better than any doctor does, and He could see the deeper problem. He knew what needed to happen for my situation to be resolved. Sometimes what seems like a curse to us is actually our greatest blessing. Only by the grace of God am I still living today. Even though I may not always understand His plans, I know that I must trust His leading.

~ Esra Eliasson

Seeing the Invisible

For ever since the world was created, people have seen the earth and sky. Through everything God made, they can clearly see His invisible qualities—His eternal power and divine nature. So they have no excuse for not knowing God. - Romans 1:20 NLT

Whoosh—the wind blew by the window rustling the bushes outside. The stalks of corn swayed back and forth while the leaves floated off the trees. The birds just sat there, hoping it would die down soon so they could fly. The streams of air had been blowing hard, on and off for four days. Sometimes it would be a nice warm summer wind with sunshine, and other times it would be a cold fall wind with rain. But either way, it was windy.

I really enjoy watching the wind as it blows by. Up, down, back and forth; it always keeps my interest. Not being able to see the air actually holds my attention even more. You can see the tall grass moving, but you can never see what is moving it. Even though we can't see the wind, we would never deny that it exists. The evidence is in the pressure we feel on our body and in the movement we see in the things around us.

God is often thought of in the opposite way. People often will say, "How can you believe in something you cannot see?" But when you think of the wind, it is actually quite easy to understand. With God, you and others around you can see Him just like you can see the wind. It is true that we cannot physically see Him, but we can often see what He is doing in our own and others' lives. If we are not looking to see the wind, we will not notice it; but if we pay close attention, we will see the amazing changes taking place in the area around us and in our lives. I know that when I look more closely, I can notice the changes God is making. I encourage you to look more closely and see if you can catch a glimpse of the amazing things God is changing in and around you.

~ Rebecca Hall

A Big Violin

*Now there are varieties of gifts, but the same Spirit; and there are
varieties of service, but the same Lord... - 1 Corinthians 12:4–5 ESV*

I'm a violist in the Fountainview Academy orchestra, and I have
played many concerts with the group. After these concerts, I am
sometimes asked what instrument I play. The conversation goes
something like this:

"I play the viola," I tell the inquirer.
"Oh, the viola. That's just a big violin, right?"
"Um, sort of. Yeah, it plays lower than a violin."
"Oh, cool," they invariably reply in a feeble attempt at sincerity.

Many people have little clue as to what the viola is and what value
it adds to the orchestra. Sometimes I ask myself, *If no one even
knows what the viola is, how can it be useful?* But the viola, like each
instrument in the orchestra, is an integral part of the chord structure.

I'm sometimes discouraged trying to discern God's plan for my life.
It can be frustrating to see the recognition of the cellos and violins, and
feel stuck in the middle as a virtual unknown. But the reality is that God
needs people in the middle. For beautiful harmony, you can't have just
a top and a bottom note! You need an intermediate tone to support the
other pitches. Paul writes, "... just as the body is one and has many
members, and all the members of the body ... are one body, so it is
with Christ. For in one Spirit we were all baptized into one body—Jews
or Greeks, slaves or free—and all were made to drink of one Spirit.
For the body does not consist of one member but of many. If the foot
should say, 'Because I am not a hand, I do not belong to the body,'
that would not make it any less a part of the body ... If all were a single
member, where would the body be?" (1 Corinthians 12:12–19 ESV).
God calls some people to be noticeable violins; but He calls others to
the equally vital work of adding harmony and support to the Christian
church. Each of us is 100% necessary—the beauty of a spiritual chord
depends on each instrument playing its part. God needs you, no
matter what your talents. Won't you play your part for His work?

~ Michael Jensen

Lucky Pete and Lucky Me, Part 1

… You shall be called by a new name, which the mouth of the Lord will name. - Isaiah 62:2 NKJV

One Sunday evening, my mom was in the garden weeding when a wet shaggy dog trotted up to her. The dog looked like a stray but didn't bark at mom or try to harm her in any way. He just stayed close to her.

"Go home, puppy dog," my mom coaxed, but the dog refused to leave. My mom walked around our neighborhood to see if the dog belonged to any of our neighbors. The dog stayed right beside her as she went to each of the neighbors' houses. None of the neighbors or the farmers living nearby had seen the dog before. When my dad got home from work, we begged him to let us keep the dog.

"Well, if we can't find his owner, then we can keep him," my dad promised. The next day, my dad sent advertisements to the radio and Humane Society.

For the next few days, we prayed and hoped that we would get to keep the dog. We took him to the vet, bought dog food for him, and even started to think of a name for him. However, on Thursday, my dad got a phone call. Someone was coming to see if this was his dog. When the man arrived and saw the dog, it was obvious that the dog was his. He said that the dog's real name was Pete.

"Would you be willing to sell Pete to us?" questioned my dad.
"Well," drawled the man, "I can see that Pete would have a good home here. I will give Pete to you." We were all so ecstatic and decided to rename the dog Lucky.

When Pete changed owners, he received a new name. When we become Christ's, we "change owners." We also are promised a new name that God Himself has chosen, and it will be given to us when we get to heaven. It is so cool to think that, when we become His children, He gives us a new name, a new life, a new identity. Don't you want to become His and receive a new name?

~ Kami Rose

Lucky Pete and Lucky Me, Part 2

The steps of a good man are ordered by the Lord, and He delights in his way. Though he fall, he shall not be utterly cast down; for the Lord upholds him with His hand. - Psalm 37:23–24 NKJV

Early one morning, after Lucky became ours, I heard the front door open and close. A moment later, I heard someone whistle and say, "Come on, Lucky." I tiptoed to the window and saw my dad walking briskly down the driveway with Lucky racing beside him. When Dad got back from his morning walk, he told us how excited Lucky was to be going for a walk. That evening, my dad took Lucky for another walk. Over the next couple days, as I would see Dad and Lucky go for walks in the morning and evening, I saw how Dad and Lucky became closer. Lucky would obey all of my dad's commands because he wanted to please my dad. Now my dad doesn't have to say anything; Lucky will start running down the driveway when he sees dad come out the door. During their walks, if they come to a "Y" in the trail, Lucky will wait to see what direction my dad points him in. Once he knows, he will rush ahead, but he will always look back to make sure my dad is following him.

I want to be more like Lucky: eager to go for my morning and evening walks with my Master. I want to give up self and be like Lucky: willing to do anything to please my heavenly Father. As Lucky and my dad spend more time together, their relationship grows. Lucky's trust in my dad grows, and he becomes even more willing to do what my dad asks of him, even if he does not yet understand why. In the same way, when I spend more and more time with Jesus through my devotions, my relationship grows. My trust in Him increases and my strongest desire is to please Him. I will want to do anything for Him even if I do not understand why. My dad won't ever ask Lucky to do something that will hurt him; and neither will God ask me to do anything that will, in the long run, cause me pain. When I come to a "Y" in my life, I can look to God to show me the direction I am to go. Don't you want to become like Lucky as well? It will be the best decision you have ever made.

~ Kami Rose

Obese

Come unto me, all ye that labor and are heavy laden, and I will give you rest. - Matthew 11:28 KJV

In November 2011, state officials removed an eight-year-old boy from his home and took him into the custody of the state because he weighed over 200 pounds. Government officials believed that the parents' inability to control their son's extremely unhealthy lifestyle was abusive and should be handled accordingly. The boy, from Cuyahoga County, Ohio, has been placed in foster care. At his weight, he is considered at risk of developing diseases such as diabetes and high blood pressure. In order to remedy his situation, he needed to be moved from the environment he had been raised in. He needed a new life.

I don't suffer from physical obesity or struggle with any eating habits like that boy did, but I do have a struggle with being weighed down and overwhelmed with the cares of this world. Occasionally, I have become so discouraged with sin that I wonder if I can go on. The burden is so heavy! I am obese with sin! Like that boy, the more sin I commit and the more I reject Jesus, the fatter I get. However, Jesus wants to rescue me from this world and give me a new life. He wants to come in, take me out of Satan's custody, and place me in His own loving and redemptive care. He wants to remove my sinful weight, and He has promised me that His yoke is easy and His burden is light. He is waiting for me to let Him take away this obesity so He can give me a new life. He's waiting for you, too. Why not give Him permission to remove the excess weight you are carrying?

~ Esra Eliasson

Rolling on a Rockslide

And we know that God causes all things to work together for good to those who love God, to those who are called according to His purpose. - Romans 8:28 NASB

Oh good! It's a rockslide chute—these are so fun! I smiled. My smile was thrust off my face by a frown though, as my sprained ankle groaned in pain. *I can't run down the chute; I'll have to be careful.*

As I carefully made my way down the rockslide, I soon found myself in the back of the group with two of my friends. While hopping down a steep part, I felt myself beginning to fall. Quickly, I dipped my shoulder, hoping to avoid face-planting. Seconds later, I found myself sitting up after rolling. The world was spinning as my friends hurried over to see if I was okay. While I was shaken and scraped up, my head and neck were uninjured. Although I was thankful for not being majorly harmed at the time, it wasn't until later that I realized how badly I really could have been hurt. What if I hadn't had a sprained ankle, which prevented me from running down the rockslide chute like I normally do? It could have been more than just a forward roll on pointy rocks; it could have been more than just bruises and cuts.

While my injured ankle has been very frustrating and a trial to deal with, I think it has in fact protected me greatly and worked out for good. Actually, every one of the trials I experience works for good. When we are surrendered to God, everything that comes our way will be under Gods' control, and be the best for us. If we could see the end from the beginning, we would want exactly what God ordains. While I wasn't thankful for it at the time, I am now very thankful for my sprained ankle. I want to do better, though. I want to be thankful for every one of my trials even when I don't understand what good they are and why they happened. I choose to be thankful.

~ Katie Sloop

A Wall of Protection

He shall cover you with His feathers, and under His wings you shall take refuge; His truth shall be your shield and buckler.
- Psalms 91:4 NKJV

My mom, my brother and I usually go to church on Friday night. Once when we were running late, we decided to take a taxi to avoid the traffic jams. The driver realized that we were in hurry, and that caused him to drive really fast. My mom noticed that it might be dangerous for us to sit by ourselves, so she told us to sit close to her and put the seatbelt on. (In Korea, we don't have to put the seatbelt on when we're in the back seat.) I was too small to put a seatbelt on, so I sat as close to my mom as possible. But my brother didn't even try to listen to her. Instead of putting his seatbelt on, he sat far away from us, leaned on the window, and he fell asleep without thinking of how my mom was worrying about him and trying to help him sit in a safer position.

We were passing many cars that were blocking our way. When the traffic light turned red, our taxi stopped on the line, which was on the biggest crossroad in our city. While we were waiting for the traffic light to turn green, we were watching the cars that were passing in front of us. Soon enough, the traffic light turned green, and our taxi started to move very fast. All of the sudden, SCREEEEECH and then CRAAASH! A truck smashed into the front part of our taxi. It quivered like an earthquake, and I almost flew out of the car. Fortunately, my mom covered me with her body, so she could keep me safe. But my brother got hurt by breaking the glass window with his head. My mom couldn't protect him because he put himself too far from her.

When we are in danger, God reaches out to help and protect us. Like a sheep that doesn't listen to his shepherd will be in danger, we also won't be safe if we refuse God's help and chose to live without Him. Let God be close to you so that whenever you are in trials and danger, He will protect you under His wings.

~ Hannah Lee

Bull Riding

*… Work hard for sin your whole life and your pension is death. But
God's gift is real life, eternal life, delivered by Jesus, our Master.*
- Romans 6:22–23 MSG

He prepared to face the next eight seconds of his life. Sitting atop
an angry bull, misgivings and second thoughts began to crowd his
mind, but he shoved them aside in favor of the adrenaline rush he
knew would follow. Prosperity, fertility, and mobility were all about to be
jeopardized for mere seconds of pleasure, but he decided that it was
worth it.

Lying in the hospital bed, he began to change his mind. The ride
was fun—while it lasted. But it definitely wasn't worth it. One moment
he was a strong, healthy man; the next, a crumpled heap of broken
bones. This had never happened before! *What had gone wrong?* At
first it had seemed pretty harmless: only a few bruises here and there,
with no major injuries. But he was riding on fate, counting on his own
ability, and forgetting that the very basis of the sport—the bull—was
dangerous.

Sin is much like bull riding. Bull riders sometimes receive prize
money for their exploits, but that money can never fully compensate
for the permanent impairments that the rider too often receives.
Similarly, sin may appear worthwhile and profitable, but it *never* pays
off. Like bull riding, sin is enticingly "fun;" but it jeopardizes spiritual
well being for a brief adrenaline rush, leaving its participants battered,
bruised, crushed or dead. In the end, it's not worth it. No matter how
enticing or harmless sin may appear, true fulfillment and joy come
only from obedience to God. Only with His strength can we conquer
the deadly allurement of sin. But when we do, God will reward us with
something boundlessly greater than sin's "prize money;" He will give
us eternal life.

~ Michael Jensen

Stumble

Thy word is a lamp unto my feet, and a light unto my path.
- Psalm 119:105 KJV

I stumbled along my way, grabbing through the air trying to find something to hold onto. The cave was pitch black, and I was enshrouded in darkness. I could feel the cold fingers clasping around me in a tight fist. I painfully inched along the ground, now on all fours. Finally, I saw a distant light slowly emerging around the bend. I immediately stood up and picked up my pace. As I came closer, the way became brighter and easier to see. Eventually, I arrived at the mouth of the cave. Once outside, I found myself on the edge of a tall cliff overlooking a bright blue body of water. It was breathtaking. I looked back into the cave behind me. *The struggle was so worth it*, I thought to myself.

Before long, I decided it was time to head back through the cave to where I came from. I slowly picked my way through and among the rocks littering the bottom of the cave. As I continued on my journey, a strange phenomenon occurred to me. It wasn't pitch black. I looked at my feet, and I could clearly see the ground I stood on. This same area had been engulfed in total darkness on the way in, but on the way out it was illuminated by the light behind me. When I turned around, facing toward the water, it was pitch black. I could see absolutely nothing. However, looking the other way, I could see where I had been, the rocks I had stumbled upon, and the walls I held onto.

As we walk on the straight and narrow path, we stumble through what seems to be darkness. We wonder why God would let us struggle through these impossible trials. However, when we look back, we will be able to see God's gentle light guiding us through. What may cause us to stumble now will only cause us to praise His name once we are through.

~ Mason Neil

Character Blind

When Jesus spoke again to the people, he said, "I am the light of the world. Whoever follows me will never walk in darkness, but will have the light of life." - John 8:12 NIV

There are more than 5,000 Chinese characters, but in China we only need 300 of them to depict our daily conversations. I have been seriously studying these characters since I was in grade one. Every day the teacher would teach several new characters to us in Chinese class and let us write each of them ten times for homework so that we would remember them.

I used to think that every Chinese person knew how to read and write Chinese, but my mom told me something that surprised me: there were a lot of people in the country who, because they were poor, couldn't send their children to school. When those children grew up, they could only become farmers or get a low-paying job. Such jobs don't require workers to be able to read or write, and we say that those people are character blind (illiterate).

But, praise the Lord, the government began to set up schools in the countryside and started a policy called "Compulsory Education," which means that all the children must go to school. The government would pay for them to be educated from primary school to middle school. The people who are character blind are becoming fewer; now more Chinese people know how to read and write, and they have a better life.

Today, there are still a lot of people who don't know what Christ looks like; they too are character blind. They still think they can have a better life with the temporary riches and pleasures of this world. But, in their hearts, they feel so empty and full of darkness.

When we are willing to learn in the school of Christ, our character will become more like His. As others see His character in us, their character blindness will vanish.

~ Bryan Chen

Red Handed, Part 1

*And they heard the sound of the Lord God walking in the garden in
the cool of the day, and Adam and his wife hid themselves from the
presence of the Lord God among the trees of the garden.*
- Genesis 3:8 NKJV

Panic swelled up in my throat, and uneasiness tormented me
like a vulture waiting for a dying animal to collapse. It all started
when I spotted a rock while walking around my family's property. The
rock, though, didn't catch my attention because it was appealing. It
was actually rather dull looking, but it gave me the brilliant idea of
painting it gold. The only paint color I could find, however, was red,
and after bringing it to my rock I realized I didn't have a paintbrush.
I was obviously not prepared, but I was on a mission, so I decided
to use my hands instead. It was kindergarten all over again. When I
became satisfied with my work, the thought, "you're not suppose to
be playing with Daddy's things" hit me. I trembled at that thought; so I
frantically went and got a bucket of water to wash my hands, and I hid
the rock. When I looked down after washing my hands, to my surprise,
they were still red. I thought maybe I didn't scrub hard enough; so I
scrubbed harder, but to no avail. At that moment, I started panicking
because I realized I must have used permanent paint. Then suddenly,
in the corner of my eye, I saw someone approaching.

Eve had a similar story to mine. She was just roaming around the
Garden of Eden when she became distracted by an innocent-looking
tree called the tree of the knowledge of good and evil. As a result, she
got both her and her husband into a fruity mess. I imagine them hiding
the fruit when they realized what they had done, just like how I tried
scrubbing the paint off my hands to remove all evidence that I was
guilty. The fact that we hide them, though, doesn't mean our mistakes
were cleaned away. By ourselves, we cannot erase the mistakes we
have made. Lucky for us, God promised Adam and Eve that He would
send Someone who would clean up our mess.

~ Shenel Cruz

Red Handed, Part 2

If we confess our sins, He is faithful and just to forgive us our sins and to cleanse us from all unrighteousness. - 1 John 1:9 NKJV

"Oh no! Someone is coming! Pretend you're playing with the water, Shenel," the voice in my head instructed me. As the person slowly passed by, my heart started to relax, but my hands were still as red as a cherry. I tried scrubbing them even harder, but nothing worked. Desperate, I began to cry, ready to surrender, because I knew I had to tell my dad or I was going to be red handed for the rest of my life. I ran into my house crying more and more with each step. The first person I saw was my sister. And when she saw my hands she started screaming and crying because she thought I cut myself and that my hands were bleeding. Lucky for me, her reaction was enough to bring my dad into the picture. I don't really know what he said when he saw me, but I do remember that he brought me to the sink. He tried scrubbing it, but of course it didn't work. Then he teasingly told me, "To get rid of the red paint, I will have to cut off both of your hands." Worry was written all over my face by this time. Just then my auntie came and saw all the commotion. She asked what was happening, and my dad told her I had painted my hands red. Her reply was music in my ears. She said, "Oh, I have paint remover; come with me, Shenel." Following her, I watched as she poured the remover over my red hands. What a relief it was to see the paint run off and have my hands clean again!

To me, the feeling of being released from the bondage of that red paint is like the feeling of being freed from the sins I have committed. This story to me never held the lesson of redemption, but now it does. That paint remover to me is like Christ's blood, which washes away my sins. Yet, Christ will not wash away our sins unless we ask Him to. He doesn't force us. He gives us the freedom to choose, and He lovingly offers His forgiveness. He is waiting for us to come to Him. I personally want to accept that offer. How about you?

~ Shenel Cruz

Painful Prejudice

He was despised, and rejected of men ... He was despised; and we esteemed Him not. - Isaiah 53:3 ASV

When I was six years old, my mom remarried. I had known Chad for as long as I could remember. He talked to me, played games with me, and went on walks with me. I loved him. But once he married my mom, something changed. In my mind, he morphed into an evil monster: a stepdad. He still treated me with love, but I never noticed. I became so blinded by my prejudice against him that I didn't see his kindness. For years, I hated him.

When I was thirteen, I realized that everyone I knew liked Chad, except me. I convinced myself that they were all misled about who he was, but I wanted to prove in my own mind exactly what it was that made him such a monster. I racked my brain, but I couldn't think of any arguments strong enough to even convince myself. I decided to study him carefully, so I could catch him red-handed in something that would prove him evil. But no matter how hard I watched him, I found nothing incriminating. In fact, I started to notice all the little acts of kindness he did for me, and how much he loved our family, including me. I was shocked. Slowly, the wall of prejudice I had built came crumbling down. Looking back, I can see that I robbed myself and my entire family of happiness and closeness. If I had given Chad a chance, I could have gained another loving father much earlier.

My story is nothing new. When Christ was here on earth, living a blameless life for everyone to see, His own people rejected Him. All too often I see people building walls of prejudice against the One who loves them most. I robbed myself of a few years of happiness with my family; but when we reject Christ, we rob ourselves of an eternity with Him. We can avoid so much needless pain if we never let the walls of prejudice go up in the first place.

~ Saraiah Turnbull

The Hanging

But as many as received Him, to them gave He power to become the sons of God, even to them that believe on His name. - John 1:12 KJV

I argued viciously and cruelly, defending my opinion with such energy and violence that I was more than committed. I had just voluntarily tied a noose around my neck. If I was wrong, then not only would I look like the greatest fool ever to grace the planet, but my credibility as an intelligent human being would evaporate. The probability of my opinion being incorrect, however, hardly crossed my mind. Me, wrong? Impossible! But I was.

It's amazing how willingly I risked my neck for my opinion. I was so self-confident that I hardly considered the option of being mistaken. Even when the trapdoor fell from under my feet, I refused to admit that I was hanging from a rope that was strangling me. To concede to my true position would have been to admit failure. Though opening my mind might have saved my reputation, I remained stubborn.

Two thousand years ago, when Jesus came to give His life for the redemption of humanity, He was rejected by the very priests who professed to worship Him. They argued with Christ, climbing the gallows from which they would soon fall. Even when Jesus lovingly warned them of their mistakes, they deafened themselves to His mercy. "Me, wrong!?" they thought. "Impossible!" When the trapdoor fell from under their feet, they still clung to their false opinions, leading the entire nation of Israel to deny their Redeemer.

To be honest, I don't believe that I would have been much different than the religious leaders of Christ's time. Based on how foolishly I have defended my faulty opinions in the past, can I imagine that I would have acted differently when it came to accepting Jesus' radical message? There's not a chance! What about you? If God calls you to some difficult task, or asks you to give up some cherished sin in your life, will you heed His call? Or will you argue with Him like the religious leaders of Israel, sealing your fate? Are you prejudiced against God's calling? Are you biased against the Truth that will set you free?

~ Michael Jensen

Be Ready

*… if you do not wake up … you will not know at what hour I will come
to you. - Revelation 3:3 NASB*

Always be prepared. It started out as a normal day with the typical
busyness of work and school. After a delicious breakfast (it was
too short!), I practiced cello and headed off to work. This particular
morning, I was assigned to work in the "tech" department, closely
affiliated with Fountainview Productions. I sat down in the office with
my laptop and a good friend, and commenced my daily labor on a
new website. Both of us happen to be amateur radio operators, and
carry our radios everywhere we go: for fun and to be prepared for
emergencies. We left the radio on in the office just in case anyone
needed to contact us. Partway through the morning, the radio came
alive: "This is KK4DSL/VE7. I have an emergency." Within seconds,
we had several staff and students mobilized and at the scene of a
car accident not too far away. Because my friend and I came to work
prepared with our radios, we were ready and able to assist in this
unexpected emergency.

We need to be prepared for Jesus' second coming. Through Bible
prophecy, we know that He is coming soon. In the book of Revelation,
He tells us that we won't know the exact time of His return and
must be prepared: not with material assets like radios, but with an
unfaltering relationship with our Creator. In addition to this relationship,
God calls us to spread the word of His soon return to the whole world.
When Jesus comes in the clouds of glory, He desires that everyone be
prepared and "mobilized" to meet Him in the air. Just as emergencies
come at unexpected times, Jesus is coming at an unknown time; let's
be ready!

~ Christian Welch

No Deceit

Blessed is the man … in whose spirit there is no deceit.
- Psalm 32:2 ESV

"Can we take her to the vet?" I begged Mom.

"Let's try one more thing. If this doesn't help, we'll take her tomorrow." Our little toy poodle, Amiga, was very sick. She had been acting strangely the last several days, and today she was much worse. She was usually very agile, climbing the stairs, jumping on and off the chairs, and playing with her toys; but today she couldn't even walk around without our help. She would not eat or drink anything and was clearly miserable.

Mom's idea sounded strange, but we decided to go ahead with it. We had been doing everything for Amiga and treating her like a little baby, but Mom wanted us to see what would happen if we ignored her. We set her on a little bed we had made for her and left her there alone. At first she whined and cried, begging us to come and get her, but Mom told us to let her go a little longer. After a couple of hours, she jumped off the chair, ran across the room, and sprang onto the couch! We couldn't believe it! Could Amiga really be making her sickness up? She began eating and drinking and playing as usual, and by the end of the day it was obvious: Amiga didn't think she was getting enough attention, so she had found a way to get more!

As crazy as this incident seems, I think I do the same thing. I use deception to gain my way and to make things easier. I need to ask myself, "Am I really too tired to help my sister with her project?" "Do I really need to eat right away?" "Can I really justify taking sick time off school and work?" In Revelation 14:5, God's saints are described as having no deceit in their mouths. I want to be one of those people; don't you? May God give us the grace to be fully truthful in all aspects of our lives.

~ Aileen Corrigan

Search and Rescue

For thus saith the Lord God; Behold, I, even I, will both search my
sheep, and seek them out. - Ezekiel 34:11 KJV

Imagine you are kayaking on the Pacific Ocean in the tourist town
of Sitka, Alaska. It's like a dream... until it starts to rain. Rain is not
uncommon in Sitka, where they get an average of 86 inches per year.
At first you may have a beautiful day, but soon the weather starts
getting worse. The rain becomes a deluge and the waves whip around
you. The current is too strong and your tiny boat flips and is lost to
sight.

This is where my dad and the Sitka Mountain Rescue team come
into the picture. In no time, boats are out searching for you. Messages
are flying back and forth between radios and the IC (incident
command) center. It may take minutes, hours, or even days to find
you; but rest assured, they will. When they find you, they will give you
the medical attention you need and make sure you are warm and safe
and back to where you belong. These people are all volunteers, and
the association relies on donations to survive. Groups like these are
all over the world, working hard to make sure people in danger will be
rescued and safe.

God is also in the business of search and rescue. Sometimes I get
lost in the storm of life, and all the temptations get so strong that I flip.
But, with one prayer to God, He will come to my aid. God is my creator
and He loves me. He never had to rescue me from Satan and sin, but
He freely volunteered because He cares for me so much that, "... He
gave His only begotten Son, that whosoever believeth in Him should
not perish, but have everlasting life" (John 3:16 KJV). Though I might
try, I can never repay all that He does for me. And He will not rest until
He has found me and brought me safely home.

~ Sarah Wahlman

Beholding the Change

… it has not yet been revealed what we shall be, but we know that when He is revealed, we shall be like Him… everyone who has this hope in Him purifies himself, just as He is pure. - 1 John 3:2–3 NKJV

All my life, my main playmate has been my sister, Megan. As we matured, we found new ways to get under each other's skin. Megan would snap, and I would antagonize. Overall, we were still close, but our different personalities created conflict.

Megan left home at the start of her junior year to attend Fountainview Academy in British Columbia, and honestly I thought it wasn't such a bad idea. I would have more time for myself (not including the time spent doing her chores), and I wouldn't have her irritating me. But after a while, that changed. I realized how much we actually did together, and I started to miss her.

When Megan came back home for break, I could tell something was different. Not only did she not snap, but she was also very kind and patient. To test her, I purposely did irritating things to see just how much she had changed, and time after time I was amazed! She really had become a different person, and I saw in her something that I wanted.

At school, Megan was surrounded by a Godly atmosphere. What I saw in her was a reflection of a different way of life. I was puzzled at first, and I tried to achieve the peaceful results of the happiness she had found. Over and over, I attempted to be like her, but I couldn't—I was doing it the wrong way. In my warped view of reaching goals, I thought that I could do everything on my own. The joy that Megan had found was only attained by having a personal relationship with Jesus, and I couldn't get it by acting like Megan. A friend, Randy Folkenberg, once said, "You can never exceed your source of inspiration." This is so true! I had to look beyond the things that I was trying to copy in order to see Who it was that I really needed. Only then, by looking to the original example—Jesus—could I find that true happiness and fulfillment.

~ Morgan Metcalf

Endless Retreat

… Eye hath not seen, nor ear heard, neither have entered into the heart of man, the things which God hath prepared for them that love him. - 1 Corinthians 2:9 KJV

"Pack your bags, we're going somewhere special for the weekend," announced Dad.

Immediately, our questions started firing. "Where are we going? What should we pack? Is it far?"

"Wait!" Dad smiled. I'm not going to tell you where we are going. You will have to wait and see. Just pack three days' worth of warm and comfortable clothing, and don't forget your hiking shoes."

As we drove, our excitement increased. Pictures of where we might be going to stay ran through my mind and our conversations. But upon pulling into the driveway, the cabin we saw was better than I could have imagined. The high, peaked roof, log walls, and sprawling veranda were beautiful. The down quilts and fluffy pillows encouraged ample rest. The time we spent there, traversing the miles and miles of trails, was invigorating. I couldn't believe how much better it was than I had envisioned.

We are going somewhere special very soon—that place is Heaven. As I think about Heaven, I see in my mind the amazing beauty, the wonderful friends, and Jesus, whom we have been longing to see for so long. I try to grasp the beauty, and just as soon as I think I understand what it is going to be like, I learn something else and realize that there is more to this incredible picture. The apostle Paul said: "… Eye hath not seen, nor ear heard, neither have entered into the heart of man, the things which God hath prepared for them that love Him" (1 Corinthians 2:9 KJV). God has planned this endless retreat for all of His children to enjoy. Praise the Lord for His magnificent gift to us!

~ Bethany Corrigan

Choosing Friends

The righteous should choose his friends carefully, for the way of the wicked leads them astray. - Proverbs 12:26 NKJV

A couple of months ago, I realized that my relationship with God wasn't as I wanted it to be. I wanted to grow closer to Him and get to know Him better, but I was having a hard time changing because of the environment that I lived in. My family is the only Seventh-day Adventist family in our town, and the nearest Seventh-day Adventist church is about three hours away. God wanted us, who knew the truth, to be an example to others; but instead, I was little by little letting other people who didn't know the truth influence me. This made me want to go to a place where I could have friends who would be a good influence on me.

So I came to Fountainview Academy and discovered it to be so wonderful that I could barely imagine something better. It has a beautiful orchard with many gorgeous trees, and there are big, marvelous snow-covered mountains all around it. But what makes this place so amazing is not the fascinating nature that surrounds it; it is the people. They are so friendly and I can see the love of God shining through them. Being in this environment helps me to grow in faith and to feel so much closer to God, and closer to Heaven.

I always knew that those I hung out with could affect my character, but I didn't realize that it could have such a big effect on my spiritual life. Now I see that being friends with someone who has the same hope as I do is really essential. "Be careful of your associates…. In choosing your friends, you should place your standard as high as possible. The tone of your morals is estimated by the associates you choose. You should avoid contracting an intimate friendship with those whose example you would not choose to imitate" (*Manuscript Releases, Vol. 4*, pg. 233).

~ Diane Carvalho

Missing the Flight

And then I will declare to them, 'I never knew you; depart from Me, you who practice lawlessness!' - Matthew 7:23 NKJV

It was a busy day of preparation. There was food to be cooked, a house to be cleaned, and bags to pack. My mom rushed around, completing task after task, feeling very on top of things. It was only a few hours before she would board a plane bound for Jamaica; and she planned on being ready. She even printed out her boarding pass the night before, so that she was guaranteed to be prepared for her trip. But as the time for her flight came, she headed to the airport, only to find that she had missed her plane. She was so focused on being "ready" that she had mistaken the flight's ETA to Jamaica as the departure time from Orlando. Suddenly, all of her preparation was rendered useless. The plane had left without her!

It's amazing how easy it is to completely miss the mark in life. To a firefighter, or a soldier, or an FBI agent, hours of training and preparation are all worthless if even a tiny part of their plan is overlooked. To my mom, it didn't really matter how much she thought ahead or how many things she did "right." She still missed her flight.

Sometimes, I get busy with the little details of my spiritual walk. I fall into the trap of trying to be a spiritual janitor, attempting to tidy up all the little messes in my life. But when that happens, I miss what's really important: my relationship with God, the Heavenly Janitor. John 5:39–40 says: "You search the Scriptures, for in them you think you have eternal life...But *you are not willing to come to Me* that you may have life" (NKJV, emphasis supplied). We search for eternal life in different places: the Scriptures, church, charitable donations, and pious deeds. But only a relationship with our Heavenly Father can lead us to true life. When we come to Him, the little details of the law will be made clear and He will begin to tidy up our hearts. But when we shift our focus off of our Lifeline, and onto our life, we will miss the flight.

~ Michael Jensen

As to a Friend

This poor man cried, and the Lord heard him, and saved him out of all his troubles. - Psalm 34:6 KJV

We sometimes get the idea that prayer is some complicated process that only well-practiced "pray-ers" should do in public, or that only set phrases can be used to talk to God. This is not the picture God wants us to have. In the book *Steps to Christ* we read: "Prayer is the opening of the heart to God as to a friend" (pg. 93). We can speak to God just like we would speak to our best friend here on earth.

When my mom was growing up, she did not know the blessing of prayer. She thought that prayer was simply repeating set phrases at certain times. When she was in college, she met my dad and his family, who were used to talking to God as a friend; and although they did not talk to her about it, she began to see that there was more to praying than she had thought.

One day, she went to the bank and took out twenty dollars for something she needed. When she went to use the money a little later, she could not find it. Being a college student on a tight budget, she did not have a surplus of money. After diligently searching her room, she remembered the simple prayers of her friends, and decided to tell God about it. Kneeling down by her bed, she prayed, "God, You know that I need this money. Please help me to find it." When she opened her eyes, the twenty dollar bill was sitting on the bed, right in front of her nose! She was elated! She knew that God had put it there, because there was no way she could have turned her room upside-down and yet missed such an obvious place.

As my mom found out that day, God is always eager to hear and answer prayer.

~ Aileen Corrigan

Endurance

… let us strip off every weight that slows us down, especially the sin that so easily trips us up. And let us run with endurance the race God has set before us. - Hebrew 12:1 NLT

Have you ever really wanted to compete in a race or accomplish a goal? These things don't happen by just hoping you will be able to accomplish them though. It takes training and hard work.

The other day, my friend and I were watching a video about dirt bike riding. This wasn't just any type of riding though; this was extreme enduro riding. Enduro riding requires the riders to cover terrain much more difficult than usual, like huge rocks or massive hill climbs. The race we watched was one of the hardest enduro races in the world. The track was designed to be so difficult that no rider could finish it.

Enduro riders have to really push themselves, as they have to complete the race in a set time to avoid disqualification. Some of the riders make it through, and they finish the race in good time. The majority of riders get stuck at hard spots along the way, and then they don't have enough time to finish the rest of the race. After all their hard work and effort, they get disqualified.

This same thing can happen in our spiritual lives. We can get bogged down with obstacles which prevent us from reaching the goal —eternity with Christ. *Steps to Christ* tells us, "Many will be lost while hoping and desiring to be Christians" (pg. 47). Just as the disqualified riders were hoping and intending to finish, but weren't adequately prepared, we must be sure we are not disqualified because we are only hoping and desiring to be Christians. We need to prepare ourselves adequately to run this race. We can only reach the finish line with the enlightenment of the Holy Scriptures and the help of the Lord. Christ can help us train to win the most important race. Let us always heed His voice, so we can spend eternity with Him.

~ Kyle Smith

Seeking the Lost

For the Son of man is come to seek and to save that which was lost.
- Luke 19:10 KJV

There was a young man who was playing basketball in his driveway when he lost his contact lens. He looked for it for a little while, then came in and told his mother. She immediately went out to search for it and before too long had found it. He then asked his mother how she found it so fast. She replied that he was just looking for a piece of plastic, but she was looking for $150.

This reminds me of the parable of the widow who lost her coin and wouldn't rest until she found it, and the story of the one lost sheep and the good shepherd who went out to save his lost sheep. It was the mission of Christ to seek and save that which was lost. It is also our duty and privilege as followers of Christ to help Him in that mission. This provokes some very sobering thoughts. How have I been treating the people around me? Like a piece of plastic, or like invaluable children of God? Have the words I've said today been spoken to seek and save that which is lost, or have they been spoken in a careless manner that wounds a person all for the sake of a joke?

The way we treat others shows if Christ is in us. If Christ is in us, then we will treat people with the love and compassion that He did. Our carnal nature doesn't let us treat people the way that Christ treated them. From childhood we are naturally self-centered and think only of self (which usually happens to be our motive for treating others poorly). The only way to be truly unselfish is to connect with our kind, caring, compassionate, selfless Savior.

~ Nolan Knuppel

Beautiful

The Lord does not look at the things man looks at. Man looks at the outward appearance, but the Lord looks at the heart.
- 1 Samuel 16:7 NIV

"Ugh, it's all dry and brown. Why is BC so ugly?"
"Excuse me? BC is not ugly!"
"Kid, have you lived in Maine? Have you been to Maine? Look, I have lived in both Maine and BC, and I am telling you BC is ugly!"

Herein lies the basis of almost all my arguments at school. As you may have guessed, I hail from the lovely New England state of Maine. When I first came to Fountainview, I felt that I was stuck in a horror land of dry grass, tumbleweed, and impossible-to-climb pine trees. I was used to the cool, damp air of Maine where moss-covered rocks gave way to an ocean filled with lobster buoys painted all sorts of bright colors. To me the beauty contest was no competition. This opinion came through very strongly in my conversations, which always seemed to morph into arguments.

Yet God still had to teach me an important lesson. I had just reached the top of a hill during a long hike. I paused to catch my breath and turned around to look at the view. All mental processes immediately stopped. In front of me loomed majestic mountains Maine certainly couldn't compete with. God created this. The thought seemed odd at first. However, it slowly dawned on me. I had been telling people that BC was ugly, yet God had created this land I was complaining about. To whine about the land was to criticize His handiwork.

In the same way, people make fun of others for anything: complexion, accent, or hair color. Sometimes I'll join in, but my conscience always gets to me. *Mason, God made these people. To criticize them would be to criticize God.* It stops me short every time. We're all made in God's image. God also made the nature around me. It may not be the beauty I am accustomed to, but it's still beautiful in a way. Even if everything is dry and brown in this part of BC.

~ Mason Neil

The Dark Tunnel of Life

Then Jesus said to them, "… Walk while you have the light, lest darkness overtake you; he who walks in darkness does not know where he is going." - John 12:35 NKJV

On a Sabbath afternoon, some of my friends and I decided to go exploring in some deserted train tunnels up on the mountain. As we approached the tunnels, they loomed before us, cold and dark, and very intimidating. We started walking through them while being careful not to trip on the rail ties scattered on the ground. Suddenly it became pitch black. The darkness surrounded me, and the air was cold and musty. I could barely see my hand in front of my face. I thought I might be stuck there forever. One of my friends, though, encouraged me to just keep walking and that it would be all right. I had to trust that I would reach the other end and see light again. In a few minutes, we were outside with the warm sun once again on our faces. Oh, it felt so good! As an added benefit, I wasn't so scared when we went through the other tunnel because I knew I would make it out safely.

At times in my life, I can feel Satan and his evil angels closing in on me. I don't know where to turn, and am held fast by the fear of never escaping. Then I hear a still small voice, telling me to trust Him to show me the way out. Jesus is the light at the end of the tunnel, and He shows me the path to take. He is the one who encourages and leads me when I don't know the way. It says in *Christian Experience and Teachings*, "In reviewing our past history, having traveled over every step of advance to our present standing, I can say, Praise God! As I see what God has wrought, I am filled with astonishment, and with confidence in Christ as leader. We have nothing to fear for the future, except as we shall forget the way the Lord has led us … in our past" (pg. 204).

When I reach the end of the tunnel, I have the assurance that I will look back and see how He has led me. Then I will rejoice that He was with me all the way.

~ Sarah Wahlman

Boundaries

Trust in the Lord with all your heart, and lean not on your own understanding; in all your ways acknowledge Him, and He shall direct your paths. - Proverbs 3:5–6 NKJV

For those of you who have had chooks (chickens), you know how stupid they can be. We used to have a few chooks, and they were very "un-smart." We started with ten, but slowly the number decreased until we didn't have any left. We kept our chooks in a nice big run where they had everything they needed. We even moved them to fresh grass daily. However, they always wanted to get out of the run and go elsewhere. This wasn't really a problem during the day, as they were quite safe if they were out then. But in the evening we would let our Rottweiler out of her run. There was nothing she liked more than chicken for dinner. If one happened to be there, she would chase it round and round the lawn until finally she would catch it and eat it. The other chooks would watch as their mate was getting attacked and eaten, but the next day they'd all try to get out too. They all had a try at it until we had no more chooks left.

How often do we push the boundaries we have in our lives, even when we know what the outcome might be? We try to see how far we can go before we run into trouble. Sometimes we might be all right and make it back safe and sound, but it only takes once for us to push too far, and then we find ourselves in big strife. We run the risk of never returning or not returning intact. We all have boundaries of some sort that we wish weren't there, but we need to realize that these boundaries are there for our protection. Just like our Rottweiler would wait for the chooks to push through their pen, away from the safety we provided for them, Satan is waiting for us to think we know better than God and put ourselves in situations God would rather we avoided. "Trust in the Lord with all your heart, and lean not on your own understanding; In all your ways acknowledge Him and He shall direct your paths" (Proverbs 3:5–6 NKJV).

~ Kyle Smith

Take the Lead

And the Lord shall make thee the head, and not the tail; and thou shalt be above only, and thou shalt not be beneath…
- Deuteronomy 28:13 KJV

"Would you like to go horseback riding today?" a friend offered.

"Sure," I replied. "That would be great. I'll meet you at the pasture at two o'clock this afternoon."

Two o'clock rolled around. We saddled up, and four of us headed off down the trail. After a little while, we came to a small creek. Although the riders in front encouraged their horses, they wouldn't budge. After several tries, the group decided to back up and let me go first. Maggie, the horse I was riding, walked straight up to and through the creek with only a slight hesitation. The other horses then gathered their courage and followed her.

As the ride progressed, the same thing kept happening. Every time we stopped or came to a steep hill, Maggie and I had to go around the other horses and take the lead. Of course, we quickly decided that I should simply stay at the head to keep our group going.

A few days later, I had a riding lesson. "What happened to you?" my teacher wondered. "You're so confident!" I explained to her the experience I'd had on the ride. "Wow," she exclaimed. "That's so exciting! Taking leadership transformed you into a more secure rider, and you will be able to progress faster."

As Christians, we sometimes are content to simply "ride" in the back, letting others lead us. This is not God's plan. When you are asked to take a responsibility at church or for a worship service—take the lead. With God's help, you will become confident in your own spiritual walk, and better prepared to witness to others.

~ Aileen Corrigan

Marathon

Rather train yourself for godliness, for while bodily training is of some value, godliness is of value in every way, as it holds promise for the present life and also for the life to come. - 1 Timothy 4:7b–8 ESV

They had no choice. Before them stood thousands of Persian soldiers in battle formation. To assail this massive army was almost certain defeat, but to wait would be to lose Athens to the Persian ships sailing around the Greek peninsula. Democracy was still in its infancy; the outcome of this day could decide the fate of freedom forever.

There were fewer than 10,000 Athenians on the small rise overlooking the Persian army—100,000 strong, covering a beach called Marathon. A messenger had been sent to request help from the nearby city of Sparta, but the Spartans wouldn't come. The Athenians had no choice but to stand their ground no matter what came their way. Miltiades, the Greek general, ordered his troops to assemble and prepare to attack the waiting Persian ranks. The command was given, and the Greeks moved forward. The Persians disdainfully watched the small group of soldiers slowly approach them. They almost laughed at the thought that so few soldiers would challenge the mighty forces of Persia. Then the Greeks began to run, picking up speed with every step. By the time the Persian archers realized that their target was in range, it was too late. They overshot the oncoming soldiers. The lightly armored Persians, who had expected the charge to be cut down by arrows, were no match for the masterfully handled spears of the Greek Phalanx. The battle ended in a complete route, halting the Persian invasion.

Those few glorious moments of triumph were long remembered by the Greek army. Yet preparation for those few moments had taken a lifetime. Daily they had practiced running 200 meters in 70 pounds of armor. What a reminder that I cannot be "suddenly" prepared to resist temptation! I cannot be prepared to do a great feat for God if I am not daily preparing and asking to be fully clothed in the armor of God.

~ Derek Glatts

1 4 9 5

Blessed is the man who does this, and the son of man who lays hold on it; who keeps from defiling the Sabbath, and keeps his hand from doing any evil. - Isaiah 56:2 NKJV

My parents started running their first pharmacy when I was born. As I grew older, they began to open more. They are all quite close together, so my parents can easily drive from one to another. When we became Christians, my parents didn't think about closing their pharmacies on Sabbath. But later, they had a change of heart, causing a big argument with their staff. My parents encouraged them to try closing the pharmacies on Sabbath, and my dad told them that God will surely bless if we follow Him. So they decided to close the smallest pharmacy on the Sabbath. Because they couldn't lose as much as they would with one of their bigger pharmacies, their staff members decided to take the risk. My parents also were not fully convinced that God would provide, but they decided to trust Him. They posted a notice on the door that said: "We are closing, not because we are lazy, but because by resting, we can walk further."

They closed that pharmacy from sundown Friday, and opened it again after Sabbath sundown. Then a miracle happened! When my dad counted up the money, he discovered that they made 1495¥ during the working hours on Friday before sunset and Saturday night. Normally they would make no more than 700¥ or 800¥ on a single business day. But now, God had doubled their profits so that they could make up for the day they were closed. This happened for three weeks, and each time the total amount earned during the working hours on Friday before sunset and Saturday night added up to 1495¥! The whole company was amazed, and they gladly decided to close all the pharmacies on Sabbath because they witnessed how God had blessed them.

One of the workers, who is now a Christian, discovered that 1495 in Mandarin is pronounced similarly to the words "Jesus Saves Me." Interestingly, he was the one who said: "If this same number occurs for three weeks, I will believe in Jesus." Now he believes.

~ Bryan Chen

Minority's Majority

The law of the Lord is perfect, converting the soul...
- Psalms 19:10 KJV

I've always been very independent—for a girl. I was home schooled, so I could manage my own time. My parents would instruct me, but nobody had to watch me because I could take care of myself. Thus life continued until I became a student at Fountainview Academy.

For the first few weeks, I felt really nervous and stressed. School was a new experience, and I determined not to blow it. But once I was settled into the routine, I felt like I was restricted. What irked me more than anything else was that somebody had to know where I was at all times. Up until then, I went where I wanted to after I checked with my parents, and they trusted me to stay safe. When it came down to having strangers tell me what to do, I was not pleased. They had just met me, so how could they know what restrictions I needed? It irritated me to the point that I considered breaking some rules on purpose.

About this time, Rosa, the head dean, stopped by to talk. She had no clue I was struggling with anything. Somewhere in the conversation, the school rules came up. I expressed some of my views, and Rosa explained. The current rules were created because somebody overstepped the boundaries. To prevent it from becoming a problem, they enforced a rule. Even though it may have only been a few people who had broken the rule, the majority had to be kept with the minority to retain harmony.

I could see the logical reasoning behind this, and I found it very similar to God's rules. Until Satan rebelled against the God's Law, no one had even known it had been in place. Everybody had been following it unconsciously, because their love for their Creator allowed no room for sin. Their focus wasn't on how restricted they were, because they were already happy. In my view of the school's rules, I saw them as my shackles; but really, they gave me the freedom to be happy. Under the Law, everything is the way it should be.

~ Morgan Metcalf

Cling to Jesus

There is a way that seems right to a man, but its end is the way of death. - Proverbs 16:25 NKJV

It was crowded, warm, and windy—extraordinarily windy—at Southaven beach. However, we didn't give this much thought as we got out of the car, brushing the hair away that now whipped about our cheeks, and with loaded arms, walked in the direction of the beach for a church picnic and vespers. Passing street after street, we finally saw the bustling traffic that caused us to park so far away—a mélange of honking cars, complete with ambulance sirens and police.

While crossing the last parking lot between our car and the beach, we noticed two teenage girls crying and shivering in the cold, frantically scanning the crashing waves. My father asked them what was wrong, then offered to help. One girl began to explain that she, her uncle, cousin, and younger siblings were swimming when the wind picked up. Suddenly, the lake became rough and perilous and they found themselves pulled by an undercurrent towards a nearby pier that stuck out far into the lake. After fighting with the waves and struggling to keep everyone afloat, this girl's uncle had everyone bobbing around the base of a small ladder suspended from the pier. With a last valiant and weary effort, he had hoisted every family member into some onlooker's outstretched arms. Looking back for her uncle, this girl could only see was the angry lake that had sapped all of the strength and energy from her rescuer. Now the agonizing minutes crept by as the family waited for a search and rescue team to come with news. Before we left, we prayed with them, later discovering that the uncle had drowned—giving up his life for his family.

Sin is an undercurrent that pulls its victims away from the safety of the shore; it engulfs their powerless efforts and they find themselves in need of a Saviour. If we are not careful, we may drown; but if we cling to Jesus, all the world's waves cannot prevail against us.

~ Esther Ferraz

Hiding or Healing?

Come unto me, all ye that labour and are heavy laden, and I will give you rest. - Matthew 11:28 KJV

"Oh, oh, ouch!" I moaned when I felt my ankle twist under me as I landed a cartwheel. I had sprained my ankle while running three days earlier, but it wasn't a bad sprain, or so I thought. Now I was attempting to do gymnastics on the lawn. Even though my ankle progressively worsened, I refused to believe I had sprained it badly, and I was too busy to let it rest. I decided to go on the school campout the next weekend, despite the fact that I had woken up in pain earlier that week. This campout included a hard hike both uphill going in and downhill coming out. When I got back to school after the weekend, I was in a lot of pain. The only reason why my ankle continued to get worse was because I didn't acknowledge it and let it rest.

Since I don't like people to see that I'm injured, I tried to hide my ankle by not acknowledging it. This failed, however, as the pain in my ankle intensified. It wasn't until I acknowledged it and decided to slow down to let it rest that it started to heal.

It isn't just this way with physical injuries—it is the same with spiritual injuries. I realized that just as I was trying to hide my ankle, I am also trying to hide a deeper problem: a problem of trying to make a savior out of my bustle of helpful activity, instead of resting in my true Savior, Jesus Christ. I feel like I need to work hard to keep up my reputation as a hard worker, and if I don't work hard all the time, I am a failure. This isn't how Christ wants me to feel; He is always with me, wanting me to surrender to Him and completely rest in Him. It isn't until I stop and let myself rest in Him that I experience healing. While I'm tired of hiding an ankle that can't support me, I'm even more tired of attempting to stand in my own "righteousness." I want to rest completely in Christ.

~ Katie Sloop

Growing Up in Love

… He is not ashamed to call them brethren. - Hebrews 2:11 KJV

As a small girl, I wanted to love my sister, and I longed for her to be my best friend; but sometimes I couldn't seem to overcome my unkind thoughts toward her. She looked up to me and wanted my acceptance, but she bugged me. Because of her, our room was always a wreck, and her disorderly habits got to me. It seemed as though she wasn't growing up. These little things bothered me until I would finally blow up and say, "Can't you just do things neatly?" or "What is wrong with you?"

My poor sister—she wanted to be like me, but instead of appreciating her good points, all I did was put her down. I felt terrible about the way I was hurting her, but I couldn't control myself. I asked God to help me, and through my parents' counsel, He did. They explained that my sister was younger than I, and that if I chose to love her just the way she was, she would grow under that love into the delightful person God intended her to be. I am grateful that God helped me to understand their counsel. Because I chose to let my sister grow up in the time that God had set for her, she has matured beautifully, and we are the best of friends. Now her room is so tidy and clean that even walking past it is a pleasure!

Jesus knows our weaknesses but is happy to call us His brothers and sisters. He thinks of us in the same way He helped me to think of my sister. "For I know the thoughts that I think toward you, saith the Lord, thoughts of peace, and not of evil, to give you an expected end" (Jeremiah 29:11 KJV). He sees us for who we can be by His grace, and His love for us makes us want to grow up to be just like Him.

~ Bethany Corrigan

Heartbroken: Treasure out of Tragedy

And we know that all things work together for good to them that love
God... - Romans 8:28 KJV

My grandpa never really expressed his feelings, but we could still see how much he loved us. He was an older man, and with every passing year, his cough got worse; so he went to see a doctor. With a solemn look on his face, the doctor told him that he would have to go to a bigger hospital with a CT scanner. He stayed with my family for a while before going to the hospital for a thorough checkup. Shockingly, we found out that the tests revealed some serious complications: lung cancer in its final stages. He had only three months left to live; however, it could be extended up to six months with the aid of certain treatments. Undergoing anti-cancer treatments, his face blanched and he lost his appetite. He slowly got weaker and weaker until he couldn't even stand up.

Prayer was our only hope; my mom and I knew it would take a miracle. A few days later, the phone rang early in the morning. My mother had scarcely put the phone down when she woke up our family. The call was telling us of my grandpa's death; my father was grief-stricken, and seeing my father cry so uncontrollably was shocking. In my whole life, I had never seen my father break down like that. After going through this heartbreaking situation, I resented God for leaving my prayer unanswered.

Why didn't God answer my prayer? It was painful for me to see my father in so much anguish; however, I realized that if my grandpa was still alive, there was no way that he would have let me go to Fountainview, my high school. Not only was he a non-Christian, but he also believed that family was supposed to live together and never separate. God led me to this school to learn how to live as a daughter of Christ. Although I wish my grandpa was alive, I see that God exposed treasure out of tragedy.

~ Ellen Yoon

85

Walking with Cabot

… What doth the LORD require of thee, but to do justly, and to love mercy, and to walk humbly with thy God? - Micah 6:8 KJV

One day while my older sister and I were babysitting our two younger siblings, we decided to take a walk up to one of the hills on our farm. It was a beautiful fall day. The hills were speckled by the changing trees; our grazing cows peacefully dotted the large grass pastures; and the fields were full of plump, ripe corn waiting to be harvested. Suddenly, we heard our little brother, Cabot, calling us. Looking back, we saw him sitting about 20 feet away amidst the swirling dust of the deeply rutted, dirt road. "Sarah, my legs are tired unto death! I can't barely take another step. Will you carry me?" Since we had only been walking for about 15 minutes, I said no and asked him to walk up to where we were. Grudgingly, he complied and half walked, half dragged his weary body up to us. Once he reached me, I held out my hand to him and walked with him the rest of the way home. By the time we arrived home, Cabot's tiredness was completely gone, and he was back to chasing kittens.

Sometimes my spiritual legs become tired in my walk with God. When I blow up at my family after a long day, make a big mistake, or do something really stupid, all I can think about is sinking down in the middle of the road of life and never getting back up again. Rather than leaving me there, Christ comes along and invites me to walk with Him. Through this invitation, Christ is not commanding me to suddenly become perfect and never make any more mistakes. No! All He requires is that I learn to love what He loves, do my best, and walk humbly with Him, realizing that it is only His strength that's keeping me going.

Are you feeling discouraged by your weaknesses? Don't lose heart! It is through walking with Him that your legs will grow stronger.

~Sarah Miller

Kite Flying

Seek the Lord and His strength, seek His face continually.
- 1 Chronicles 16:11 KJV

There are few things more refreshing than flying a kite on a windy day. I love taking my brother's traction kite and letting it drag me along the ground as it arcs back and forth with huge, sweeping motions. It's such a satisfying feeling to be in complete control, pulling on the handles to direct the kite's every action. Loops, turns, stalls, and dives are all executed at my command. But as soon as I fly outside of the wind zone, the fun is gone. A kite can't fly by itself! Without wind, it falls from the sky like a limp piece of tissue paper.

Even though God has given us control of our lives, we don't make them fly. Without the wind that comes from seeking His face, we're left with a grounded, powerless kite that has almost no purpose for existence. This is why we are supposed to "Seek the Lord and His strength, seek His face continually." On our own, we have no strength. But His strength is perfect, and when we seek His face by pursuing a relationship with Him, God will impart to us His infinite power.

To me, the value of accomplishing various goals comes from my dad. If I overcome some obstacle or complete some difficult task, I tell my dad about it. If his approval doesn't rest on what I did, then I might as well not have done it. Without his face smiling on my achievements, their value is greatly diminished. So if I'm working on a project, I can find strength through the knowledge that my father's face is smiling in acknowledgement and approval. Ephesians 5:10 says, "Try to learn what pleases the Lord" (NCV). If I can obtain strength from the approval of my earthly father, how much more can I get from pleasing my Heavenly Father? Infinitely more. When I seek the Lord's face, and receive His strength, my life is transformed from a limp piece of tissue paper into a thriving, powerful kite that's ready to fly high.

~ Michael Jensen

Time of Testing

I, the Lord, search the heart, I test the mind... - Jeremiah 17:10 NKJV

This may seem weird to some people, but I enjoy large academic tests. Not just the chapter review tests, but final, end-of-year exams. But when it comes to other types of tests where I have to do something physical, like piano recitals, I don't appreciate them very much. I get nervous, jittery, and my legs feel like water-logged ramen noodles. The dread that I will fail makes it almost impossible for me to continue; I lose my concentration and end up making mistakes. In my mind, I know it's not something I should worry about, but I can't help it.

When Satan was forced to make our world his permanent home, God had to let the human race make a choice. Either they could choose to reject Satan and his lies so they could continue living in their perfect Eden home, or they could choose to question God's law by thinking that God was withholding knowledge and power from them. In order for the other worlds and angels to see how wicked Satan was, the test had to be given.

Adam and Eve were prepared to meet the temptation. The basic instructions were: stay away from the tree of the knowledge of good and evil, don't separate from each other, and call for help if you ever need it. But Eve disregarded all of these warnings and was led into temptation by a snake. When I first read this story I thought, *How could she be so stupid? Didn't she know it's not normal for a snake to talk? If it was me, I wouldn't have failed the test.* But then I considered how many times I have failed daily tests that come my way. Because these tests are so small and seemingly insignificant, I think I can handle them on my own. In response to my thoughts, Philippians 2:12 had the perfect answer. It says, "Work out your own salvation with fear and trembling."

My mind may deceive me into thinking I can face little tests on my own, but in reality, I should be shaking from head to toe! The answers to these tests can be decided in a split second, but they affect more than just my school grades. They determine my eternal destiny.

~ Morgan Metcalf

Pause, Part 1

*We give thanks to You, O God, we give thanks! For Your wondrous
works declare that Your name is near. - Psalm 75:1 NKJV*

Up, up we hiked. With Uncle Ken as our leader, we took step after
step up the steep trail into the Wallowa mountains. Our unusual team
of backpackers included cousins, aunts, uncles, moms and dads,
brothers and sisters, nieces and nephews, and even Grandpa Harvey.
We tromped amidst rich green foliage, beautifully arranged among
tree trunks and rocks. The work of our intelligent Creator was clearly
visible.

Even with this scenery to encourage us, Auntie Nellie started
slowing down. Tiredness began to set in, one hiker at a time. My
muscles started to burn. Everyone was ready to relax around a warm
fire. Yet, we trudged on, trying to motivate each other, until we reached
our campsite. Once we had plopped our backpacks on the ground,
we looked around us at the scene: a calm stream wound its way
along beside us, majestic pines rose up on the valley sides, and the
mountain named Eagle Cap rose like a fortress into the sky.

It was in this serene wilderness that we gathered as a loving family
around a crackling fire. Together, we worshiped God and sang as with
one voice *I Want To Go To Heaven.*

Worship complete, we stood around the fire as Uncle Ken talked
about the plans for our next day. "Tomorrow, we can start at 7:00 A.M.
and head for the summit of Eagle Cap."

Hardly had he finished speaking before several of us jumped in,
exclaiming, "What? No way! I'm not going tomorrow. We've gotta
rest tomorrow. Tomorrow is not a good day to climb that 9,000 ft.
mountain." The tones of voice were annoyed and upset. Feelings were
on edge. The air intensified.

~ Andrew Sharley

Pause, Part 2

*So then, my beloved brethren, let every man be swift to hear, slow
to speak, slow to wrath; for the wrath of man does not produce the
righteousness of God. - James 1:19–20 NKJV*

Quietly, Uncle Ken replied, "Okay, we can wait 'til the day after
tomorrow." He left to ready himself for bed. Friction still hung in the
air. The loving, praise-filled atmosphere had disappeared. Sides had
been taken. Uncle Ken's careful plans had been stuffed down in quick
anger. Unresolved tensions continued as we dispersed. I went to my
tent, miserably full of regret for my hasty response to Uncle Ken's plan.

The absolutely joyful time God had given us together had been
instantly destroyed by our hasty and angry words. Though a grueling
hike on the very next day seemed very unreasonable, so much pain
could have been avoided by simply pausing to seek God's attitude.
Then we could have calmly responded to Uncle Ken's rather shocking
announcement. We could have mentioned our concerns in a humble
manner, willing to be wrong. While lying in my tent, I realized that no
matter how upsetting the plans ended up being, nothing was worth a
hasty, relationship-destroying response.

Thankfully, God's forgiving attitude was very plentiful and we
continued to have a peace-filled family retreat. It is clear that there
is no situation so bad that it is worth an angry, quick response. How
much better is Jesus' way of gentle, unselfish words! The next time
someone irks us, we can pause and ask Jesus to remove our anger
and give us His attitude.

~ Andrew Sharley

Yellow Snow

But evil men and seducers shall wax worse and worse, deceiving, and being deceived. - 2 Timothy 3:13 KJV

It was Sunday morning, and there was a fresh layer of powdery snow. My friends and I had gotten up early so we could go sledding. Today was extra special because my friends were not very used to snow, at least not in this quantity. They had spent most of their childhood as missionaries in Africa. However, even though they hadn't seen much snow before, I was still surprised when they asked why there was a spot of yellow snow. "I've never seen yellow snow..."

I stared in disbelief. How could one not know what yellow snow is? This was definitely a chance I couldn't miss. "Well, it's kinda complicated. Like chemistry!" I replied. "You see, when the snow is still in the air it undergoes a strange transformation, sort of like how a caterpillar turns into a butterfly. Sometimes the transformation has a problem, and the snow turns yellow." My friends' eyes grew big. ... I added, "it also tastes AMAZING!" After some time, I had them holding some of the "yellow snow" in their hands on the verge of eating it. Slowly they opened their mouths. They brought the snow closer and closer. Then... "STOP!!!" Why is my sister always there to ruin the fun?

"Mason Elliot Neil, what on earth are you doing? These poor kids had no clue what they were getting themselves into!"

It was true—I was being very unkind. But it was for a good cause, right? Well, after my friends discovered I was a fraud, sledding wasn't fun any more. I had destroyed their trust in me.

In life we get all kinds of mixed messages. Whether through the television or through our peer group, we're always being told what we should do. However, these messages are not always right. We need to remember to look to the Lord and follow Him, not our peers. We can always trust that He knows what is best for us. When we do, who knows what kind of mess we will avoid?

~ Mason Neil

Torn Away

In His providence He brings these persons into different positions and varied circumstances that they may discover in their character the defects which have been concealed from their own knowledge ... Often He permits the fires of affliction to assail them that they may be purified. - Ministry of Healing, pg. 471

My heart sank as I pulled open my blue striped curtains and saw the drenching rain, dying grass, squishy mud, and melting, rotten snow. Why did it have to rain? Why couldn't the snow stick around? I wrinkled up my nose and stared at the water cascading down my window. The six inch deep, glittering snow had blanketed the ground until that morning. It had concealed the rocks, weeds, and mud, covering the filth in a smooth blanket of white fluff. It was just fluff, though; under that blanket the mud, weeds, and filth still existed. Now, the rain had torn away that covering, exposing the mud and yellow grass. It looked so sad, so dead, so ugly.

Often a smooth blanket of snow covers us, concealing our mud and filth. The only thing visible is a sparkling Christian exterior. It looks so beautiful, so sincere, so perfect. But, then the rain comes—drenching rain, tearing away the snow and exposing our muddy actions, untruthful words, dying love, and rotten characters. It is disgusting; it is ugly.

We hate the rain; we want a blanket of snow to conceal our mud and filth, and we vainly try to hold onto the snowy fluff hiding our bad side. But Jesus lets it pour. It's the only way we will acknowledge those faults we don't even want to think about—the ones we shove down immediately when they surface. It is painful and ugly, but because Jesus loves us, He lets it rain. He cares about us so much that He wants to refine us for Heaven. I want Jesus to make it rain and take away my white fluff; I want Him to show me all my faults and take them away.

~ Katie Sloop

Who is God?

"Lord, show us the Father, and it is enough for us." - John 14:8 ESV

My mind raced across an ocean of thoughts, bouncing from idea to idea in an attempt to answer a seemingly simple question: who is God? I soon realized that solving this mystery would be a challenge, especially considering that absolutely nothing on this Earth can be used as an example. Humans are weak and sinful; God is infinitely powerful and sinless. Nature is flawed, selfish, and imperfect; God is immaculate, selfless, and perfect. So I can't compare God to anything that I'm familiar with. How could I grasp an understanding of something so infinite and far beyond my mind's feeble reaches? I decided that the only way was to examine God's closest encounter with fallen humanity. Maybe seeing what He was like as a human would help me to disperse the fog of ambiguity that arises when a finite human tries to comprehend an infinite God. So I turned the focus of my quest to the life of Jesus.

Jesus stood in marked contrast to the rest of mankind. He spent His life serving a wayward and crooked race, only to be murdered by the very same people whom He had dedicated Himself to saving. Yet His boundless compassion could not evaporate; He prayed that His Father would forgive the very men who had just stripped, scourged, spat on, and mocked Him, driving spikes through His hands and feet to secure Him to a lifeless tree. Throughout His life on Earth, Jesus manifested the same passionate, tender affection towards those around Him as He did on the cross. He suffered long and was kind. He did not envy, did not seek His own, and did not rejoice in iniquity. He bore all things, believed all things, hoped all things, and endured all things. He never failed. So in my search for an answer to the great question of who God is, I stumbled upon the simple yet profound answer: God is Love.

~ Michael Jensen

The Choice is Yours

How long will you hesitate between two opinions?
- 1 Kings 18:21b NASB

I am very indecisive. Whenever I go shopping it takes me a long time to decide if I am going to buy something or not. With food, it can take me a long time to choose what to eat, and I often rely on other people's opinions. I remember my mom telling me one time not to be so indecisive, but I didn't see a reason for it. If I eventually made a decision or someone else made a decision for me, I figured I would be fine.

Time went by and I didn't really think very much about my indecisiveness until I had an interesting conversation with my friend. It got me thinking about how my hesitancy could affect my spiritual life. In my walk with Jesus, there is no room for indecision. I cannot please both God and this world; therefore, I must ultimately choose between life and death. On Mount Carmel, Elijah asked the people: "How long will you hesitate between two opinions? If the Lord is God, follow Him; but if Baal, follow him" (1 Kings 18:21 NASB). Even though people were confronted with that question more than two thousand years ago, it still applies to us today. You probably don't have to literally choose between God and Baal, but you may have a worldly idol that keeps you from spending time with Jesus. If so, a decision must be made, because "No one can serve two masters; for either he will hate the one and love the other, or else he will be loyal to the one and despise the other..." (Matthew 6:24 NKJV). "This is a matter to be settled between God and your own soul, settled for eternity." "What we do not overcome, will overcome us and work out our destruction" (*Steps to Christ*, pg. 35, 32). In this case, I have overcome my indecisiveness: I have decided to follow Jesus and please Him only. Have you decided who you're going to please? Time is short because Jesus is coming soon. Don't get stuck in the valley of indecision.

~ Diane Carvalho

Comfort in the Dark

I will not leave you comfortless: I will come to you. - John 14:18 KJV

The pressure was just too much for me to hold in. I couldn't help but cry. Two people had invited me to their house for lunch, and I simply couldn't choose where to go. They both were really good friends, and I didn't like the feeling of choosing one instead of the other. I asked my other friends what to do, but their solutions didn't agree. One said I should go to my friend who had asked me first, and my other friend pressured me to go to the other one because she had been invited there too. This made making a decision harder for me. Then at last, after thinking about it for a few hours, I made a decision to go to the ones who invited me first. Although I had made this decision, I still didn't have peace. So that night, with puffy eyes, I prayed. I asked God to give me peace about my decision and to help me know where to go. Then it happened. I had never felt anything like it before. It was like someone gave me a hug. Peace and comfort surrounded me with warm arms. It made me feel that Christ was there comforting me.

Before Christ ascended into heaven, He promised His disciples that He would not leave them alone. He assured them that He would send them the Holy Spirit to be their Comforter. From my experience, I can testify that Christ keeps His promise. Now, whenever everything seems like it's going wrong and I feel helpless, I know where to go. I have learned that if I just ask Christ for comfort, He will give me His peace.

Perhaps you're behind in homework or you have a big decision to make. Maybe you're hurting from the sorrows of life or have been rejected by a friend. Whatever it is, if you rely on and trust in God, you don't have to worry any more. When you ask Him to take away your fear, worry, or sorrow, He will do so, and in its place, He will give you His perfect peace. What are you struggling with today? Don't be afraid to talk to God about it. Give it to Him to hold, and I promise you that He won't fail you in your time of need.

~ Shenel Cruz

Dead—Then Alive!

*For I know the thoughts that I think toward you, says the Lord,
thoughts of peace and not of evil, to give you a future and a hope.
- Jeremiah 29:11 NKJV*

Sirens raced down the street and came to an abrupt halt outside a little house. My sister Stephanie and her crew leapt out of the ambulance and rushed inside. There they found a man in full cardiac arrest; he had no pulse and he wasn't breathing. One man immediately started CPR. Another crew member slid a ventilation tube down the man's throat, and yet another medic gave him a shot with drugs that were supposed to help restart his heart. Second after second and then minute after minute ticked by, and still there was no response. Frustration came over the crew as they realized that this man was not going to come around. The medic reluctantly called the doctor for orders to officially pronounce the man dead, which the doctor gave. After ending the call, the paramedic half-heartedly decided to check one more time for a pulse.

"This man's pulse—it's—it's back!" he cried, astonished.

Immediately, everyone began working at their original tasks. Without stopping, they loaded him in the ambulance and sped off to the nearest hospital. On the way there, the man miraculously started moving his hand and breathing on his own. He even started opening his eyes and trying to talk. All the medics were amazed! This man should have been dead! He was dead! But now he was alive again!

God had a purpose for restoring that man's life. He could have easily let him stay dead, but He didn't. If you let God work through you, you will come to see that God have a purpose for your life too.

~ Julie Kelly

Who Will Open the Door?

*Submit yourselves therefore to God. Resist the devil, and he will flee
from you. Draw nigh to God, and he will draw nigh to you.*
- James 4:7–8a KJV

Once there was a little girl who was questioned about how she
triumphs over Satan. "Well," replied the little girl, "when Satan comes
and knocks on the door of my heart, I let God answer the door. When
Satan sees God, he says, 'Oops, I must have the wrong place,' and he
goes away."

I love this story because it illustrates how we can have victory over
Satan. To have that victory, we must have a personal connection with
Jesus, because only through a relationship with Christ are we able to
receive the power we need to resist the Devil. It is necessary for us to
daily submit ourselves to Christ so He can answer our heart's door for
us.

Ellen White wrote: "The tempter can never compel us to do evil.
He cannot control minds unless they are yielded to his control. The
will must consent, faith must let go its hold upon Christ, before Satan
can exercise his power upon us … Every point in which we fail of
meeting the divine standard is an open door by which he can enter
to tempt and destroy us" (*Desire of Ages*, pg. 125). We must totally
submit ourselves to God if we are to be out of Satan's grasp. If we do
not do this, our door is left open, and Satan is able to come in without
knocking.

For the little girl to defeat Satan, she had to have God in her heart.
Jesus says, "Behold I stand at the door and knock. If anyone hears
My voice and opens the door, I will come in to him and dine with him,
and he with Me" (Revelation 3:20 NKJV). The little girl had opened her
door and let Jesus in. When we let Jesus into our hearts, we become
His. It makes me so happy to know that I belong to such a loving
heavenly Father who gives me the power to gain the victory over
Satan. "But thanks be to God, who gives us the victory through our
Lord Jesus Christ" (1 Corinthians 15:57 NKJV).

~ Kami Rose

Keep Your Eye on the Goal

I press on toward the goal to win the prize for which God has called me heavenward in Christ Jesus. - Philippians 3:14 NIV

There I was. It was my first day in orchestra and I felt like I was constantly lost. I had only been playing cello for about a month and a half when I decided to join; my teacher thought I was not ready, but I had a goal to improve my cello playing as much as I could while I had the opportunity to be in an orchestra.

The first few weeks of orchestra were the hardest. Every time I left a practice, I reevaluated my decision to be there. I felt like there were so many reasons to stop: I could only play double bass music, and maybe I was just not good enough yet. No matter what reasons came up, I decided to keep pressing on.

As time went by, I discovered a good way for me to learn. Whenever I got lost, I would just watch the lead cellist to see what he did. One of the main things I noticed was that he watched our conductor very closely and didn't seem to get lost as easily as I did; so I decided to try watching the conductor closely as well. From that day on, I did my best to watch our conductor intently to see if it would help me like it helped our lead cellist. At first it was really hard to remember to watch him, but slowly as time went by it started to become a habit. Eventually, I noticed that I did not seem to get lost as easily. Keeping my eye on the goal by watching our conductor really helped.

Since I have learned the secret of keeping my eye on the goal, I have tried to apply it throughout my life. In work, school or play I try my best to keep my eye on the goal. When I was just looking around the orchestra while I played, I lost sight of my goal; but when I found a place to watch, I no longer got lost. I encourage you to keep your eye on your goals so you can reach them, too.

~ Rebecca Hall

Promises Broken

For all the promises of God in Him are Yes, and in Him Amen, to the glory of God through us. - 2 Corinthians 1:20 NKJV

My energetic grandfather, Paul Smith, was only 53 years old when he was diagnosed with melanoma. Because it was a rapidly growing cancer already in his body, the melanoma was beyond remedy when diagnosed. Grandpa Paul had lived very healthfully and joyfully, a caring physician who went out of his way to bring people to total health. He loved Jesus as his most precious friend and was constantly trying to bring others to his Savior.

My mom and her family began praying for a miracle. As they kept praying, his condition changed—for the worse; but they kept praying, laying before God His promises for healing. But Grandpa Paul only grew weaker and sicker. Then came the heart-rending day when miraculous healing was no longer an option. "Why?! What went wrong, Lord?!" my mom cried. "You did not keep your promises. Your Word says that whatever we ask in Jesus' name will be given. Why this?!"

An uninvited anger welled up in my mom's mind. *Why did God not keep His word?* Her relationship with God strained as the dismal weeks passed. It seemed God could not be trusted—His promises were mocking words. One day she was struggling through Hebrews 11. Reading about heroes of faith, she came upon this startling verse: "And these, having obtained a good testimony through faith, *did not receive the promise,* God having provided something better for us, that they should not be made perfect apart from us" (vv. 39-40 NKJV, italics supplied). Suddenly something clicked. Mom's grief did not disappear, but she realized that God hadn't broken His promises. Her faith-filled father had died without receiving God's promised reward. But God had a better plan. He was saving His best blessings for my mom and her family to receive *together*—at His coming.

I still don't know why God allowed Grandpa Paul to die, but I am convinced that: "… all things work together for good to those who love God…" (Romans 8:28 NKJV). God never breaks His promises.

~ Andrew Sharley

Copy, Paste

But put on the Lord Jesus Christ, and make no provision for the flesh, to fulfill its lusts. - Romans 13:14 NKJV

I sometimes get sick of being me. Growing up, I have always wanted to be someone else. I have wanted to dress like someone else, have the standards of someone else, and I've even desired the friends of someone else. If someone had bought something new, I would beg my parents for the same thing. Then I would show the person how cool it was that we had the same taste. I was constantly living someone else's life.

Lately, that is what has been going on with me and my best friend. She does a little better than me in almost everything. She runs faster than I do, gets up earlier than I do, and always looks better. So, because I became jealous, I did what I used to do: I copied her. However, this did not work. Outfits that brought out her best features brought out my worst. Hairstyles that looked amazing on her made me look like a wreck. While this was going on, I didn't give God a chance to talk to me, and I didn't take time to talk to Him. Then one night, when my jealousy was wearing me down, I heard God whisper in my ear. He said that He had created me to be me, and I shouldn't try to copy my best friend, but try to be more like Him.

When we try our best to copy Jesus, we can be sure that it will work. Jesus doesn't have any outfits that bring out our worst features. His outfits look amazing on us all. If we always try to copy other people, we can be sure that it will make us look awful. And by focusing on this, we'll miss out on the beautiful outfit Christ has just for us: His robe of righteousness.

~ Agnes Grétarsdóttir

One-Up or Build Up?

… encourage each other and build each other up.
- 1 Thessalonians 5:11 NLT

"My grandpa was a rocket scientist," my friend Derek informed me. "He invented things that go to the moon." I thought about that for a minute. What had my family done that was as impressive as that?

Suddenly, it dawned on me, and I blurted out, "My great uncle invented Cheez Whiz™!"

My friend stared at me for a moment, trying to grasp if I was serious, and finally burst into a fit of uncontrollable laughter. Once I thought about it, I had to agree that it was kind of funny. After all, his grandpa had invented a rocket, while my claim to fame was a relation who had invented spreadable cheese. I must admit, I sounded rather puny in comparison.

My whole life I've always found myself trying to one-up people. Someone would say, "My daddy's a doctor."

Of course, I had to counter them. "My daddy was a football player, and then he was an Air Force pilot. Beat that!"

Why is it that whenever someone states something good about themselves, I feel the need to counter it with something better about myself? In my self-centered heart, I always feel the need to build myself up to be better than those around me. I think that it makes me look better in others' eyes, when in reality it merely makes me appear self-absorbed and insecure.

Instead of constantly breaking each other down, shouldn't we be building each other up? When Jesus was on earth, He didn't seek fame and glory for Himself. He was the most humble, others-centered man ever to walk the earth, and we are to follow in His footsteps.

~ Moriah Mays

Walking Bibles

… the Lord does not see as man sees; for man looks at the outward appearance, but the Lord looks at the heart. - 1 Samuel 16:7 NKJV

I won't deny it. I like clothes from a few name brand stores. Not for the logo, but because the style is either cute or the fabric is comfortable. One problem is that those clothes are expensive. An easy remedy, though, is for me to shop at my favorite store: Goodwill. Since I can always find nice clothes for really cheap, it's like the ultimate yard sale!

To me, used clothing is great because it's already comfortable and you don't have to spend a lot of money. When strangers see me, they don't know who I am or why I do what I do. The only thing they know about me is what they gather from my appearance. To them, I look like an average teenager wearing expensive clothing. They don't know the truth about my clothes.

Whether we consciously recognize it or not, we are all gauged, compared, evaluated, or judged by others. What they see on the outside is not always the same as the inside, though. Unless they take the time to get to know me, their only opinion of me is gathered from what they have observed, for better or for worse.

But what if these people watching me know I am a Christian? What if they have never met a Christian before? What if, in their mental dictionary, they forever equate the word "Christian" with me? In a lot of circumstances, that is exactly what happens. Whether the person they met was Christlike or not, the impression they received is emblazoned on the entire group. For me, this is a very intimidating thought. Since I claim to be trying to live a Christlike life, it is valid to say that my life is an example of the God I serve. For a lot of people, my life will be the only Bible they will ever read. It makes it paramount that every day I wear who I am, because what I really believe in my heart is what shows through. "So live that those who know you, but don't know Him, will want to know Him, because they know you" (Unknown Author).

~ Morgan Metcalf

Decrease?

Therefore this joy of mine is fulfilled. He must increase, but I must decrease. - John 3:29b–30 NKJV

I don't know about you, but I tend to become a little bit competitive when it looks like someone else might obtain my favorite position. Whether in trumpet-playing or in schoolwork, I begin to become upset and jealous toward my peers. I do not like this competitive tendency of mine. Do I have to keep living with these grudges?

In the Bible, John the Baptist was tempted with similar thoughts. He reacted very differently though. As Jesus began to teach publicly, more and more of the people who had been listening to John started following Jesus around. John's position was being taken over by Jesus. But John wasn't envious. He told his disciples, "Therefore this joy of mine is fulfilled. He must increase, but I must decrease" (John 3:29b–30 NKJV). He was willing to fade from view. He only wanted to accomplish the task God had for him. He was then filled with joy as Jesus became more honored and favored than himself.

How did John have such a selfless attitude? Is it possible for me to view others as John viewed Jesus? Can I be free from jealous grudges? Jesus said, "And I, if I am lifted up from the earth, will draw all peoples to Myself" (John 12:32 NKJV). We can choose to lift Jesus up. We can think of Him often. We can pray that God will constantly draw our thoughts to the Lamb of God. With our focus only on our Redeemer, our thoughts will gradually be replaced by His. Realization of our helplessness will become more apparent. As with John, God's honor will gradually become most important to us.

We may not be changed as quickly as we wish; but the Author and Finisher of our faith will enable us more and more to gladly say of our peers: "They must become more admired, I must fade from view." I choose to think on my Savior more often. Are you interested in such a choice?

~ Andrew Sharley

Plane Rides

For He who has mercy on them will lead them ... He will guide them.
- Isaiah 49:10b NKJV

My grandpa has an airplane that is affectionately called "Charlie." Countless times I have had the thrill of riding in the plane with him and seeing my world from the air. Taxiing down the airstrip behind my grandparents' house, I would get a feeling of joy and excitement that I simply cannot explain. My heart would pound with excitement as soon as I heard the engine start up, and I would anticipate the fun ride I knew I would soon enjoy. Many times it would just be the two of us up in that little Cessna 180, and on those occasions I would sit in the passenger seat and pretend that I was the one flying. I would grab hold of the steering wheel that was in front of me. In my mind, it seemed as though I was the one in charge, "steering" the plane, but in reality my Grandpa was sitting right there beside me. He was the one making the plane run: pushing all the right switches, buttons, and pedals to ensure that we were safe.

Many times in my own life, I feel like I am in charge, just like I felt in control of the plane. I grab hold of the steering wheel and fly through life barely noticing that the One who created me is actually the One who is guiding each aspect of my life. Even though it seems to me that I am the one steering and pushing all those buttons, God is actually sitting right next to me making sure I don't come crashing to the ground.

It is so easy to think that we can control our own lives, but the fact is that we can't do anything of ourselves. When we take control, our lives will quickly fall apart, but when we allow Jesus to sit in the driver's seat of our "plane," we will undoubtedly soar. He wants to steer us through the hard and the easy times to the ultimate goal which He has set before us—Heaven.

~ Elizabeth King

Hope

I go to prepare a place for you. And if I go and prepare a place for you, I will come again and receive you to Myself; that where I am, there you may be also. And where I go you know, and the way you know. - John 14:2–4 NKJV

We will probably never fully understand how blessed we are. So often, we forget the simple gifts God has given us: health, friends and family, food, a place to sleep. More importantly, we forget our greatest blessing: hope. But every once in a while, we experience something that makes us realize just how much we really have.

The town I live in is colored with scenes of utter hopelessness. The destitute beg for money in the grocery store parking lot. Parents abandon their small children at the city's annual fair. People try to drown their despair with alcohol, but instead of fixing anything, it makes their problems multiply. How different would their lives be if they had the hope of a better life—one with Christ?

My mom is a nurse, so I've spent plenty of time around sick people. Each time I visit a hospital or a nursing home and see the pain and despondency that is etched on the faces of so many patients, I'm reminded of how fortunate I am to have my health, my youth, and a bright future before me. I have my whole life in front of me, and after this life, I can look forward to an eternity with Christ in heaven.

But how many people don't have that hope? How many don't know that they have a Savior who wants to help them with every struggle? That they only have a short time left before Christ comes again to take His people to live in heaven with Him?

You and I have something that so many people don't: the precious hope in our Savior. I want to share that with everyone. What about you?

~ Saraiah Turnbull

Don't Settle for Mud Pies

My soul will be satisfied as with fat and rich food, and my mouth will praise You with joyful lips. - Psalms 63:5 ESV

"These are just right. Mommy is going to think that they are real pies!"

My sister and I had just finished making mud pies and were carrying them to the front porch to show Mom. We were sure she would like them and were quite proud of ourselves for making them look so nice. We set them down on the first step and ran into the house to call Mom. We excitedly escorted her to where we left our pies. To our dismay, the pans were scraped clean. There was not a trace of our beautiful creations left. We looked around to see what had ruined our pies and found the tell-tale marks on my baby sister's happy face. She had eaten them!

If my sister had waited for lunch time, she would have been able to enjoy a more satisfying meal; but instead of waiting for real food, she went ahead and ate the play pies that we had made. I would never eat a mud pie, even if it looked just like a real one; but I sometimes do essentially the same thing in my spiritual life. When I am in too much of a hurry to find peace and enjoyment from God through His Word, and instead choose to seek satisfaction through what I can accomplish in this world, I am eating a "mud pie." It doesn't make me feel good though; it eventually makes me sick. I become disgusted with life and find that I am not satisfied at all.

If we take time to search the scriptures and find the true joy and satisfaction that comes from a relationship with God, we won't be hungering for things of this world. God offers the real food—don't settle for mud pies!

~ Bethany Corrigan

Chess!

But you are a chosen generation, a royal priesthood, a holy nation,
His own special people, that you may proclaim the praises of Him who
called you out of darkness into His marvelous light…
- 1 Peter 2:9 NKJV

"I'm hungry!"

That is the third time he has said that in the past five minutes, I
thought while rolling my eyes. Then a thought flew into my mind: *If he's*
hungry… if we eat at the pizza place… we could play with the gigantic
chess set there! My brother must have been thinking the same thing,
because we both took off sliding across the slippery pool-side surface.
Soon my brother and I were lugging around black and white knights,
horses, and pawns half our size while scheming up our next moves.
This knight is valuable, and I don't want to let him get it. Oh, I could get
his king cornered here, but I'll probably lose another pawn doing that—
but who cares? And so the game went.

When we moved away from that giant chess set, I missed it. There
is another giant chess game that I am part of though. This chess game
is meaner than the one I used to play, and you're part of it whether or
not you want to be. In this game, if you aren't decidedly on one side,
you're on the other. This chess game isn't actually a game, it's real;
it's the Great Controversy. The two sides are good and evil, Christ and
Satan. The two sides are quite different–one is a dictatorship, the other
is a loving kingdom. We are under Satan unless we decidedly choose
to be part of Christ's kingdom. Under Satan, we're pawns—we have
no choice and we aren't valuable—he just uses us as he pleases, and
he is pleased to squash us dead. We see his rule in the governments
of Hitler, Mussolini, Zedong, Pinochet, Hussein, and Idi Amin. On the
other side, we are Christ's knights. As knights, we are valuable—He
doesn't just want to use us; He loves us, cares for us, and wants the
best for us. His love is demonstrated in His sacrifice on Calvary. We
have a choice between being Satan's pawn or Christ's knight—I want
to be a knight.

~ Katie Sloop

Reaching Goals

… stand fast in one spirit, with one mind striving together for the faith of the gospel… - Philippians 1:27b KJV

Do you remember holding a helium balloon and wondering whether a gust of wind from the nearby carousel would whisk you up and blow you away? I, myself, have entertained such imaginations, but there is a man who didn't just dream about flying with balloons—he actually made it happen.

Nothing would stop the adventurous 47-year-old Kent Couch. He decided to build a lawn chair that would enable him to fly out of Oregon. First, it would take plenty of balloons. Not the birthday ones you'd pick up at the dollar store, but the jumbo-sized kind. It would also require a lawn chair, water weights, and, among other things, lots of rope. Soon he had built his contraption and was ready to try it out. The first try was successful, yet a little dangerous. Settling in his lawn chair with a cluster of balloons floating above him, four water weights strapped underneath his chair, as well as a GPS, parachute, and BB gun to shoot balloons, he floated away. But then, having popped too many balloons, Couch began to descend rapidly and quickly made use of his parachute. He tried again, and this time tied the balloons within reach so that he could release air rather than blasting off a balloon here and there. The ride was much more peaceful, and towards the end, with only eight pounds of water weight left, Couch descended—in his lawn chair—and soon landed on terra firma, just short of Idaho. What an achievement! Although it was dangerous, this man poured a lot of energy and effort into accomplishing something he really wanted to do—something he had dreamed of.

What about us Christians? Do we have a goal that we are striving for in the same way? Jesus gave everything to make sure that we could be lifted heavenward. Shouldn't we now be pouring energy, heart and soul, into preparing ourselves and others for the ascent?

~ Esther Ferraz

Hid in My Heart

Thy word have I hid in mine heart, that I might not sin against Thee.
- Psalms 119:11 KJV

"Supper time!" My mother called down the hall.

"Yes!" I muttered to myself as I dashed towards the table. "I'm starving!"

For the last hour, my stomach had felt like it was fighting a war. The smells of the delicious food threatened to shatter my already impatient nerves. Plopping down at the dinner table, I eagerly eyed the dishes of steaming food. I was secretly hoping that the meal prayer would be short, allowing me to satisfy my appetite sooner. However, my dad suggested that before we pray, we should repeat our memory verses. My heart and stomach seemed to drop to the floor in disappointment. *Couldn't we forget it just this one time?* I thought.

When I was younger, my family would memorize many verses from the Bible. We would select various scripture verses and repeat them before our meals and at family worship. As you might guess, I wasn't always the most supportive of this ritual. Quite often my impatience would get the better of me and I would grumble and complain about having to repeat the verses over and over again.

When we are a humble learner of Christ's words, He will be to us a refuge and defense from Satan. By His strength alone we can overcome Satan's attacks. Now those verses that I memorized back then are very precious to me. Whenever I feel like I am in a place where I can't see the way out, the Lord brings to my memory an encouraging promise. It's almost as if God is right there beside me, wrapping his arms around me in a big hug and saying, "I'm here for you, whenever you need Me."

~ Sierra Buhler

Generations

For as by one man's disobedience many were made sinners, so by the obedience of one shall many be made righteous. - Romans 5:19 KJV

My family runs a dairy farm that is nestled among the peaceful, green rolling hills of Vermont. Arthur L. Miller, my great-great-grandfather, bought our farm around 100 years ago and began farming with a handheld plow, 20 milk cows, and a family to provide for. Since then, the family farm has been passed down through five generations of Millers, and is currently supporting four families, 130 milk cows, and eight tractors. My fondest memories will always be of running through endless fields of waving grass, stomping in the brown, weed-filled water of our dearly beloved "Cow Pond" and sharing special family picnics of graham crackers and milk on the hill as we watched the sun slowly streak its closing rays over the tired world. To think of the impact that our farm has had on our lives, our church, and our community is astounding. All of this was made possible by the choice of one man.

My great-great-grandfather was not the first man who has had a significant impact on my life. Over 6,000 years ago, a man named Adam decided to make the first move in a rebellion against God. Since that choice, every generation for thousands of years has progressively degenerated. When we were at our absolute lowest point, another man, Jesus Christ, also had a decision to make: would He go through with His plan to redeem this fallen race? Was it worth it to Him to be rejected and killed by the ones He had come to save in order to spend eternity with them? All of humanity hung on His answer. Jesus answered the question with a resounding "Yes!" It was worth it.

You too have the decision on how you will influence the generations that will follow you. You are given the power to pass on a curse or a blessing to people that you may never meet. What will you do with that power?

~Sarah Miller

Secrets

*"For My thoughts are not your thoughts, nor are your ways My ways,"
says the Lord. - Isaiah 55:8 NKJV*

In many grade school classrooms there is a rule against telling
secrets. There is good reason behind this rule. Imagine with me that
a little student is watching his playmates whisper to each other. I can
see him yearning to know what they are saying. The little boy walks
crying to his teacher, and he tells her that his playmates wouldn't tell
him their secret. The teacher sighs inwardly as she works through this
frequently repeated situation. She then decides to make an official rule
banning all secrets.

Why would a student be so upset because he is excluded from
a secret? I believe we all have intense curiosity, especially when we
think we're missing out on something exciting. We want to know what's
going on and be where the fun is. Almost subconsciously, we wonder:
"Am I missing out on something? Is there some excitement that I don't
know about?" We want to know everything that's going on.

The first woman ever created had this same curiosity. When Eve
was at the tree of the knowledge of good and evil, the Devil convinced
her that God was concealing a more abundant life. He told Eve
that God was keeping secrets from her to keep her from the fullest
happiness. Eve suddenly wanted to know the secrets that God was
keeping from her. She wanted to know everything that God knew. So,
she ate the fruit purported to give her greater knowledge. In this action,
she made the most consequential mistake of human history. Her
mistake not only ruined her blissful existence, but it also led to every
sorrow and grief on our planet. All this pain came from the human
desire to know everything. Whether it creates tears in kindergarten or
brings sin into the world, the desire to be a know-it-all always causes
trouble. If only Eve had allowed God to be the all-knowing One. God
wanted to shelter the first couple from the griefs and fears of sin
because it is not our job to know everything. We do not want to make
the mistake of trying to know all that God knows. Let God be the all-
wise One. He lovingly whispers: "Trust Me, I am all for you."

~ Andrew Sharley

111

A Selfish Heart

Keep your lives free from the love of money and be content with what you have... - Hebrews 13:5 NIV

"Look at my new doll!" My little friend exclaimed, holding up her hundred-dollar toy. My jaw dropped open. I had never seen, much less owned, such a beautiful and expensive doll. I had been perfectly happy with the rag doll my grandma had made for me, but now that I had seen this one, jealousy sprang up inside my little heart. It wasn't fair that my friend should get a new doll when I didn't!

I grew up on a little farm in Tennessee for most of my childhood. The woods were my home, so I never even thought of new toys and clothes. Who needs toys when you have a whole farm of animals to play with? But when we moved off the farm, I began to see all the things the world was trying to convince me I was missing out on. I even had the audacity to pray for my selfish wishes. I found myself wishing I had things that I didn't need: the new clothes, expensive electronics, and fancy toys.

However, when I directed my thoughts towards Christ's sacrifice, I realized how selfish I was. When Jesus came to earth, where did He come to? Did He choose to be born into a wealthy, influential family? No, He was born in a stable, to a poor couple who probably didn't know where their next meal was coming from.

I take so much for granted. Here I am looking at someone else with jealousy because they have better shoes, when there are so many people who don't have shoes at all! When Jesus was on earth, He didn't go where it was most comfortable; He went where He was needed. As I go through life, do I just float along living for myself and taking His sacrifice for granted? Christ's sacrifice wasn't only in His death, but also in the unselfish life He led to give us eternal life.

~ Moriah Mays

The Grandfather

*By this we know that we love the children of God, when we love God,
and keep His commandments. - 1 John 5:2 KJV*

A frail old man once lived with his son and his son's family. Being
an older gentleman, his vision was blurry and his hands were shaky.
At the dinner table, the grandfather's trembling hands would frequently
make things difficult for the other family members. Peas would
sometimes roll off his spoon and drop to the floor. His shaking hands
would spill his glass of milk on the tablecloth. Plates were frequently
broken when he accidently dropped them. After a while, the family
became irritated with the grandfather. The son and his wife agreed
that they had had enough of the old man's accidents. A small table
was placed in the corner of the kitchen. There the grandfather would
eat his meals alone. Sometimes, a tear would roll down his wrinkled
cheek, unnoticed by the rest of his family. His small grandson had
been watching what was happening to his grandfather. One day, he
announced to his parents that he was making small tables for them
too. After all, if Grandfather had his own table, why shouldn't they?
The parents were stunned by their son's proclamation. With tears
in their eyes, they led the grandfather back to the table. There he
happily ate his meals, surrounded by his family. No more harsh words
were spoken when he spilled his milk. No one yelled at him when he
accidently dropped his plate. Instead, his unsteady actions were met
with love and patience.

How often do we treat those around us as if they are "spilling peas
at the table," or "spilling milk on our nice Sabbath tablecloth?" I find
that I am often judging others on how they act, whether it is in their
Christian life or in their social interactions. Just like the Grandfather,
people are ostracized to the small table in the corner simply because
our love for them is based on their actions. Just as God's love for us is
impartial and infinite, so should my love as a Christian be for everyone
around me.

~ Sierra Buhler

Keep Pressing On

*I press on to reach the end of the race and receive the heavenly prize
for which God, through Christ Jesus, is calling us.*
- Philippians 3:14 NLT

"Just keep pedaling!" My dad exclaimed as we biked up the big hill on our way home. Every day, in almost any kind of weather, my dad and I biked to and from school. The way there was downhill and easy; however, that meant that the way home was all uphill. Since I was only six, I became exhausted easily and my dad had to help me get home.

I remember one day in particular when the hills seemed steeper, and the way seemed longer. As we biked, my dad was always right there in front of me, encouraging me. He told me to keep on pedaling or else I wouldn't make it. I did my best to pedal constantly. However, this day I just couldn't make it. "Dad! I can't keep on going!" I yelled through the wind. Without hesitation, he turned around, came back to me, and placed his hand on my back to push me up the hill.

That day, I knew I was on my way home, and I wasn't going to let the hills or the wind stop me. When I felt like giving up, the realization that my dad was right there to help me gave me strength.

The hills might seem steep in your life, the wind fierce, and everything just too overwhelming. Maybe you feel like giving up; but I want to ask you to not let things of this world stop you from making it home. Remember that God is only a call away, and if you call on Him, He will be right there to push you up the hill.

~ Agnes Grétarsdóttir

Content with Little

Keep your lives free from the love of money and be content with what you have, because God has said, "Never will I leave you; never will I forsake you." - Hebrews 13:5 NIV

I am 17 years old and in 11th grade. I have lived in Bend, Oregon for most of my life, and my God has provided for all of my needs. My family has always had plenty of food, clothes, and a warm house to live in. God has provided several opportunities to visit different countries such as Thailand, Israel, and Mexico. I am very blessed. But something happened that made me see just how blessed I am.

Two summers ago, I had the privilege of participating in the Ultimate Workout outreach program in southern Mexico. While we were there, we built a Seventh-day Adventist church, supported a Vacation Bible School program, and tried to help in any way that we could. I noticed that these people who we were serving didn't have many of the things that we take for granted in the United States. They were living in small stucco houses with dirt or concrete floors, yet they were so joyful. Animals lived in their yards, and trash was everywhere. Yet they found time to generously help our cook make meals for our large group.

Most of the native people there had a better walk with God than I had ever seen before. Their lack of earthly possessions was actually a blessing. It occurred to me that the many things that I have are sometimes a distraction from a closer walk with God. I learned that when I am filled with the joy that comes from the Lord, my joy "spills over" on the people around me and makes them happier too. The more generous I am with the blessings and talents that God has given me, the more joyful I'll be.

~ Anna Ford

A Strong Hand to Hold

For I the Lord thy God will hold thy right hand, saying unto thee, Fear not; I will help thee. - Isaiah 41:13 KJV

One blustery morning, my mom, brother, and I went to town to get some groceries. It was raining and the parking lot was particularly wet. Mom tried to find a parking place that was close to the door, but everyone else must have had the same idea, and we ended up parking on the far side of the parking lot. Since I was only two, my mom had my brother, who was fourteen months older than I, hold one of my hands while she held the other to steady me. As we neared a large puddle, I got the great idea to lift both of my legs and swing from their hands. "Whee!" I squealed, pulling my brother down into the puddle with me.

I still hold great confidence in my brother, who has grown tall and strong since then. He has not only grown physically but also in his relationship with God. I know that I can trust him to make good decisions, and experience has shown me that his outstretched hand will always reach to help me in my greatest times of need.

His strong hands remind me of another hand that is stretched out to save me. As a result, this quote came alive to me in a recent time of discouragement: "… if you keep looking up, not down at your difficulties, you will not faint in the way, you will soon see Jesus reaching His hand to help you, and you will only have to give Him your hand in simple confidence, and let Him lead you. As you become trustful, you will become hopeful" (*Messages to Young People*, pg. 63). My hope was renewed! Will you take His hand and let Him lead you, too?

~ Bethany Corrigan

Thirsty

… whoever drinks of the water that I shall give him will never thirst.
- John 4:14 NKJV

A young marine corporal named Joey Mora was aboard an aircraft carrier that was patrolling the Iranian sea. One day, he fell overboard. It was 36 hours before anyone noticed he was missing and a search and rescue mission was initiated. But it was abandoned after an additional 24 hours had passed. Joey was presumed dead. But 72 hours after his fall, Joey was rescued by four Pakistani fishermen. He was found in a state of delirium, treading water in his sleep. His tongue was cracked and dry after spending so many hours bobbing in the salty sea. The only thought on his mind was "Water!"

To Joey, water had become the most valuable thing on Earth. After so many hours spent languishing in the salty ocean, he was absolutely desperate for something to drink. The water that he had taken for granted mere hours before suddenly became infinitely more valuable because he was desperately thirsty.

As Christians, we are called to carry the gospel to a desperately thirsty world. Each and every soul on this planet is thirsty from their long lives spent languishing in the salty sea of sin. Everyone is looking for something to satisfy that emptiness inside of them; and Christians are the only ones who know what they need! We are supposed to be a light shining in the darkness. But by our torpid indolence, millions are perishing in their thirst, never having been led to the water of life. Jesus is the only one who can satisfy the longing of the world; but have we led them to Him?

~ Michael Jensen

Duet Living

If the whole body were an eye, where would the sense of hearing be? If the whole body were an ear, where would the sense of smell be?
- 1 Corinthians 12:17 NIV

The most exciting event of the year for piano students had come. The piano recital was organized by Mrs. James, our teacher, who divided most of the students into groups of two or four. I found out who my partner was, and I felt kind of discouraged: it was Brock.

"Yes! Bryan is the one who plays with me!" Brock yelled after his piano lesson. "It's gonna be great!"

Can he stay in tune and cooperate with me at all? I don't really trust him, Lord, and I really want to do well on the duet. Tell me what to do. But God didn't answer right away; maybe He wanted me to wait for a little while, and let me to figure it out. Oh well, I really didn't know.

So I left the answer to my prayer with God, and I practiced my own part. That was not a bad thing to do because soon I could almost play my part with my eyes closed. I kept wondering, *What about Brock?*

"Hey, Bryan, let's practice together," Brock announced, "The recital is getting closer." After playing a few bars, he said, "Ah man! I need to practice more on this!" And then Brock left. It was kind of a short practice together, but it was better than I expected. As we practiced, our piece became more and more perfect, and we were beginning to trust each other more.

Finally the day came. All the people clapped after our performance, and we bowed proudly.

We are all different, but we are all united in Christ, as parts of His body. "... there should be no division in the body, but that its parts should have equal concern for each other" (1 Corinthians 12:25 NIV). When we decide to work together, there is harmony.

~ Bryan Chen

God's Grace Goes On

Oh, give thanks to the God of gods! For His mercy endures forever.
- Psalms 136:2 NKJV

When I came home this past summer on break, I met the newest addition to my family: a middle-aged man named Nate. He eats meals with us, takes showers at our house, and wears my step-dad's clothes. He has several dogs, one leg, and no home.

Nate started to drink when he was very young, and over time, the alcohol seriously affected his mind. As a teenager, he walked out into traffic and was hit by a car. He sustained a head injury and lost his left leg. His injuries keep him from getting a job or even caring for his own basic needs. Every month he gets a disability check, but promptly wastes it on alcohol. By the end of each month, he is back at our house, hungry and cold. The cycle is incredibly frustrating to watch because Nate repeats his mistakes over and over, without seeming to learn anything from them. Everyone pities Nate, but it's hard to want to help him. Not only did he bring his problems upon himself, but he still continues to waste what meager resources he has.

In reality, each and every one of us is like Nate. We have a free will; God allows us to make our own decisions. Yet we abuse our privilege. We cause our own problems by choosing to sin. And even after we've seen the trouble that results from sin, we often repeat the same mistakes. 2 Peter 2:22 says, "It has happened unto them according to the true proverb: The dog turning to his own vomit again, and the sow that had washed to wallowing in the mire" (NKJV).

However, the amazing thing about God is that, no matter how many times we mess up, He'll never give up on us. It's impossible to exhaust His grace. Every time we fall, He is there to pick us up and show us a better way.

~ Saraiah Turnbull

Go and Sin No More

… For if through the offence of one many be dead, much more the grace of God, and the gift by grace, which is by one man, Jesus Christ, hath abounded unto many. - Romans 5:15 KJV

There was once a well-to-do gentleman who had a lovely flower garden with the most wonderful flowers you could dream of. As he was sitting in his seat by the garden gazing on its beauty, he saw a boy come by the outer path, stop, and steal a beautiful flower from his garden. The man couldn't believe his eyes. The boy kept walking, so the man hopped out of his seat and took a roundabout way to meet the boy on his way out. When he met the boy he asked him, "So which is the prettiest flower in my garden?"

The boy was surprised to see this man who came out of nowhere. He thought a while and then concluded, "That rose over there, sir." The man silently went over to where the boy had pointed (with his hand still on his shoulder) and plucked the very rose he pointed to and handed it to the boy. The boy stared into the face of the gentleman and asked, "Ain't you gonna have me punished, sir?"

The gentleman looked at the boy clutching his two flowers and answered, "No, but answer me one thing: are you ever going to steal flowers out of my garden again?" The boy didn't hesitate in assuring him that he wouldn't. So the gentleman was satisfied to leave it at that.

Sometimes we deserve a stiff punishment, and grace is extended in its place. When we share this with others, many times it inspires them to try harder—I know it has for me. Christ has done the same for us—His friends. Although our sins killed Him, He still offers us eternal life by His grace. He offers it to us as sinners that we may repent and follow in His footsteps. "But God commendeth His love toward us, in that, while we were yet sinners, Christ died for us" (Romans 5:8 KJV).

~ Nolan Knuppel

120

Dye to Self

*For jealousy and selfishness are not God's kind of wisdom. Such things
are earthly, unspiritual, and demonic. - James 3:15 NLT*

One day, my friend suggested that we dye our hair. At this thought,
my eyes shone with excitement. This, of course, was against my
mother's will. She explained to me that my hair would be damaged
and would grow back with funny streaks. I begged and pleaded with
her, but nothing worked. Finally, I decided that I would dye my hair
secretly. But I had one problem—where would I get the money? Our
family's piggy-bank caught my eye. To my great joy, I found it almost
full of loose change. Stealthily breaking it open, I surveyed the mound
of coins. Luckily, my mother was in the shower, and had no idea what
her little girl was up to. Immediately, I made the short dash to the
hair salon with my friend. Back at home the inevitable happened: my
mother discovered the empty and broken piggy-bank on the floor.

She immediately marched over to the salon, where she found
a very chagrined daughter, perched on a tall chair, her hair already
plastered with foil. Just by looking at my mother, I could tell that her
blood was boiling. But it was too late to change anything, and my
mom, not having any other choice, gave in to the idea of having my
hair dyed.

Long ago, Lucifer, the most honored angel in heaven, made a
very selfish decision. He had become very jealous of Jesus, who was
second under God the Father. Lucifer began to incite rebellion against
Jesus in the hearts of the angels. Because of this rebellion, Lucifer
was thrown out of Heaven. He lost everything that he had, his honor
and his beauty, just because he wanted something he couldn't have.

After I dyed my hair, I regretted it. The color grew back differently,
and my hair was damaged. Often, when we get what we want for
ourselves, it ends up bringing us pain. As Christians, we need to have
the unselfishness of Christ in our hearts. The battle against our selfish
wants is the greatest war we will ever fight, but with God by our sides,
we will become conquerors.

~ Ellen Yoon

Speak No Evil

Keep your tongue from evil, and your lips from speaking deceit.
- Psalm 34:13 NKJV

Oh no, did I really say that? It was too late to take it back; nothing I could do would erase the words I had just spoken. My best friend and I had a fight; it was my fault, and it could have been easily prevented if I hadn't slipped up. What I said was the truth, but I said it without love, and because of that, it offended her. She burst into tears and left the room. We stopped talking all together after that.

All my life I have found myself slipping up and saying things that offend and hurt people. I have lost friends and have had friendships drawn apart because of this. I tried so hard to overcome this bad habit of speaking before thinking, but it seemed hopeless. Finally I realized that because I am a human being, I am sinful and can't overcome evil tendencies on my own. It was then that I started giving my words to God and letting Him help me find the right words to say. I still slip up often, but with God's help, I am able to swallow my words and think of something more uplifting to say.

Trying to accomplish things by myself never seems to work out the way I want it to. It isn't until we accept God's help that we can finally accomplish what needs to be done. Philippians 4:13 says: "I can do all things through Christ who strengthens me." Ask Christ for His strength, and see what He does for you.

~ Raina Walker

Upside Down Logic

… learn from Me, for I am gentle and lowly in heart…
- *Matthew 22:29 NKJV*

Has it ever occurred to you that the life of a Christian is twisted? It's twisted because we are called to live in a way different from how the world thinks. Of course I've known this, but my mind hadn't totally grasped this idea until today while I was having my morning devotions. I was reading in Luke 14:7–14 where Jesus tells a parable about a banquet. He was telling the people with Him that, instead of them going to the best seat at the table, they should go to the lowest seat; and by doing so, they would be exalted. Yes, that's right. It says that by being the lowest, we will also be the highest. Weird, eh? Then in verse 12, He talks to the host of the party and tells him that he shouldn't invite his friends, family, and rich neighbors to his party since they can pay him back by inviting him to their house. Instead, he should invite the poor and the needy, who are unable to repay him. I don't know about you, but I think that's interesting. A party to me is supposed to be filled with presents, and the people you love are supposed to be surrounding you.

The way Christ wants us to live is so different from how we really do. It doesn't even seem humanly possible, but maybe it seems that way because it isn't appealing to our human nature. I mean, who likes sitting in the worst seat and inviting a bunch of random poor people to their house for a party when instead, they could have it with the people closest to them? Why did Jesus tell this story anyway? Well, in *Desire of Ages* it says: "The work of God is not to bear the image and superscription of man" (pg. 182). To me, that is what the story is trying to show. The way God works is nothing like how we work. Everything He does is selfless and includes being a servant—He does it out of love. As a child, when Jesus saw someone hungry, He gave them the little food He had. He didn't even expect to be paid for it. The interesting thing is that this is how Christ wants us to live. It's very different, but this is what makes us stand out as Christians. So, I have one question for you. Are you ready to live a twisted life?

~ Shenel Cruz

Lesson of Trust

The fear of man bringeth a snare: but whoso putteth his trust in the Lord shall be safe. - Proverbs 29:25 KJV

We were on our way home from a long day of shopping. It had been pouring rain all day, and the roads were quite wet. I was concerned they would get slick with the cooling night temperatures, but my dad was driving and wasn't worried, so I tried to calm my fears.

My uneasiness resurfaced, however, when I saw a sign that warned, "Watch for black ice." I then realized that I wasn't trusting God. I was choosing to let fear rule my heart in the place of Him. Sensing our anxiety, Dad assured us that the sign was just a general winter warning; it was not likely that we would run into black ice on this trip, since the temperature had been above freezing for quite some time. As I chose to let God take control, I felt somewhat calmed, but I was still struggling to trust Him fully.

"Let's have worship," Dad suggested. As we sang one of my favorite hymns, I noticed a huge rock in the middle of the highway. My heart lurched, and I could feel fear rise up inside me. By the time Dad realized what it was, we were too close to swerve around it, and the only other option was to try to straddle it. We stopped singing and stared at the rock, knowing that it was too large to clear. Whizzing over the top, we didn't hear any scraping at all! I realized that God had kept us and our van safe.

Instantly, I recalled the words we had just sung about our Heavenly Father's care for His children: "… from all evil things He spares them, in His mighty arms He bears them." As we sang the next verse, my heart filled with joy: "Praise the Lord in joyful numbers. Your Protector never slumbers."

~ Bethany Corrigan

Oma and Opa's House

Let not your heart be troubled … In my Father's house are many mansions… I will come again, and receive you unto myself; that where I am, there ye may be also. - John 14:1–3 KJV

My grandparents' house in Germany is very special to me—like a second home. With all the moving I've done in my life, their house has always been a familiar landmark in time, a home base that I can always refer back to—wherever I am. Through the years I've made many a happy memory at that house, and when I visited last year, it was like old times once again. It reminded me of all the many happy Christmas celebrations spent there: curling up in the living room and playing board games with my sister and Grandpa, helping Grandma cook up the tastiest meals on earth, and hammering away on a birdhouse with my cousin in Grandpa's immaculate workshop. I remembered the nearby walnut trees we raided like squirrels, the black pump in the vegetable garden which provided for our many water fights, and the bulging hammock we'd sit in and savor homemade ice-cream.

When I discovered that Oma and Opa were selling the house, I felt very sad. They weren't going to move very far away, but the house with all its memories and familiar nooks and crannies would no longer be there to welcome me.

Thinking about this makes me long for a permanent home: a place I will never have to leave, a place that will always be there for me. When talking about this to my parents, they reminded me that Jesus is building a place that will someday be my permanent home: a home where there will never be a teary goodbye or feelings of homesickness. I will make better memories in that home than in any place here on earth. It helps me to remember that this world isn't my home, and that I'm just passing through.

~ Esther Ferraz

Hazardous Trails

Let us fix our eyes on Jesus, the author and perfecter of our faith…
- Hebrews 12:2 NIV

Here at Fountainview Academy, there is a trail that goes from the school building to the girls' dorm. This path is very steep and can be hazardous in the daytime and even more so at night. As the days get shorter, it becomes necessary for the girls to hike to and from the school building in the dark. One moonless night when I was hiking up the trail, I found that if I looked at the trail right in front of me, I started to stumble. It was only when I looked up and kept my eyes on the lights at the end of the path that my steps became sure.

Ellen White's first vision was about a straight and narrow path that led to heaven. On this trail traveled the Advent believers who were being led by Jesus to heaven. They were safe only when they kept their eyes on Him. There were some who said, "This is too hard. We should have reached the City before this … they stumbled and got their eyes off the mark and lost site of Jesus, and fell off the path down in the dark and wicked world below" (*The Early Years - Volume 1*, pg. 57).

I have found that it is very easy for me to take my eyes off of Jesus. I spend time with Him in the morning but then don't talk to Him for the rest of the day. Often it is only when I stumble and fall that I remember to talk with Him. I realize that it is so important for me to keep my eyes on Jesus; He is the light shining before me, and I know when I keep my eyes on Him, He will keep me from stumbling and falling off the trail.

~ Kami Rose

Domino Effect

Let no corrupt word proceed out of your mouth, but what is good for necessary edification, that it may impart grace to the hearers.
- Ephesians 4:29 NKJV

"Ewww… that soup looks so gross!" I muttered under my breath as I went through line in the cafeteria. Behind me, I noticed a girl about to ladle some of the soup into her bowl. Then she glanced at me, the pot of soup, and back to me before sheepishly returning her bowl to the stack of dishes and mumbling her agreement. Behind her, a couple guys saw us avoiding the pot of soup, and, assuming there must be something wrong with it, they skipped it, too.

I've been noticing little incidents like this a lot lately. Without thinking, I'll say something negative, and people around me will agree and start complaining about whatever it was that I mentioned. Like a row of dominoes, the influence of my careless words causes a chain reaction of discontent.

Lucifer was only one angel out of the entire heavenly host, yet his dissatisfaction created a wave of unhappiness throughout heaven that was far greater than he could have imagined. He caused bitter discord to take the place of the sweet harmony that had characterized heaven. His discontent spread, evolving into the wild epidemic of sin that we see all around us today.

Although I certainly don't try to cause others to be discontent, that's not enough. Satan can use me without me even noticing. I have to make a conscious and decided effort to guard what I say and do, so that my words and actions won't cause others to become unhappy. With God's help, I'm starting to be more aware of the effect I have on others, and beginning to use my influence for good.

~ Saraiah Turnbull

Solid

How can … [I] stay on the path of purity? By living according to your word. - Psalm 119:9 NIV

"Look out below! There's a rock coming!"

I quickly jumped to the right of the narrow chute and watched as my dean Rosa narrowly dodged the small avalanche of rocks headed her way. A group of students and I had decided to go on a Sabbath afternoon hike with our deans. Since there weren't any trails that led to the ridge where we wanted to go, Jay, Rosa's husband, cut his own path and began hiking. On the way up the mountain, we stumbled upon what looked like an old avalanche chute. As we began to climb it, rocks were dislodged and fell dangerously close to those further behind. Before long, it became apparent that the route we were taking was not safe and that we would not reach the top before dark. Although we were disappointed to turn back, we were still thankful to arrive in one piece.

Often I find myself doing the same thing in my walk with God. By allowing my selfish character to lead my life, I discover that my path has suddenly become so difficult that I can't keep walking it by myself. The consequences are too demanding, and the debt I have accumulated from my pleasure is too expensive for me to pay. Instead of allowing the avalanche of penalties to swallow me, Christ offers a solid road out: His Word. The principles outlined in the Bible are tried and true. When I follow them, changes begin to show in the way I act, think, and live my life. Before long, I am once again on the right road.

Jesus desires for you to leave the downward path, and instead follow the simple, upward way that He has planned for you in His Word. Won't you make the choice to follow His path today?

~ Sarah Miller

Grace

… the Lord is very compassionate and merciful. - James 5:11b NKJV

I was homeschooled from first grade through eighth grade. For a couple of years, I was tutored by a retired school teacher. Her house was heated by a wood stove, and in the winter we were very cozy.

One day, as I was sitting at the table doing my school work, I heard something going on in the kitchen and went to see what was happening. As I dashed around the corner, I started to fall and put my right hand on the nearest thing to steady myself. Unfortunately, the nearest thing was the sizzling hot wood stove. Instantly, I felt an intense pain in my hand and I jerked it away from the stove. The skin on the palm of my hand was all shriveled up. I was afraid to tell my teacher, but the pain was soon unbearable. She called my parents, then proceeded to get out bandages, ointment, and a couple of other things. When I saw her pull a pair of scissors out of the drawer, I was very nervous. I was sure she was going to cut the skin off my hand. I asked about them and was relieved when she said they were for cutting the gauze.

Just like I didn't want to tell my teacher that I had hurt my hand, we, by nature, don't want to confess our mistakes; especially if they are willful. Mine was not intentional, but I was still afraid that my teacher would be angry with me for not looking where I was going. Instead, she was very compassionate. We also, when we have sinned, are afraid that God will be angry if we trouble Him. Yet God is not angry with us at all. He is often very sad that we have done wrong, but He is gracious. When we make mistakes, even willfully, and confess them to God, He will have compassion on us. He is very willing to help when we come to Him with our problems. I am so glad we serve a compassionate God. Aren't you?

~ Kami Rose

The Sail Head of Perfect Character

Now for this very reason also, applying all diligence, in your faith
supply moral excellence, and in your moral excellence, knowledge;
and in your knowledge, self-control, and in your self-control,
perseverance, and in your perseverance, godliness; and in your
godliness, brotherly kindness, and in your brotherly kindness, love.
- 2 Peter 1:5–7 NASB

I stood at the mast, waiting for the right moment to ascend to the head of the flaked mainsail to secure the cover. My hands were numb from the cold water and balked at the thought of climbing partway up a carbon-fiber pole without the aid of a halyard and harness. Finally beginning my ascent, I grabbed hold of some lines to elevate me within reach of the footholds. As I arrived at each one, the next one always seemed to be just close enough to get to without encountering excessive difficulty. Soon, I arrived at the head of the sail.

In a similar way, we need to climb the mast of character. We fail to realize the importance of our characters as witnessing tools and as something we will keep for eternity. If we choose to begin our climb by exercising faith in Christ, each foothold along the way will come within reach. At this moment, many are standing at the bottom of the character mast, waiting for an opportunity to begin their ascent. There's no better time than now to begin that difficult journey. We must start by building a relationship with God and ask Him to impart His character to us. As Paul says in Romans, "... tribulation brings about perseverance; and perseverance, proven character" (Romans 5:3–4 NASB). Each foothold of tribulation and character building we encounter along our journey is a step toward another. For example, in Galatians 5 Paul proclaims, "... the fruit of the Spirit is love, joy, peace, patience, kindness, goodness, faithfulness ... against such things there is no law" (Galatians 5:1 NASB). If we start with love, our love for others will end in joy. Joy can lead to peace, and peace to patience. This continues the entire way up the mast until we arrive at the "sail head" of a perfect character.

~ Christian Welch

Incredible Offer

Being justified freely by His grace through the redemption that is in Christ Jesus… - Romans 3:24 KJV

My sisters and I needed laptops. Most of our homeschooling was on the computer, and our family's one laptop just didn't meet our needs. So, my parents got on the internet and started searching. Eventually they found the right computers for us. The problem was that none of us had enough money to buy a good laptop, and Dad and Mom simply couldn't afford to help us.

Mom had been talking on the phone with my grandpa about which computers we should get. When she got off the phone, she was smiling. Grandpa had told her that he and Grandma would buy the laptops for us. I was so excited! Because of my grandparents and their love for us, we would be able to have the computers we needed. We also had the opportunity to use our resources towards a laptop for my brother.

This is like what Jesus did for us. Because of our sins, we had a great debt that we couldn't pay. But because of His great love for us, He paid the price on Calvary. We can have salvation through accepting His blood in place of our sins. We also are given the opportunity to use our time and energy in bringing others to Christ.

But just like my grandparents' offer, we have to take advantage of God's grace. My sisters and I could have told our grandparents, "We don't need you to help us. We just won't get laptops." Then, although the funds were available, we still would not have been able to have computers. It's the same way with God's grace. We must accept it into our daily lives for it to make a difference in us. Let's choose today to accept God's incredible offer!

~ Aileen Corrigan

Clean and Free

A faithful man will abound with blessings, but he who hastens to be rich will not go unpunished. - Proverbs 28:20 NKJV

My grandfather has been a scientist all of his life, and he has worked as a rocket scientist for many years. One of his greatest achievements was working with the team that built the propulsion system for the 'Eagle' that landed on the moon in 1969. In his later career, he worked as a test engineer for a leading jet engine company.

One day he began testing an anti-icing system for a jet engine. He then noticed that the system was flawed and that ice had begun to form on the engine. He put this on his report and gave it to his supervisor. The next day his supervisor came to him very angry, demanding that he change his report. My grandfather knew that if he changed the report, the lives of thousands of people would be put at risk. After refusing, my grandfather went home and wrote a letter to his chief administrator about the incident. He almost lost his job, but when he threatened to give the letter to the Federal Aviation Administration, he was not fired. His supervisor then asked him if he had any suggestions about what to do about the flawed anti-icing system. My grandfather, with his keen, analytical mind responded that he did have an idea. He proceeded to design an anti-icing system for his company that is still used on most commercial airliners to this day. When the company registered a patent for his design, they did not put his name on it because of his refusal to change his report. If he had changed his report, he would have received recognition, power, and most likely, riches from holding the patent, but instead he was content to have a clean and free conscience.

Being free in your heart is one of the greatest feelings. If your conscience is clear, your life is at peace and you are free. God is the only one who can give us a clear conscience and freedom.

~ Derek Glatts

Eat Until Your Smile Comes Back

When your words came, I ate them; they were my joy and my heart's delight, for I bear your name, Lord God Almighty.
- Jeremiah 15:16 NIV

I grew up being very healthy. However, about five years ago I came home from school feeling a little under the weather. Even though I felt this way, I decided to help my mom cook supper. She told me that she didn't need help, so I then decided to take a little nap. I don't know how long I slept, but I woke up with a weird feeling. I felt like I was on fire and yet freezing cold at the same time. The whole world seemed like it was spinning, and I couldn't talk or get out of my bed. Finally, my mom came into my room to wake me up, and discovered that I had a fever of 40.3°C (about 104.5°F). As soon as I saw my mom, I fell asleep and didn't remember anything until the next morning.

The next day, I was totally fine, except a little weak. My mom told me that she had called my uncle, who is a doctor, and followed his directions to make my fever go away. I didn't feel hungry at all. Although my mom was happy to see me recovering, she was worried about my lack of appetite. To satisfy my mother, I did my best to eat and managed to have a few spoonfuls at a time. My mom was worried, but she couldn't do anything about it. After a week passed, I still had no strength, no energy, and no smile. I thought I was fine not eating any food, but my body didn't agree. My body needed energy. Slowly, I began to force myself to eat until the day came when I was hungry again and my smile came back.

God's Word, the Bible, is the food for my spiritual body. I need to eat, chew, and digest God's Word to grow and get energy for my spiritual life. When I am healthy, I feel hungry when I need food; but when I am sick, I don't feel my need of nutrition. Sometimes I do not feel hungry for God's Word, but I have learned to recognize that this is the time when I need it the most.

~ Hannah Lee

Here Am I; Send Me

Also I heard the voice of the Lord, saying, Whom shall I send, and who will go for us? Then said I, Here am I; send me. - Isaiah 6:8 KJV

When I was in seventh grade, the students of our church traveled to India for a mission trip. In preparation, we memorized hymns and catchy tunes in English so that the children could easily follow us.

Before we went to India, my mind was filled with worries because most of us could not speak English well, and I was also concerned about India's religion. Most Indians are Hindus, which made me fearful about spreading the gospel there. How dare we share God's Word among the Hindus? No matter how ready we were for this trip, we still didn't know what to do. With all this worry, we flew to India. For three weeks our goal would be to do our best to show them what a Christian's life is like. Our primary project was to run a summer Bible camp. At first I had thought that fewer than ten people would come to the camp, but more than fifty people came to enjoy the Bible camp with us! Women, children, and even elderly men joined in the fun. Each day was a blessing, and we felt privileged to share Jesus with them. When these guests started to pray with other students, I was so happy that I could've spread my wings and flew. When the Bible camp ended, students hugged me and said that because of me, they found Jesus. I was amazed! During only three short weeks, God worked through me. That summer I experienced His power, and, through my class, God introduced His plan of salvation to the young Indian people at Bible camp.

There are a lot of people who don't know about God, but the harvest of souls is ready, and I believe God sent me to India to lead some of them to Him. The voice of Jesus is calling. He is calling loud; He is calling long; He is calling now. The reward He offers is rich and free. Won't you answer the call of your Master now, with "Here am I; send me, send me!"?

~ Ellen Yoon

Uphill Climb

The Lord is my light and my salvation; whom shall I fear? the Lord is the strength of my life; of whom shall I be afraid? - Psalm 27:1 KJV

Every day we face an assortment of mountains that take on different forms. Homework, relationships, personal goals, or just getting out of bed in the morning are all different summits that we must conquer. In these struggles, many apply the self-reliant "do or die" mentality of free-soloing rock-climbers—people who climb without ropes or harnesses—relying only on their own hands and feet.

Many see the road to Heaven in a similar light. They imagine Christianity as a daunting obstacle in their path, but believe that they can climb such a mountain with their own strength. However, such an achievement is impossible. The route is far too treacherous, technical, and difficult. There is only one way to make it to Heaven: aid climbing. An aid climber relies entirely upon ropes, harnesses, and his other gear to scale the mountain. He is not trusting his life to his own holds, nor ascending completely by his own strength. His safety is placed entirely in the integrity of the rope he is hanging from.

Jesus, through His death, became our rope, enabling us to climb the otherwise insuperable cliff to Heaven. Next time you find that you're solo climbing for all you're worth, ask yourself why you decided to scale an impossible route without a rope. Are you hanging thousands of feet above the ground by nothing but your own hands? Has pride or selfishness or doubt caused you to abandon your lifeline? Take advantage of Christ's gift and clip back into the rope of His grace. With every step you climb, your load will be resting completely on the sacrifice that Jesus made for you. When you reach the summit, you will find that Heaven is cheap enough. After all, Who was really bearing your weight the whole time?

~ Michael Jensen

Crooked Perfection?

Therefore, if anyone is in Christ, he is a new creation; old things have passed away; behold, all things have become new.
- 2 Corinthians 5:17 NKJV

I was sitting in my best friend's cozy, pink chair while doing my homework, when all of a sudden, I felt a need to go down to the junkyard, pile up some wood, and build a shoe rack.

Leaving my homework and the cozy, pink chair behind, I walked down to get some wood. I roughly measured what I needed; however, it was hard to find equally sized wood. After half an hour of searching, I started to walk back to my room with my material. Grabbing a hammer and some nails, I proceeded to make my shoe rack. When I was done, I was very proud of what I had made; but when I stepped back to see the full view, I noticed that it was crooked, and very lopsided. Despite these obvious faults, I was still very proud of my masterpiece. It was the first shoe rack that I had ever made, and it actually worked.

Just like the shoe rack wasn't perfect, we aren't perfect either. However, Christ wants to use us to finish His work here on earth. He takes us, imperfect human beings, and puts us together with other imperfect human beings, creating a work of perfection. Even though we may be crooked, He can still use us; He will look at us and tell us we are perfect in His eyes as long as we trust Him to be the Master Builder.

~ Agnes Grétarsdóttir

Giving up and Getting Back

… He shall give you the desires of your heart. - Psalm 37:4b NKJV

School-hunting was hard: my local Academy had offered me a piano scholarship and great academics; homeschooling was another option—it would be cheap and practical. Then there was Weimar, another possibility; but among all the options, my heart had been drawn to a faraway school in British Columbia. This school, Fountainview Academy, had a focus on music ministry. Music was important to me. Lately I had been thinking about my own music experience: classical music, competitions, nerve-wracking tests, and countless recitals. I loved it all, but what was the point? I'd look back on life and see only a blur of self-glorifying notes. Knowing this could never give me deep satisfaction, I wanted something else—I wanted my music to glorify God and point others to Him. This was exactly what Fountainview offered. At first, Fountainview seemed to end my school hunt; but when I started to think practically, I felt a conviction that homeschooling must be the answer. Did it make sense to go so far away from home and pay for expensive plane tickets and tuition? If Fountainview wasn't God's will, I didn't dare enforce my own desires. Yet how my desires hollered back at this conviction! I still wanted to go to Fountainview! In a state of turmoil and tears, I dragged myself to my parents' bedroom and blurted out my conflicting thoughts. They patiently listened to me, and we decided to sleep on it. That night my pillow was soaked before I made a decision. I wanted to be in harmony with God's will, and the only way I could was to give up my own desires in order to see what His desire really was. I surrendered to Him, and with a clear conscience, fell asleep.

The next day, after much praying and reading, my parents came to a consensus: Fountainview was the place! I couldn't believe it—I'd be going to the school I had so hoped to attend, but then surrendered—only to have God give it back to me! My inexpressible joy came from the peace of surrendering and knowing that I was in harmony with God's will. This is perfect peace.

~ Esther Ferraz

Faithful

*But seek first the kingdom of God and His righteousness, and all these
things shall be added to you. - Matthew 6:33 NKJV*

I am a Korean Seventh-day Adventist, and in my country we have
school on the Sabbath day (which is Saturday). When I was in middle
school, keeping the Sabbath was one of the hardest things for me to
do, but I had faith that God would take care of everything for me. I had
to miss the first day of school, different fun activities, and even my own
middle school graduation because these events fell on Sabbath. This
was very hard for me, especially since I love being around people, but
there was something much harder: the week of tests. In Korea, we
have a week of tests for every term. I had to miss two very important
subjects (socials and Korean) on the first test week of middle school
because they were on Sabbath. Since I didn't attend, I received zero
percent in both of those subjects, but I determined to never give up.

When the second week of tests came, I was told that they would be
held on Sabbath again. After school, I dragged my heavy feet from the
classroom. My teacher called me back and asked me if I was going to
miss this test again because of church. I said that Sabbath is a day to
not just go to church but to spend time with God. My teacher paused,
then told me to continue studying for the test scheduled for Saturday.
On the way home, I prayed the whole time that God would help me to
stay faithful to Him no matter what happened.

The next morning, I went to school as usual. While all the students
were busy studying for the test, my teacher came into the classroom.
I saw a little smile on his face, and then I heard the most amazing
announcement in my whole school life. The announcement was that
the weeks of tests were moved from Saturday to Tuesday and Friday. I
knew that it was a miracle for me! From that day, for as long as I went
to school there, they never had a test on Sabbath until I graduated.

If we are faithful to God, He will work everything out for us. Even
though sometimes it seems like He isn't going to do anything, when I
stay faithful to Him, He will come through in His timing.

~ Hannah Lee

The Lady with Good Water

So in everything, do to others what you would have them do to you, for this sums up the Law and the Prophets. - Matthew 7:12 NIV

In upper Manhattan, a giant old homeless man came into the local thrift shop one day. Looking very thirsty, he asked, "Lady, may I have some water?" The lady had compassion for the man, but she would have to go to the other side of the room to get water, which would give him an opportunity to steal something. So she decided she would give him some of the lemonade that she had prepared for a meeting. She gave him a big glass of lemonade and he drank it right down. "That was the best water I ever drank. May I have some more?" She poured him another big glass and ended up giving him the whole pitcher. When he was done, he smiled, "That was the best water I've had in a long time. Thank you!"

A few months later, the same lady was in lower Manhattan, walking down the stairs to the subway, when she heard some young men approaching from behind. She knew that they were going to give her a push and run up the stairs with her purse. A ragged figure was sitting on the platform of the subway. He saw what was happening, jumped up and ran straight for the thugs. Knife in hand, he shouted, "You touch her purse, and I'll cut your throat!" The petrified thieves took one look at the giant of a man and ran right back where they came from. Then the man smiled, "You're the lady with the good water."

This is one of my favorite stories that my grandpa used to tell my sisters and me. It taught us that if you sow kindness, you will reap kindness. Today, will you sow kindness? You will definitely be rewarded.

~ Anna Ford

Behind the Scenes

Every good gift and every perfect gift is from above...
- James 1:17 NKJV

I have a three-year-old cousin named Joshua who loves cars. He loves them so much, in fact, that he names most of the cars that drive past us whenever we go for a walk. Whenever he cries, a nice toy car will take care of his problems. One day, Joshua's dad (my uncle) decided to buy him a fabulous toy car. He spent lots of time looking for the best one, and finally ordered it. Three days later, the mailman came and dropped off the big package for Joshua. He was so excited; the present made him happy the whole week. While he was playing with his car, his mom asked him if he knew who bought that car for him. He said with great confidence, "The mailman bought it just for me!"

I thought that was very cute, but at that moment God taught me a lesson. My cousin didn't know all the work his dad did to buy him that toy car and how the mailman only delivered it. All he knew was that since the mailman was the one who brought the toy to him, that man must have been the one who bought it. That part really impacted me, because the way Joshua thought was the same as the way I think every day. I thank God when He answers my prayer or when He reminds me of encouraging Bible verses. However, He does more than that for me each day. The oxygen I breathe in, the water I drink, the sunlight that keeps me warm, every heartbeat that keeps me alive— we accept all these gifts without thinking of the effort God put into making us happy at every moment. What we see is not everything. We need to grow up and be more observant of the things we don't see on the surface.

~ Hannah Lee

Time to Wake Up

And do this, knowing the time, that now it is high time to awake out of sleep; for now our salvation is nearer than when we first believed.
- Romans 13:11 NKJV

One morning, my mom was feeling really tired, and she told my oldest sister, Becky, who was six years old at the time, that she wanted to take a one-hour nap. Mom asked Becky to wake her up when both hands on the clock were pointing to the 12, and then they would eat lunch. She gave Becky some books and toys to keep her occupied, and then went to sleep. Becky looked at all her books and played with her toys. She looked at the clock and saw that only 20 minutes had passed. Becky waited, andthen waited some more.

To her six-year-old mind, time seemed to move at a crawl. Ten minutes seemed like a million years. Would it ever be 12 o'clock? She was starting to get hungry; no, she was starving! She must have food now! Suddenly it was too much for her to bear. She ran to Mom's room and called, "Mommy, its time to wake up! It's 12 o'clock! Can we eat lunch now?" My mom got up, but felt so tired that she looked at the clocks just to be sure. Only one of the clocks said 12—all the rest had a different time. Becky admitted then that she had gotten tired of waiting, so she moved the clock's hands to 12.

Jesus is coming back to this Earth. We don't know exactly when, and sometimes we feel impatient and think that we cannot wait any longer in this sinful place. Although we cannot turn the hands of time forward to that great day, we can hasten His coming by daily preparing to meet Him and sharing His love with others, so they will be ready, too. Then Jesus will come in all His glory, and we will sit down together at the marriage feast. Oh, how I long for that day! Don't you?

~ Sarah Wahlman

Warnings

… But he that taketh warning shall deliver his soul. - Ezekiel 33:5 KJV

Have you ever wondered why God cast Satan and his angels out of Heaven after they rebelled? Wasn't it against God's character to punish them?

I remember one day I was supervising some children as they were playing together. After a while, one child started to say unkind things to the others. I explained that if he continued to be mean, he would not be able to play any longer. When he persisted in his thoughtlessness, I informed him that he would have to go and find something else to do. It wasn't that I was dealing harshly with him; I was only doing what was necessary after he had refused to heed my warning.

This story illustrates how God dealt with Satan after his transgression and fall. Satan was trying to change things in Heaven so that he could have his own way. God warned him that if he continued in this course of action, he would have to leave Heaven. Even after God's warning, Satan persisted in following his rebellious path, and because of this, God had no choice but to cast him and his angel friends out of their heavenly home. God wasn't doing anything out of character; He was just allowing the natural consequences of Satan's way.

It is the same for us. If we are not willing to accept God's warnings for our waywardness, in the end He will have no choice but to leave us out of heaven, where our presence would make everyone, including ourselves, miserable. It's going to be our own fault if this happens. Let's choose to heed God's warnings today, instead of willfully losing out on Heaven and all its joys.

~ Aileen Corrigan

Potholes

... For He Himself has said, "I will never leave you nor forsake you."
- Hebrews 13:5 NKJV

When I have a bit of spare time, I love to go for a dirt bike ride. One of the places I enjoy visiting on my rides is a failed subdivision that's full of straight, level, broad grassy roads. There are no unexpected twists or turns, and I can see a long way ahead of me. In places like this, I often succumb to the temptation to open the throttle and fly down the trail at a high speed. Unfortunately, some of these grassy roads have huge potholes and ruts that are nearly invisible until it's too late. When I decide to abandon good reason, shooting down these roads like a rocket, I sometimes encounter an unwelcome pothole or rut. Thankfully, I have yet to be killed by one of these obstacles. Nonetheless, the close calls I've had are slowly teaching me to be more cautious on these trails, because I've realized how easy it would be to become maimed, crippled, or annihilated by self-confidence.

Some stretches of life are very similar to the roads of that failed subdivision. They appear smooth, safe, and level. They invite a person to ignore the Holy Spirit's guidance in a mad drag race across the rut-riddled ground. Consequently, many have experienced the traumatic shock of crashing into a rut or hole in their lives. Just as Christian tumbled into the slough of despond in *The Pilgrim's Progress*, so are many Christians tremendously injured or discouraged in their spiritual walks. When things seem to be going great, an unforeseen obstacle brings their racing to an instant stop. However, just as in Christian's situation at the slough of despond, there are always steps or a bridge around the traps that the devil has laid for us. The danger comes when we take our eyes off of the light. When we ignore the Holy Spirit's guidance, unclasping our hand from His, and self-confidently opening the throttle, we will eventually fall. So each and every day, hold onto Jesus. Even when the "good" ground looks tempting, always remember that He knows best. Never let go of His hand.

~ Michael Jensen

Who is God?

… the love of Christ controls us… - 2 Corinthians 5:14 NASB

I once had the opportunity to tell someone about Jesus for the first time. I was reading a Bible story to my kindergarten class of gypsy girls in Albania when one little girl raised her hand and asked, "Teacher, who is Jesus?"

I responded, "Well, He's God's Son"

She paused, "Teacher, who is God?"

"He's like a father." Then realizing her perception of a father, I quickly added, "But a good father, the best one in the whole world."

"Like your Daddy!" she responded.

Suddenly I realized how good my life is. Not only do I have a father, but I have a warm place to sleep, food, family, and friends. But what if all those things were taken away? If I had been born into a family like the one this child came from, would I still want to serve God? Am I serving God for my own selfish reasons, or do I truly love Him?

I remember the first summer I was away from home. I came to Fountainview and was out in the carrot fields angrily accusing and questioning God. "Why did you bring me here?" I asked. After praying for quite a while, I finally ran out of words and fell silent. Almost as if through an audible voice, I heard the words: "Because I love you."

God loves me, so shouldn't that be the reason I love Him? But sometimes I base my love on what God gives me. This love centered on myself in fact isn't love at all, but merely self-worship. The only way we can have true love toward God is by looking to Christ. By beholding His goodness and love, we will become changed. Christ has shown a perfect picture of love in His death on the cross. By looking to the cross, our carnal love is changed into the likeness of His perfect love.

~ Moriah Mays

Free Fall

Whether you turn to the right or to the left, your ears will hear a voice behind you, saying, "This is the way; walk in it." - Isaiah 30:21 NIV

I was always the only girl. All my life I grew up with guys as friends; not because I chose to, but because there weren't any girls my age. After a while, I preferred to be with the guys because being rough and tough, getting dirty, going outdoors, and working with machinery was more interesting to me. Anything a guy could do, I could do, too.

When I joined Pathfinders, I wasn't content with doing crafts with the girls. I wanted to be outdoors and marching. To fulfill the hardest marching honor, I had to attend a night at a neighboring club that only had guys. The instructor never showed up that night, so the guys and I went outside. We were doing normal… stuff when my friend Jeremy saw this window well. Another guy commented that when he was little, he used to walk on the grate that covered the opening. Automatically, Jeremy climbed onto the grate. I started to get on as well. In the back of my head there was this Voice that said, "This is scary and not a good idea," but since I was the only girl, I didn't want to look wimpy. A few moments later, I wished I had listened. With our combined weight, the rusty nails holding up the grate gave way. We both crashed fifteen feet down onto the cement slab below. I landed on my feet. Jeremy didn't. The grate had hit him and broke his jaw, knocking him unconscious. He lay in a pool of blood on the cement. Instantly, I regretted my choice. Inside, I screamed at myself, wishing that I had listened to the Voice in my head.

The moment had been mine to decide. If I had said something to discourage the idea, the guys would have listened to me. I feared that my disregard to the Holy Spirit's prompting could have caused Jeremy to be paralyzed or killed. But I had been more preoccupied with what others would have thought of me, rather than the safety of my friends.

That day I learned two lessons: number one, don't ever walk over grates; and number two, always listen to the voice of the Holy Spirit.

~ Morgan Metcalf

Washing Away My Shame

It shall come to pass that before they call, I will answer; and while they are still speaking, I will hear. - Isaiah 65:24 NKJV

It was my kindergarten graduation day, and I was very excited because I felt like I was the center of attention. Yummy food, pretty decorations, lots of people, fancy gowns—all of these things made me feel like a star. After the excitement of graduation, my family left and my classmates gathered in a classroom to have a nice big farewell party.

Just then, I realized two things: all my friends had received flowers from their parents, except me; and I really needed to go pee! All the excitement made me totally forget to go to the restroom, and now I was about to wet my dress! The fact that I hadn't received flowers wasn't very important at that moment because I couldn't think of anything else. So, I ran back to my house, which was not too far away from school. It seemed like my bladder was about to explode! I don't remember how I got back home, but once I saw my house door, I could not hold it any longer. I started to bang on the door, but my mom took forever to open it. Well, just right before my mom opened it, I wet my dress. When I saw my mom, I started to cry. Of course, my mom asked me why I was crying, but I couldn't say that I wet my dress. I was so embarrassed and ashamed. Instead of asking for help, I said, "All my friends got flowers except me!" and started to complain. But, guess what? Once I was done complaining, I realized that my mom had already washed me and cleaned my mess.

This is how it is with God. We are sometimes embarrassed to ask God for what we need because we feel dirty and ashamed. Yet, we don't need to hide or try to cover our shame. My mom knew about my mess without me telling her, and likewise, God already knows everything. He is already prepared to wash us and clean our mess before we even ask.

~ Hannah Lee

Needles

Beware of false prophets, who come to you in sheep's clothing, but inwardly they are ravenous wolves. - Matthew 7:15 NKJV

I can remember a time when my family went cross-country skiing in the backcountry of Montana. It was a beautiful day as the snow fell lightly onto the trail ahead of me. In awe, I gazed at the snow-covered trees. We passed many kinds of evergreens: fir trees, which have always been my favourite because of their soft needles, and many different pine and spruce trees. But then I discovered something odd. I noticed a tree that, from afar, looked like any other evergreen, but when I looked at it more closely I saw that its needles were turning gold and falling off.

Later in the day I asked my mom about this, and she told me that these trees were called Tamarack pines. In the summer you could not tell them apart from the rest of the forest. However, when the storms of winter approached, they lost their needles, and you could truly see that they were deciduous trees and not evergreens.

Among us are many evergreens that God has sent to guide us down the narrow way. These men and women of God are lights to those who are lost in darkness and are leaders who will help us through dark times. However, there are often men and women who are among us and were not sent by God. They teach us and tell us about what to believe, but do not have the power of the Scriptures behind them. Sadly, they are often able to lead many astray with their false teachings. If I do not have a firm foundation in the only reliable source of knowledge that God has given me, then I will be easily swayed into their darkness. It may seem easier to simply follow where my pastor leads me, but when the storms of winter come, I might find that the evergreens in my life have lost their needles. Then who will I turn to? It is only through the diligent study of Scriptures that we can stand when the storm comes.

~ Derek Glatts

Drainpipes

If we confess our sins, He is faithful and just to forgive us our sins, and to cleanse us from all unrighteousness. - 1 John 1:9 KJV

When I was young, but still old enough to know better, one of my neighbors and I went down the street to another friend's house and "borrowed" two of her Bratz® dolls without asking. We proceeded to take these little dolls back up the street to my neighbor's house and climb on their flat concrete roof. Soon after we started playing, we spotted one of their drainpipes. Since this drainpipe was on the very edge of the roof, it didn't go through the concrete blocks to the ground, but opened below the six inch block roof. Thinking it would be grand fun to have the dolls go down a "water-slide," we put the dolls through the little drainpipe. Since it was just wide enough that we could slip the dolls through, we decided to try the long drainpipes reaching to the ground. The first two drainpipes we tried worked really well and the dolls came shooting out the slippery, scummy pipes at the bottom. Then I tried a third drainpipe…but this time the doll didn't come slipping out the bottom. We hurriedly climbed down to try and pry it out, but it was stuck. We never got it out and ended up sneaking back with only one doll. Although our friend missed the other doll, neither of us told her about our crime until years later. Eventually, I apologized to her and she willingly forgave me even though we had hurt her greatly. As far as I know, that poor little Bratz® doll is wedged in that scummy drainpipe to this day.

A life of disobedience is like that. We think it is grand fun as we are shooting down the slippery water-slide of sin. Since we usually pop out at the bottom just fine, we keep hopping in—only to get stuck in the scum at the bottom. We then realize our mistake, and when we can't get out, we panic. Only when we confess our sins and repent can Jesus—our Friend—forgive us. But He does more than just forgive us—He climbs into the scummy drainpipe we are wedged in and pulls us out.

~ Katie Sloop

Fingerprints of Love

The heavens declare the glory of God, and the firmament shows His handiwork. - Psalms 19:1 NKJV

In the southern state of North Carolina, I frequently experience beautiful sunsets. Each evening brings an enchanting display of brilliant colors. Like a painter's palette, vibrant mixtures of strawberry, peach, aquamarine and violet swirl into a striking patchwork, bordered by the Blue Ridge Mountains.

Often, I eagerly wait for the evening's cool, feathery fingers of wind to arrive, and bring the night's performance. Ever so slowly, an unseen Artist selects a few colors, blending them into patterns. Since they are constantly changing, my eyes are riveted to the sky. I don't want to miss a single moment. The mood changes as the sun departs, and the colors swirl into one last finale. The sun dips below the horizon, drawing with it the fading splendor. The shadowy night has arrived.

Night skies like this always leave me with a sense of awe. They captivate my soul and draw my spirit heavenward. During these moments, I am permitted to witness a private performance of the lights, clouds, and colors all mingling together in unison. But no canvass can paint itself. Behind this delicate masterpiece of art is an Artist. This Artist is the Master Artist. His amazing creations can reach the depths of the human heart. In them I can sense God's presence reaching out to me, calling me to a higher place. It's like He is right there with me.

Even though I can sense God, I can't see Him. However, through being in nature I can be with God. That's why He gave me His creation. Not only can I enjoy the beauty of nature, but I can also see God's character and love portrayed through creation. The beauty of nature is a reflection of His love and even every leaf, beetle, and flower shows how much He cares for me. Nature shows me God. His fingerprints of love are there, yearning to touch my heart.

~ Morgan Metcalf

Disappointed

You may be perplexed in business; your prospects may grow darker and darker, and you may be threatened with loss; but do not become discouraged; cast your care upon God, and remain calm and cheerful. Pray for wisdom to manage your affairs with discretion, and thus prevent loss and disaster. - Steps to Christ, pg. 122

My family was affected by the severe decline of the housing market in 2007. We lost a lot of money, a house, and friends. My dad's business went from having twenty employees to three; however, this could have been avoided if we had sought God's guidance in buying an additional home.

I was 13 years old at the time, and we were considering buying another house. Being the practical child that I was, I didn't see why we needed a new home. I was hoping that we could finally settle down after having moved around so much during the previous two or three years. God had come to my dad in dreams several times, telling him to buy a farm, but he didn't listen. My parents loved warm Southern California, and they didn't want to move away from my grandparents, so they bought a more expensive house on a golf resort. They did not seek God's guidance in this, and because of that, we got into trouble later on. Two years later, the economic crisis occurred, and we could no longer afford to pay for the house. We had to sell it, meaning that we lost all we had invested in it. God had something better in mind for us, but we didn't consult Him first. "For I know the thoughts that I think toward you, says the Lord, thoughts of peace and not of evil, to give you a future and a hope" (Jeremiah 29:11 NKJV).

Even though we lost so much, God still provided for all our needs, and He continues to take care of us today. God had an extra supply of grace for my family. He allowed us room to grow and to learn from our experience. What a gracious God we serve!

~ Anna Ford

Forgiveness

If we confess our sins, he is faithful and just to forgive us our sins, and to cleanse us from all unrighteousness. - 1 John 1:9 KJV

Holly was 14 years old when she spent part of her summer in Saskatchewan with her aunt and uncle. She desperately wanted to learn how to drive standard, so her uncle George decided he would take her out around the farm to teach her. Holly was having fun learning to drive, and her uncle George was very proud of her. After a little while she started feeling more comfortable with her new ability. One particular day, as Holly was trying to shift into another gear, she wasn't paying attention to steering or her uncle, and she crashed right into the side of the barn. She was horrified, felt awful, and couldn't think of what to say. Uncle George started laughing, turned his head towards Holly, and said, "OK, you can park here." She couldn't believe it: even though she had just put a hole in the side of his barn and dented the front of his truck, he forgave her and wasn't angry at all.

We go through life asking God to teach us and help us through our experiences. We feel like everything is going well until we suddenly mess up big time. I always expect God to look down from Heaven and tell me how stupid my mistake was. Instead, if I ask for His forgiveness, He comforts me and helps me grow from the experience. He wants us to truly repent; then He forgives us for our sins and forgets all about them.

~ Raina Walker

Love Your Enemies

Be not overcome of evil, but overcome evil with good.
- Romans 12:21 KJV

Bruce was a lonely boy, a misfit at school, and neglected by his parents. Bruce was also 6'4" and grossly overweight. Every day after school he would come home, lock himself in his room, and listen to screamo and heavy metal rock. He was a dark, intimidating person, and he would make fun of what was positive.

When I was 12 years old, I started playing basketball with other kids my age in the town close by. That's where I met Bruce for the first time, and I was quite intimidated by his appearance: he would wear disgusting looking t-shirts with decaying faces on them. Once he realized I was a Christian and a vegetarian, he made fun of me. I told my parents about how he was treating me, and they told me that I should invite all of them home for dinner and games. So I went and talked to my friends and invited them each one by one. Bruce had heard about this, but he wasn't expecting to be invited. So when I invited him, he was so shocked that his face lit up with excitement. He couldn't believe that after everything he had done to me, I still was going to invite him home.

When people treat us badly, we might be tempted to just ignore them or treat them badly in return; but we should look at Jesus and think about how He forgave His persecutors while He was on the cross. Jesus says in Matthew 5:44, "But I tell you: Love your enemies and pray for those who persecute you" (NIV). And even when the soldiers were casting lots for His clothes, He said: "Father, forgive them, for they know not what they do" (Luke 23:34 ESV). Those little things make a difference. I recently heard that Bruce was doing well and losing weight. I'm thankful for the opportunity that I had to reach out to him. Every time we see someone in need, we should go out of our way to treat them as Jesus would. The difference that you can make will amaze you!

~ Esra Eliasson

What Are Words?

But God demonstrates His own love toward us, in that while we were still sinners, Christ died for us. - Romans 5:8 NKJV

I recently read a news report about a singer named Chris Medina, who was engaged to a beautiful young woman named Juliana. They planned to get married two years after becoming engaged, but shortly before their wedding, Juliana was critically injured in a car accident. She sustained a severe head injury, and doctors doubted she would survive. Because of a crushing injury to her face and skull, Juliana's beauty was permanently marred. Chris refused to give up hope that Juliana would recover, and two years later he's one of her main caregivers. Juliana has made remarkable progress, and Chris states that when she can walk down the aisle, they will be married. On the date they had originally set for their wedding, Chris sang a song to Juliana, in which he expressed his undying commitment to her.

Chris has received a lot of admiration for sticking by Juliana, though she is forever changed. Although as Christians we talk about loving others selflessly—as God loves us—when we actually see selfless love in action, we think it remarkable.

In the Garden of Eden, Adam and Eve lived in perfect harmony with God. They walked and talked with Him daily. Their world and everything in it was perfect. Then tragedy struck, leaving humans with horrible handicaps. Adam and Eve suddenly thought of God as cruel, selfish and unjust. They no longer wanted to obey their Creator. Adam, Eve, and the entire human race were horribly marred by sin. But God still loves us! Though we are no longer recognizable as His perfect creation, He hasn't given up on us. He came to earth and died on the cross for us; He saved us from the death we deserve. He is our caregiver now—our Daily Help to overcome the handicaps of sin. When He comes again, He will transform us into His image, and we will be joined to Him for eternity as His perfect bride.

~ Sarah Wahlman

True Love

Greater love hath no man than this, that a man lay down his life for his friends. - John 15:13 KJV

My father is a very practical man who shows through his actions that he loves and values my life more than his own. When I was thirteen, I contracted an eye infection that left a large opaque scar across the very center of my left cornea. Because the only option for bringing vision back to that eye was to replace it with someone else's, my doctor thought that it would be best to wait before taking such a drastic step. Three years later, I was struggling on an overdue essay when I phoned my dad for ideas. In an effort to help me, he brought up my scar. He told me that he had been seriously considering giving me his cornea so that I would be able to see again. He explained that it was more important to him that I would be able to see through both eyes than for him to have his complete sight. When he shared this with me, my heart melted. Although I knew that my father loved me, I hadn't really thought of how far he would go for me.

You know, there is Someone else who has done even more for me than giving up His vision. Jesus gave me His life. When the virus of sin was first contracted in Heaven, the only way to remove it was by utterly destroying all that was associated with it. Jesus offered to take sin's eternal consequences upon himself so we could be rewarded with His eternal benefits. Of all the angels of Heaven, only Jesus' perfect life could atone for our debt of sin. His love is utterly selfless; He sacrificed himself to save us.

When you recognize someone's deep love for you, the barriers in your heart go down. When even a small glimpse is caught of Christ's infinite love for us, our hearts respond in answering love. We love Him because He first loved us. Compassionately, willingly, and freely, Jesus offers you Himself. Will you accept His gift of love?

~ Sarah Miller

Never Give Up!

Howbeit when He, the Spirit of truth, is come, He will guide you into all truth: for He shall not speak of Himself; but whatsoever He shall hear, that shall He speak: and He will shew you things to come.
- John 16:13 KJV

When I first came to Fountainview as a freshman, I started having my devotions in English. Because I'm Icelandic, this proved to be quite a challenge. I would wake up in the mornings and pray to God to help me comprehend what I was trying to read in my devotions. Page after page I would read, but to my dismay, I found that I could not recall or comprehend anything I had just read. It went on like this for pretty much the whole year. As you can imagine, I would get very discouraged at times; but I did not give up, though time after time I would walk away with nothing to contemplate throughout the day. Today, I can read a passage from the Bible and actually get a clear glimpse of the deeper meaning. The reason why I can now understand is that I stuck to it and didn't give up. God continues to teach me more and more every day, and I praise Him for that.

You might feel that, like me, you read the words but don't understand the concepts. Maybe you go through page after page without grasping the meaning or you feel you're not uncovering the hidden treasure that you sought so fervently for.

Though the Bible can be hard at times to understand, and you might feel that it is of no use to have your devotions, don't give up. Jeremiah 29:13 promises, "if you look for me wholeheartedly, you will find me" (NLT). You may have to search with all your heart, but in the end you will be repaid a thousand fold. Stick to it, and God will reveal to you more lessons than you ever would have dreamed of.

~ Esra Eliasson

Father

*Let your conduct be without covetousness; be content with such things
as you have. For He Himself has said, "I will never leave you nor
forsake you." - Hebrews 13:5 NKJV*

I often wondered what it would be like to have a father who was
there for me; a person who would show me how to ride my bike, play
ball, and teach me whatever other things dads are supposed to. My
dad left when I was two, so I never knew what it was like to have a
father. As the years went on, I just pushed away the idea of having a
father to do daddy-daughter things with. Still, sometimes the thought
would cross my mind, and I would wonder what it would be like to
have a dad, and I would wish I could have one.

When I was older, I realized how much fun my friends had with their
dads and again began to wish I had one too. When I was ten years
old, I started going to church and learning about God. It was then I
realized that I do have a Father, and that He has been with me all the
time. This thought amazed me; I had no clue that I did have a Dad who
watched out for me and comforted me. My mind was blown away as I
realized that God was my Father, and He had always been.

I did get to know my biological dad, but God is the one who has
always been there for me. I learned that even though some earthly
fathers can be great and show us an image, on a much smaller scale,
of how loving our Heavenly Father is, God is the ultimate Father who
will never let us down.

~ Raina Walker

Life's Roosters

Surely He will save you from the fowler's snare and from the deadly pestilence. He will cover you with His feathers, and under His wings you will find refuge… - Psalm 91:3–4 NIV

We lived in the country and had a menagerie of pets, including several chickens and one large aggressive rooster. He wasn't really ours; we were just keeping him for a friend. He had decided that he was in charge of the property, and thus he could rule over us. He bullied us kids, our mom, and even our dad. We knew he was dangerous, and we were always supposed to carry something to fend him off with. He wouldn't try to hurt us if we had something to protect ourselves with. One day I somehow found myself in the backyard with the rooster and no means of protection.

"MOM, help! Let me in!" I screamed at the top of my lungs. I raced around the house, faster than I thought I could go. Being chased by a man-eating rooster made the adrenaline pump through my veins. He was getting closer to me. I ran several times around the house shrieking as loud as I could, hoping to be heard. Thankfully someone heard me and opened the door to safety.

Satan is like that rooster. I know how dangerous he is by all the sadness and sin in the world. I can protect myself with things like prayer and God's Holy Word, the Bible. Sometimes, though, I forget to be on guard and find myself face to face with the devil and all his temptations. He is out to destroy us, and we cannot outrun him. God hears our cries for help and comes to our rescue. He will open the door to our salvation and let us in where we can rest in His protection and love.

~ Sarah Wahlman

He Made Up for the Rest

… whatever you do, do all to the glory of God.
- 1 Corinthians 10:31 NKJV

The idea of playing piano in front of an audience for my eighth grade graduation was not something that made me nervous. No, it terrified me. It seemed that no matter how hard and long I practiced, I would always make mistakes in front of others. My hands always shook, my face always felt hot, and my heart always pounded at breakneck speed.

Graduation steadily drew near, and I used every spare moment to practice. I really wanted to do well for once. The melody should sound sweet, the tempo should be kept, and my fingers should actually hit the right notes! But there was something that I neglected to consider as I practiced my heart out. What was my reason for playing? Was the point to show off one of my "talents" so that everyone could be proud of me? Was that why my piano instructor patiently coaxed me into a commitment to play? Was that why I had accepted? Hmmm… I needed to rethink this. The slow progress I was making frustrated me. I was trying to do everything in my own strength. That's the problem, I realized. I decided to let go of my selfish motives and give my piece to the Lord. I wanted to do it for His glory so that others could be blessed.

At graduation, I was extremely anxious. Even when I practiced a few hours before the performance, my piece wasn't perfect. It still needed to sound better and there were certain parts that were a challenge. In my cap and gown, I walked toward the piano feigning calmness while praying that God would be glorified. I sat down, turned to the right page, placed my hands on the keys, and began. My fingers moved, and the piano sang with such beauty—it absolutely amazed me. Before I knew it, the majestic sounds of the last chord diminished. God was glorified! I did my very best, and He made up for the rest.

~ Ashley Wilkens

Almost Gone

*But encourage one another daily, as long as it is called "Today," so
that none of you may be hardened by sin's deceitfulness.*
- Hebrews 3:13 NIV

"Agnes, I don't think I can handle this anymore. I just want to die."
Kristy told me.

I was shocked and didn't know what to say. As this went on for
days, then weeks and months, I felt like all of my energy had been
drained. I was at the point where I almost gave up our relationship
because I was too tired and stressed. I didn't need another thing
on my plate—one more thing to drag me down the drain. But then I
realized that that was when she needed me most, and that was when
I needed to show her true love and commitment. So I tried. I stayed up
late to comfort her, and we talked daily about what was going on.

Little did I know the results of my efforts until the day she handed
me a letter. I opened it. She wrote of how she often had picked up
the knife, but then put it back down because I had been there for her,
because I had reassured her she was loved. At the close of her letter
she said that, had I not been her friend and helped her, she probably
wouldn't be here today.

As I thought about this, I realized how selfish I am. Had I given up
this friendship, she could have killed herself—just because I was too
tired to care for my friend. So often I only think about myself and don't
realize that by forgetting myself for a second and putting others first, I
can make a difference.

~ Agnes Grétarsdottir

Don't Wait!

Do not boast about tomorrow, for you do not know what a day may bring. - Proverbs 27:1 NIV

When I came as a freshman to Fountainview Academy, I had a hard time keeping my room clean. Day after day I would be so busy; I would put off little things like making my bed, folding my clothes, and putting stuff away after I used them. It was no surprise, then, when I found a yellow note on my door almost every day reminding me to clean my room. To pass room check, I would do the minimum. I kept ignoring the note on my door, and it didn't have a lasting effect on me. Deep inside I knew that I should keep my room cleaner, but it became harder and harder the longer I allowed my habit to metastasize.

So often we do this in our own lives. We put off different tasks such as homework, dusting the house, feeding the dog, or doing laundry; putting off what we think are little things. But before we know it, we often end up with an overwhelming pile of tasks to accomplish.

Don't put off the things of today until tomorrow. Procrastination is one of those little decisions you face each day that influences your character. *Christ's Object Lessons* says, "The importance of the little things is often underrated because they are small; but they supply much of the actual discipline of life. There are really no nonessentials in the Christian's life. Our character building will be full of peril while we underrate the importance of the little things" (pg. 356).

Repeated actions form habits, habits form character, and by our character, our destiny for time and eternity is decided. When you ignore the little tasks set before you, it's easy to get sucked deeper into the habit of procrastination. It's a lot harder to get out of a hole once you're in it; but with God's help you can conquer life's struggles, one little thing at a time.

~ Esra Eliasson

Tick, Tock

And that, knowing the time, that now it is high time to awake out of sleep: for now is our salvation nearer than when we believed. The night is far spent, the day is at hand: let us therefore cast off the works of darkness, and let us put on the armor of light.
- Romans 13:11–12 KJV

It has been a very busy day, filled with music lessons, phone calls, and homework. As I stumble into my room, my mind swirls with endless thoughts. When I drop to my knees beside my bed, I have to fight to keep my eyes open. "Dear Lord, thank You so much for today. The snow is so pretty…" my thoughts trail off into oblivion until I jerk myself awake again. "Dear Lord," I try a second time. Once again my mind strays. As I stare into the blackness, I hear a faint ticking sound. Harnessing my thoughts, I try to figure out what's making the noise. Suddenly I remember: it's my clock. "What time is it?" I wonder. Switching on the lamp, I squint through bleary eyes to see that it's… eleven! This realization gives me the energy to finish my prayer and crawl up into my cold bed.

In the same way that I kept falling asleep, I find myself sleepwalking through life by not living up to the potential that God has for me. He's called me to unite with Him and be a warrior against sin, but too often I shrink from my duty and seek something less difficult. But I am getting tired of being mediocre. When I recognize how far I have drifted, I am motivated to get back on track.

Sleepwalking through life is not a problem unique to me. Many are being lulled into the false belief that this world is all there is—that their everyday actions don't matter. They don't realize that Jesus is going through the records right now to see who will be saved. In Romans 13:11–12 Christ is giving us a wakeup call: it is past time to awake, for now is our salvation nearer than we realize. Salvation begins today if we so choose. God's clock is ticking. I don't want to be found asleep!

~ Sarah Miller

Seeing Past the Crack

This is my commandment, That ye love one another, as I have loved you. - John 15:12 KJV

One of the annoying things about winter in Canada is the number of cracks and stone chips you get on your car's windscreen caused by the rocks that are left by the sand trucks. My parents had hoped to get through the winter with our windscreen staying intact, but to no avail. The crack started out small, but over time grew in size until it had spread its way right across the driver's line of sight and reached over to the passenger's side. At first, the crack was annoying and got in the way, hindering my vision when I drove. I used to find it difficult to focus on anything other than the crack and see past it to the road ahead – it was distracting. It got to the point where I didn't want to drive because all I could see was the crack.

I discovered rather quickly though, that if I wanted to get where I was going, I had to learn to see past the crack and not let that be my focal point. So I did; I trained myself to look beyond it to the road that lay ahead. The crack is still there; I just don't notice it so much anymore.

We are all a bit like our windscreen: we all have cracks and chips, imperfections and character flaws. I would like to say that I never notice other people's cracks, but that would be lying. Unfortunately, I tend to see their cracks and imperfections, and this becomes my focus. If I am not careful, their 'cracks and chips' will become all I see, and before I know it, I will be judging them based on these issues. Sometimes I get so caught up on a person's character flaws that I would rather not spend time with them.

This is when I need to apply the same principle I used with the windscreen. I need to look past their imperfections and see them for who they are. Jesus does this for me: He sees past my flaws and cracks and still wants to be my friend. I need to do the same. In doing this, I will enjoy being with others so much more. In the same way, I enjoy the drive now that I have learned to see past the crack.

~ Kyle Smith

June 12

The Green-Eyed Monster

*… Take heed and beware of covetousness, for one's life does not
consist in the abundance of the things he possesses.*
- Luke 12:15 NKJV

I was a very popular girl in my elementary school. Smart and
talented, my personality caught everyone's attention. When I
graduated from elementary school, I was still quite popular, but things
started to change when I met Sumin. She was very smart, kind,
talented, and pretty. At first, I enjoyed hanging out with her, but slowly
I began to realize that she was better than I was. When I got 100%
on my test, she would get 102%; when I drew a creative picture for
art class, her picture would have just one more detail to make it more
appealing. Because of her, I was losing the attention of the people
around me. I knew that she was better than I was in everything she
did, but I couldn't accept that fact. My envious thoughts towards her
turned into spiteful actions. Even though she was genuinely nice to
me, I started to ignore her. I tried to put her down to make myself look
better.

The chief priests and leaders of Israel treated Jesus like I treated
my friend, Sumin. They knew that Jesus was loving, kind, and
encouraging. But "they incased themselves in prejudice" and "they
rejected the clearest evidence of His Messiahship," (*The Great
Controversy,* pg. 595) because they were losing their popularity.
They saw Jesus' power and influence over the people and coveted it.
Because of their jealousy, they lost a saving relationship with Jesus
and their position in Heaven.

Sometimes we are covetous of other's talents and have envious
thoughts towards them. Instead, we need to be content with what God
has given us already. "Let nothing be done through strife or vainglory;
but in lowliness of mind let each esteem other better than themselves"
(Philippians 2:3 KJV).

~ Hannah Lee

Live or Live

"All right," Jacob replied, "but trade me your rights as the firstborn son." - Genesis 25:31 ESV

Have you ever noticed how important context is? Take the words live and live for example. When you are reading a sentence like, "I live down the road," if you only read the word "live," you might think I was meaning "live," as in "there was a live concert in town last night." Or take the words "right," "right" and "right." Four ways you can read these words are "turn right at the next street," "you are right," "come right now" or "it's my right." All four words are spelled and sound the same, but it is seeing in context that lets you know exactly what I am saying. This is especially true if you are reading this out loud right now.

When reading, context is important. Whether you are reading signs, books, notes, or the Bible, you need to understand what the words are saying. When I am reading a book, I do not take a sentence from one book and mix it with a sentence from another book or only read half a sentence before going to the next one. That wouldn't make sense. There are times when people do that with the books in the Bible and think it is OK.

When studying the Bible, understanding a verse in context first before mixing it with others or skipping parts is really helpful. Reading in context means reading the verses around it and taking time to think about what you have read. This will help you to not get confused. As I bring this to a "close," I encourage you to draw "close" to God by reading His words in context.

To be a-"live" in Christ, we need to "live" our lives in context.

~ Rebecca Hall

164

Worries

Casting all your care upon Him; for He careth for you.
- 1 Peter 5:7 KJV

My eyes grew wide as my hand sank into empty pocket of my pants. Oh great! I frantically sorted through all my drawers, boxes, and cupboards. Nothing. I flew down to the school building, crossing my fingers for luck. I slid into the cafeteria and looked into the empty trash can. Nothing. I looked into the dumpster. Nothing. I interrogated the cafeteria worker who was on duty at the time. "Have they taken out the trash? Where did it go?" Still nothing. My retainer was gone.

I painfully told my mom the news over the phone. I felt so bad about losing something so valuable. My mother patiently listened and encouraged me to pray about it. I fell on my knees and gave it all to God. I still couldn't find my retainer, but I wasn't going to worry about it.

Two months later, I was dressing up in my New Englander attire for my school's International Supper. I put on my moss-green mud boots and zipped up my matching rain jacket. My hand slid into my pocket as I walked toward my New England booth. I felt something bulky touch my hand. I gently fingered it, trying to decipher what it was. It was my long-hoped-for retainer! I immediately sent up a prayer of thanks to God for helping me find my lost retainer.

Some things in life seem too small for God to care about. Or maybe we just haven't given Him our worries and cares. We stress out over things in life we can't control, but if we give our worries to God, He will take the load for us. We may not see immediate results; our problems may not vanish in an instant, but if we are trusting God to take care of our problems, our lives will be so much easier. Let me encourage you not to hesitate to give God all your worries today.

~ Mason Neil

Afraid of Death?

Bless those who persecute you; bless and do not curse.
- Romans 12:14 NIV

In the year 1569, Dirk Willems, a faithful follower of Jesus Christ, was apprehended at Asperen, Holland for being re-baptized as an Anabaptist. Dirk knew exactly what awaited him if he did not escape. Therefore, he made a rope with strips of cloth and slid down it over the prison wall. The police chased him through the forests until he came to the edge of a sizable pond. A thin layer of ice had formed on the surface of the pond. Dirk rushed across and made it to the other side, but the thin ice broke under one of his pursuers, who was running close behind him. Dirk immediately turned back and pulled the floundering man from the frigid water. Dirk risked his life for his pursuer, even though he knew that he would now be burned at the stake. But he couldn't bear the idea that his pursuer would die without knowing Christ.

When Jesus was hanging upon the cross, He was bearing the weight of the world's transgressions on His shoulders. However, He wasn't thinking about His pain and the guilt that He felt; He was thinking about the souls of those who had just nailed Him to that cross. Even while the guards were still gambling for His clothes, Christ was praying for their salvation. Jesus had the power to destroy all who had beaten and tortured Him, but He knew that in doing so He wouldn't have fulfilled the plan for their salvation.

Each one of us has a mission on this earth: to bring the message of Christ's love to as many people as we can, even if those people want to kill us.

~ Esra Eliasson

Daddy, Daddy

*If you then know how to give good gifts to your children, how much
more will your heavenly Father give the Holy Spirit to those who ask
Him! - Luke 11:13 NKJV*

When I was a kid, Father's Day was my favorite holiday besides
my birthday and Christmas. When Father's Day was just around the
corner, my little brain began to think of all the things that I could do
with my dad. Playing catch, watching baseball games, going shopping,
or just hanging out with him were a few activities we might do together.
My dad was always busy working, so this Father's Day was the only
day that I had the opportunity to do anything with him. My brother and
I enthusiastically poured many hours, much artistic talent, and lots of
love into making special cards for him. Regardless of where we went
or what we did, it has become a precious day that reminded both my
dad and I of how much we love and care about each other.

Everybody needs a father. Fathers provide guidance,
encouragement, and most importantly, love. When Jesus' disciples
asked Him to teach them how to pray, He started with "Our Father."
God, who created each one of us, wants us to call Him "Daddy!" When
you realize that God loves you infinitely more than anyone can, you
will make Him the first One to whom you take all of your concerns, all
of your joys, and all of your burdens. He becomes your primary source
of comfort and hope; through prayer and the study of His Word, you
will receive the guidance you need in your struggles. He has been
knocking on the door of your heart, asking you to open up to Him.
He is the Father who will never leave you nor forsake you, and He is
waiting to shower you with the affection that only a daddy can give.

~ Ellen Yoon

The Top

The Lord is my strength and my shield; my heart trusts in Him, and I am helped. - Psalms 28:7a NIV 1984

Crash! More rocks tumbled over the edge of the cliff. I grasped at a tree root and pulled myself up onto a narrow ledge. I turned and looked down the nearly twenty-five foot face that I had just climbed. I took a deep breath and continued up, this time not on a cliff but a steep rocky slope.

I continued climbing, passing boulder after boulder, tree after tree. After about thirty minutes of placing foot in front of foot, I stopped to take a break. Turning around, I sat cautiously on an old, fallen tree, and looked down at the small portion I had just climbed. I was only about a quarter of the way up, so the view was not very spectacular. I turned my head and looked back up the mountain. It seemed too rough and too difficult for me. At that point, it did not seem worth it. However, I heaved in some of the thin air and continued up the mountain. One hour passed, and I was starting to get close to the top. Still, the view was not very nice. By that time, the forest had closed around me, and when I looked closely, I could see a small brick building up ahead. After another brief break, I continued my trek to the top. When I finally summited, I looked over the other side of the ridge. It was beautiful: colorful forests, winding streams, and towering boulders. Even though the trip was difficult, it was worth it in the end.

What if, when sitting on the fallen tree near the bottom, I had decided to turn around and go back? What if, instead of continuing to the top, I had decided that, though beautiful, it was not worth it? What if, in your spiritual walk along the narrow path to heaven, you find the road too steep and too difficult and consider it not worth the work? When you reach those tough spots in your walk, will you turn back? Or will you press onward to the heavenly city with the pearly gates?

~ Ben Dietel

Baking Soda Cake

*re is a way that seems right to a man, but its end is the way of
eath. - Proverbs 16:25 NKJV*

The sun peeked in through the kitchen window early that summer morning to find two seven-year-olds peering into the oven. It was my mom's birthday, and my sister and I decided to wake up early to make her a surprise birthday breakfast, complete with a cake. The cake was my idea, so I decided to make it while my sister prepared the rest.

I browsed several of my mom's cookbooks before I found the perfect recipe. Feeling very grown up, I gathered all of the ingredients and started measuring. We didn't have quite enough flour, but I knew that sometimes my mom substituted ingredients, so I just added enough baking soda to make up for the missing flour. What's the difference between two white powders, anyway? Soon my batter was done, and I slid my cake pan into the hot oven. I was very proud of myself for making a cake without any help, and I couldn't wait for it to finish baking. Soon the timer dinged, and I dashed to the oven to retrieve my masterpiece. But instead of the perfectly round, beautiful cake I had pictured, I saw a bubbly, drippy mess hardening onto the inside of the oven. My cake had exploded like a volcano, spewing batter all over the kitchen. Instead of the wonderful birthday breakfast I had hoped to greet my mom with, she had to spend the first several hours of her morning cleaning up the mess I'd made, while my cake sat on the counter, unfit to eat.

I'd sincerely wanted to please my mom by doing something special for her. But regardless of how earnest I was in my intentions, I did not follow the instructions exactly, so the end result was a total failure. It's the same in our lives. If we don't carefully follow the instructions in God's word, we can't expect a happy ending either.

~ Saraiah Turnbull

From First Place to the Last Position

"He must increase, but I must decrease." - John 3:30 KJV

It was a very hot, sunny day. 34 students, including myself, were running around the school field making wheezing, huffing, and puffing sounds. It was PE testing day! It wasn't a hard test, but it wasn't easy either. I did my best on every test, even though I was dizzy and felt like throwing up. Finally, we had one test left, which was a 400-meter run. By the time I got to the finish line, I felt very happy with the fact that I completed PE testing and that I got a pretty good grade.

I started to look around after I caught my breath, and I saw that my friend was still running the last lap. She usually gets excused from running because of her asthma, but this time, she had to do it to pass the class. She looked like she was in pain, but the only help that I could give was to encourage her. Then I saw something interesting. I thought my friend was running by herself, but I saw that someone else was running with her! And the most surprising part was that I recognized the person who was running with my friend. This girl was one of the best athletes in PE class. Instead of being in first place, she had chosen to help my friend make it to the end. She even let my friend finish first, and this top athlete became the last person in the whole class to finish the race.

When I saw that, I felt so ashamed of myself. I realized that if I was that girl, I would have never given up my place at the top. But that girl was different, and through her actions, I saw Jesus.

Before Jesus came to the earth, He was in the highest place: He didn't have to give up His position. However, instead of keeping His place, He came to this earth and put Himself in the lowest of places to encourage us and bring us to the end of our journey, which is Heaven—our home!

~ Hannah Lee

Missed Blessings

*A faithful man will abound with blessings, but he who hastens to be
rich will not go unpunished. - Proverbs 28:20*

I once read a story about a young man who was getting ready to
graduate from college. For many months he had admired a beautiful
sports car in a dealer's showroom, and knowing his father could well
afford it, he told him that it was all he wanted.

As Graduation Day approached, the young man awaited signs
that his father had purchased the car. Finally, on the morning of his
graduation, his father called him into his private study. After telling him
how proud he was of him and how much he loved him, he handed his
son a beautiful wrapped gift box. Curious, but somewhat disappointed,
the young man opened the box and found a lovely, leather-bound
Bible. Angrily, he raised his voice, "With all your money you give me a
Bible?" and stormed out of the house, leaving the Holy Book.

Many years passed and the young man was very successful in
business. He had a beautiful home and a wonderful family, but realized
his father was very old, and thought perhaps he should go and see
him. He had not seen him since that graduation day. Before he could
make arrangements, he received a telegram telling him his father had
passed away and willed all of his possessions to his son. He needed
to come home immediately and take care of things.

When he arrived at his father's house, sadness and regret filled his
heart. He began to search his father's papers and saw the unopened
Bible, just as he had left it years ago. With tears, he opened the Bible
and began to turn the pages. As he read, a car key dropped from an
envelope taped behind the Bible. It had a tag with name of the dealer
who had the sports car he had desired. On the tag was the date of
his graduation, and the words "PAID IN FULL". How often do we miss
God's blessings because they are not packaged as we expect?

~ Kyle Smith

171

Free Falling

Let us hold unswervingly to the hope we profess, for He who promised is faithful. - Hebrews 10:23 NIV

Early one morning, my grandfather called my dad to tell him that either both he and my uncle needed to come back to the family farm, or else he would have to sell it. At that time, my dad worked at a Christian high school where he taught Bible as an ordained pastor, while my mother stayed home to take care of my sister and me. After much prayer, my parents felt that God was leading them to go back to the farm, where they moved shortly thereafter.

Once we arrived at our farm, Dad had no peace about being there. For years, my father wrestled with the fear that God was not pleased with his decision to leave the pastoral ministry. In the midst of all his turmoil, God taught my father that regardless of what he felt, he could have peace in the knowledge that God had led his decision and faith that He would continue to lead him in the future.

When God calls you to follow Him, He doesn't show you from the beginning to the end of your journey. Instead, He just shows you how to take the next step. When the path you are following seems to drop out of sight, you are left with the choice to either turn around and hightail it back to where you came from, or to continue on through the sheer grit of believing that He who has called you is faithful. The decision to go forward does not come with a wave of warm and fuzzy feelings. Instead, it comes with the calm, quiet assurance that, with the call of duty, there is His promise to see you through. It is when you are free falling that you will learn to use your wings of faith.

~ Sarah Miller

Jump

*… Yet lackest thou one thing: sell all that thou hast, and distribute
unto the poor, and thou shalt have treasure in heaven…*
- Luke 18:22 KJV

Slowly my friends and I scaled the sharp rocks and steep incline, our eyes locked on our destination. I wiped the sweat from my forehead, sighing in relief at the sight of the last ledge. My eyes cleared the top, and I swung my arm to grab the last hold in the long chain of steps and handles up the cliff. As I sat down and caught my breath, I peered over the edge. "Whoa. It looks a lot taller from up here!" I yelled to some of my less adventurous friends down below. They smiled back at me and assured me it would be worth it. They looked so peaceful swimming around in the clear blue water. Slowly, I backed away from the edge. *The more I hesitate, the harder this will be.* I took a deep breath, then sighed. Without a second thought, I ran.

The ground disappeared from under my feet. *Wait, I take it back! Don't do this to me!* A soft groan escaped my lips as my body plunged through fifty feet of air. My legs kicked, trying to find something to hold on to. They weren't used to not having anything to stand on. Less than a second later, I plunged into the mountain water. The feeling was one of pure joy. My arms spread out as I began swimming back to the surface. I felt the cool water flow around my head as I emerged from the blue depths. I beamed a huge smile and exclaimed, "Let's do it again!"

God calls us to jump. He is calling us to jump out of ourselves and into service. In the world's eyes, living for someone else other than ourselves is crazy. "Why on Earth would you do that?" they may say to us. But we know that a life spent in service will be much more rewarding in the end. We can choose to lend an ear to those around us, cautioning us not to make any changes to our sinful lives; or we can look to God and give up everything that may be holding us back from a life with Him. Make the jump—it's so worth it!

~ Mason Neil

Bumper Sticker Religion

*Let your light so shine before men, that they may see your good works
and glorify your Father in heaven. - Matthew 5:16 NKJV*

Last spring, we moved to a new house. Since the backyard was
not fenced, one of our first projects was to create a trolley for our dog,
Rex, allowing him to run safely in the yard. We also cleaned out an old
shed to make a warm, dry space where our dog could go to get out of
the rain. We put a thick, old blanket on the floor for a bed and set up
his food and water dishes inside, along with some of our dog's favorite
toys. Rex sniffed around and curled up on the bed.

Just then we noticed one of our neighbors, whom we'd not met yet,
watching us. "I'm calling Animal Control on you!" she yelled. "You can't
lock that dog in there!"

"We're not," we reassured her. "We are making a place where he
can get out of the sun and rain." Instead of listening to our explanation,
the woman continued to yell. My mom decided the best thing would
be to go over to the fence and talk to her face to face. She knocked at
the gated backyard fence, but the lady yelled, "Go away! I don't want
to talk to you!" As my mom walked away, she noticed a bumper sticker
on the woman's car: "God has blessed America: has America blessed
God?" If this woman believed the words she plastered on her car for
all to see, why didn't she act in a way that blessed God?

If we fear God and want to go to heaven, we need to reflect His
character. "The strongest argument in favor of the gospel is a loving
and lovable Christian" (*Ministry of Healing,* pg. 470). To show others
the love of Christ, we need to love, too. How is it possible to be loving
even when others around us are unlovable? We can only achieve
this goal by letting Jesus into our hearts and allowing Him to lead
us through our everyday lives. He must be the decider in everything
we do, whether it be large or miniscule. Is your religion more than a
bumper sticker religion? Does your Christianity shine through your
actions and everyday life?

~ Sarah Wahlman

Doors

… looking unto Jesus, the author and finisher of our faith…
- Hebrews 12:2 NKJV.

Imagine two doors in the Christian life. One door is 15 feet to your left and the other is 15 feet to your right. Both doors swing open, out and away from you. Behind the door on your left is the Devil and his tricks. If you open that door, you will enter into Satan's sinful paths. But for some reason, that door's latch does not hold well. Behind the door on your right is Jesus with His righteousness. If you enter that door, Jesus will welcome you and bring you into His likeness.

You quickly decide that you want to do the right thing, and you definitely do not want to open the left-hand door. Therefore, you grab onto the handle of the left-hand door and pull, to keep it closed. You even push against the door jamb with one hand while clenching the door handle in the other. Although it is tiring, you want to make sure you do not enter into sin.

"I wish I could see Jesus," you think. But, you can't because you have to keep sin's door shut. Finally, you collapse, totally worn out. This is your fatal mistake. In your fatigue, you had forgotten that you had been leaning toward the door. As you collapse, the poorly functioning latch gives way, and you painfully realize that you have fallen into sin.

In horrible shame, you crawl to the other door and knock fearfully. The door swings open. "I am so glad you're here!" Jesus exclaims. "It's dangerous out there." He envelops you in a huge bear hug.

Everything now becomes clear: instead of straining to avoid sin, focus on coming closer to Jesus—His friendship, His will, His grace, His power.

~ Andrew Sharley

Following His Path

Trust in the Lord with all thine heart … and He will direct thy paths.
- Proverbs 3:5–6 KJV

The moment I checked my email, I almost threw up all the noodles I had just eaten for lunch. The letter of acceptance from Fountainview Academy, which I had been waiting several months for, was in my inbox! I couldn't hold in my excitement, and I ran screaming around the house.

The excitement was short lived; the process of preparing to go to Canada from Korea was very stressful. The hardest part was getting a student visa. We needed to wait at least three weeks to get a visa, and registration day was only a month away! Getting a visa wasn't the only complication. While I was waiting for the visa, I needed to buy a plane ticket; however, we couldn't find a direct flight to Seattle. Without knowing English very well, getting off one flight and finding the connection would be nearly impossible. During all this planning, my church family was praying for everything to work out. God definitely answered their prayers. Shortly after, my dad called and said that he had finally found a direct flight. Unfortunately, the visa didn't come before I left for Canada, but my family still decided to send me to school. As I expected, going through security at the airport without proof of my true intentions was difficult; but after a long wait at the Canadian border, I finally received my student visa. Although it was quite challenging to come to Canada, I knew that attending Fountainview was part of God's plan for me because I saw how He overcame all of the obstacles.

Through that experience, I realized that God *does* have a plan for my life. Without God's help, I would be like a child who had lost her parents and didn't know what she should do. The path God is leading me on may seem hard at times, but I must remember that His way is the right direction for my life.

~ Ellen Yoon

Run

*I have fought the good fight, I have finished the race, I have kept the
faith… - 2 Timothy 4:7 NKJV*

Becky and I kept a steady pace, each step thumping in unison
as our feet hit the ground. Running outside was good: the beauty of
nature surrounded us, we talked about meaningful things, and our
blood was circulating. But as we ran longer, the once easy pace began
to call for more effort. My heart and lungs expanded and contracted
in vigorous ways to meet my body's growing demand for oxygen.
By now, sweat was removing toxins from my body, and the slight
uphill grade of the road gave my legs an excuse to groan. I began to
experience the sick feeling that running always brings.

Running makes me feel weaker, but at the same time it builds my
strength. I felt sick and wanted to stop, but having Becky there pushed
me on. We worked together. We talked about pleasant things to take
our minds off our disgruntled bodies, and we empowered each other
with encouraging words.

Our Christian experience is more than just a run—it's a race. Our
goal is to meet Jesus and live with Him forever. As a "baby Christian,"
faith seems effortless at first, but the longer we run, the more we
realize the difficulties and feel the struggles. Trials and temptations
make running harder; they make us hurt and "sweat" in a way that
is healthy—purifying our characters. Prayer is our energy and we,
as fellow Christians, push one another onward and help each other
ignore the pain.

Don't doubt that this race is difficult—it is! But we need to realize
that we are only the runners; our job is solely to run. Christ gives us
the strength, courage, and endurance. He already ran this race!

His coming is soon!

The finish line is near—keep running!

~ Ashley Wilkens

Time

See then that ye walk circumspectly, not as fools, but as wise,
redeeming the time, because the days are evil.
- Ephesians 5:15–16 KJV

Time is the measurement for our lives. Therefore, using time wisely is essential. Using time is easy, but making full use of your time is the hard part.

As a ninth grader at Fountainview, I had a lot of time on my hands. The one thing every upper grader would say to me was "use your time to the fullest." Yet despite all their loving persuasion, I blew it. Instead of practicing my instrument, going to the gym or for a swim in the pond, I would end up in a minor conflict with my friend, or I would engage in verbal warfare with the deans about the rules.

I now try to use every second I have in the most effective way. The time isn't mine; it's God's. 1 Corinthians 6:20 says, "For ye are bought with a price: therefore glorify God in your body, and in your spirit, which are God's" (KJV). God made time and life. If God owns me, and I waste His time on pointless things, then I am stealing from the One who gave me the chance to live. John 14:6: "Jesus saith unto him, 'I am the way, the truth, and the life: no man cometh unto the Father, but by me'" (KJV). If God is life and He made time, then using time correctly is truly living; whereas if I choose to squander it, instead of living, I'm doing evil. Now that I have made this discovery, instead of lying around trying to wait for time to pass, I try to find something productive I can do with my time. My spare moments are now filled with learning new things and widening my knowledge by reading.

Winston Churchill once said: "Time is one thing that can never be retrieved … the hours that are lost in idleness can never be brought back to be used in gainful pursuits." We all have time given to us, and it's our choice how we use it. Whether I choose to waste it on pointless pursuits or use it for God's benefit, is really my choice. So, how are you going to use your time?

~ Chris Donatelli

The Scriptures a Safeguard

*To the law and to the testimony: if they speak not according to this
word, it is because there is no light in them. - Isaiah 8:20 KJV*

The first Adventist missionary to Iceland founded a publishing
house that started printing a newspaper. This paper soon became
the most read newspaper in the country because it contained new
religious ideas, and many people debated these controversial
subjects in their own publications. The spiritualists argued especially
hard against the missionary's articles. To answer their arguments,
the missionary began to study spiritualistic teachings. This was a
dangerous move. Through the study of spiritualistic doctrines and by
dwelling on satanic themes, the man became a spiritualist. He never
worked in Iceland for the Lord Jesus again.

We never need to study error to prove truth. The answer to every
false doctrine and misleading delusion is found in God's Word. Jesus
met each of Satan's arguments with a "Thus says the Lord." He found
the answers in the Scriptures, and we can still find them there today.

"The people of God are directed to the Scriptures as their
safeguard against the influence of false teachers and the delusive
power of spirits of darkness. Satan employs every possible device
to prevent men from obtaining a knowledge of the Bible; for its plain
utterances reveal his deceptions… he is now putting forth his utmost
efforts for a final struggle against Christ... So closely will the counterfeit
resemble the true that it will be impossible to distinguish between them
except by the Holy Scriptures. By their testimony every statement and
every miracle must be tested" (*The Great Controversy*, 593.1).

We must study the Word of God to have victory over Satan. In the
ancient days, Christ's disciples cast out demons, simply by trusting
God and His Word. We are to do the same.

~ Esra Eliasson

Paralyzed

Fear thou not; for I am with thee: be not dismayed; for I am thy God: I will strengthen thee; yea, I will help thee; yea, I will uphold thee with the right hand of my righteousness. - Isaiah 41:10 KJV

I hated sleeping by myself. Whenever I went to sleep, I always had nightmares. In my dreams, demons and ghosts came to try and hurt me. One night I dreamed I was reading a book in my room, and my mother came in and turned off the lights. I tried to stand up and turn the lights back on, but I couldn't move at all. It felt like somebody was pressing down on my chest. Suddenly, a girl's voice screamed my name. I heard her voice echo around the room, becoming louder and louder. Her voice was so high that it could have shattered glass. All I wanted to do was to wake up and call for my mother, but I felt paralyzed. I must have moved in my sleep because with a struggle I awoke. Every night, these same kinds of dreams would haunt me, and I was terrified to sleep at night. I needed help.

I told my piano teacher about the nightmares. She is a good Christian woman, and she advised me that I should pray to God for protection before I went to bed. I was not a Christian at that time, and I didn't even know how to pray; but following her advice, I started to pray before I went to bed. "Please God," I prayed, "protect me from evil so I can go to sleep." After I prayed that night, I was able to go to sleep feeling safe and reassured that God would protect me from any evils.

From this experience, I learned that God really does protect and care for us. I never believed in God before this experience happened to me. But after praying to Him every night, and seeing how my nightmares disappeared after I prayed, I realized that there really is a loving God. If we pray to God for protection, He will give us the power to resist evil. Satan's forces dare not take one step towards us with Christ by our side.

~ Ellen Yoon

Waiting Patiently

… This same Jesus, who has been taken from you into heaven, will come back in the same way you have seen Him go into heaven.
- Acts 1:11 NIV

When I was a little girl, I enjoyed doing things with my mom and dad so much. We used to read stories, my mom and I made meals, and dad and I played fun games. It was so nice just to be with them and spend time together. But unfortunately my dad had to go to work, and I would miss him while he was gone. I remember that I would call him just to see where he was, what he was doing, and when he was coming home. Sometimes it seemed like forever until he would be back.

During the time he was away, my sisters and I would keep occupied doing the things that my mother asked us to do. We had a nice time, but we would always wonder when Daddy was coming home. Sometimes I would call him up to five times a day to ask for his help or have a question answered. And upon his arrival home I excitedly shouted, "Daddy's home!" and ran to the door to give him a big hug.

The Bible tells us that our Father in Heaven is sending Jesus again someday to take us to our heavenly home to be with Him forever! He also is there for us, to listen to us, and answer our questions. In fact, He wants us to talk to Him several times a day, even every hour or more. The Bible also tells us that Jesus is in Heaven now, preparing us a place (see John 14:2). And just like I patiently and excitedly waited for my daddy to come home, now I am waiting for my Heavenly Father to take me home to be with Him. Won't you wait with me?

~ Anna Ford

Relief from Suffering

… Behold! The Lamb of God who takes away the sin of the world!
- John 1:29 NKJV

We were driving home from church one Sabbath when we saw a deer on the road. It looked dead, but turned out to be a little fawn that had been hit by a car, but was still alive. To our horror, a dog was eating it. My dad stopped the car and chased the dog away while we rushed to the fawn. The poor thing was in horrible pain; I held the little fawn's head in my lap and stroked its head, crying for its pain. I wanted so badly to make it better, but my mom told me there was nothing I could do. Soon, its eyes closed and it stopped breathing—it was dead. This experience is one of my saddest memories.

Although this happened many years ago, I still feel like crying when I remember it. To see something suffering, and not be able to do anything to help it, makes me feel so helpless. I can only imagine how Adam and Eve must have felt after sinning. Having never seen death, they were told to sacrifice a helpless lamb.

"This ceremonial offering, ordained of God, was to be a perpetual reminder to Adam of his guilt, and also a penitential acknowledgment of his sin. This act of taking life gave Adam a deeper and more perfect sense of his transgression, which nothing less than the death of God's dear Son could expiate. He marveled at the infinite goodness and matchless love which would give such a ransom to save the guilty. As Adam was slaying the innocent victim, it seemed to him that he was shedding the blood of the Son of God by his own hand. He knew that if he had remained steadfast to God, and true to His holy law, there would have been no death of beast nor of man. Yet in the sacrificial offerings, pointing to the great and perfect offering of God's dear Son, there appeared a star of hope to illuminate the dark and terrible future, and relieve it of its utter hopelessness and ruin" (*The Story of Redemption*, pg. 50).

~ Sarah Wahlman

Wolves in Madrid

Resist the devil, and he will flee from you. Draw nigh to God, and He will draw nigh to you. - James 4:7b–8a KJV

Have you ever been disappointed by deception? Jesus warns us in Matthew 7:15 to beware of wolves in sheep's clothing. Let me tell you how my family was deceived by "wolves" in Madrid.

We were on our way back from our yearly visit to our relatives in Portugal. Our SEAT van zipped through the arid Pyrenean Mountains that stood tall and rolling on either side of the highway. Just after passing through the city of Madrid, a policeman waved us over to an empty parking lot. He approached us and presented his police license. After asking to see my parents' wallets, the policeman proceeded to search the car. But after poking through a few things, he asked to see the wallets again. Now the confusion as to why we were stopped turned into uncomfortable apprehension. His dark figure outside my mother's window was intimidating, and he repeated his demand. She handed over the wallets. We watched with bated breath and pounding hearts as he carefully picked through the wallets a second time.

The seconds seemed to morph into hours. Then in a sudden flurry, he snatched the cash from the wallets and made a mad dash for his car, which was already started with three of his accomplices waiting inside, one of them at the wheel ready to take off. Shouting, my parents raced after him. We'd never had as much as €1000 in our wallets at one time before, but we had just received it from relatives. We were baffled, angry, and very disappointed to find that a "policeman" we had trusted was just a wolf in sheep's clothing.

But there is another, more dangerous wolf lurking, disguised and waiting to deceive me at any moment. The only way I can be safe from the crafty wiles of this wolf is by staying close to the Shepherd. He puts it this way: "Abide in me…" He has promised that He will keep us under His care if only we will listen and obey His voice.

~ Esther Ferraz

Not a Clown

You search the Scriptures, for in them you think you have eternal life; and these are they which testify of Me. - John 5:39 NKJV

When I grew up in Communist China, I used to believe whatever I was told. Before I became a Christian, I heard the name "Jesus" a lot. But when I heard the name "Jesus," it was a joke. In kindergarten, the children would always sing, "Jesus can kill, and because he knows you're stupid, he is going to look for you tonight." So in my mind, "Jesus" was a silly and horrifying clown who never existed. This type of thinking stayed with me from kindergarten to age eleven.

Then one day, my parents became Christians, and I was shocked. How could my smart parents become idiots? How could they believe in a "god?" I believed that there was no god at all because that's what I was taught. Even though my parents were explaining to me about Jesus and telling me the truth, I kept ignoring them. Day after day, I could see the changes in my parents. They became more humble and gentle, and much more kind to the people around them. That caused me to ask the question: Why have their lives changed so much?

"We studied the Bible," said my mom, "and this is how Jesus treats us, and how He wants us to treat others."

So that motivated me to look at the Bible and see what "Jesus" is really like. While I was reading, I found the words of Jesus so full of wisdom, and I thought, *Jesus is really smart!* Then I gave up believing in the thoughts of others, and now I believe that Jesus is real. He is the real God. After I became a Christian, there were still a lot of people misusing the name of Jesus, but I chose not to listen to them anymore. Instead, I chose to live out the character of Christ through His power within me, as my parents had shown me.

~ Bryan Chen

An Icon of God

*Now then we are ambassadors for Christ, as though God did beseech
you by us: we pray you in Christ's stead, be ye reconciled to God.*
- 2 Corinthians 5:20 KJV

I'm an American. This naturally means that I've inherited a bit of the
civic pride common to many from my country, and that I've heard a lot
about how to treat our flag. Since the famous stars and stripes are a
representation of America—its government, people, and history—it's
important to treat the flag with respect. This is especially true when
the flag is being flown in international meeting areas, or in foreign
countries, because the flag is an icon of America. So a "flag code" has
been developed, a set of rules that explains how to fly our flag in such
a way that it shows respect to the nation that it represents.

Even though I'm an American, my true citizenship lies in the
kingdom of Heaven; and Heaven has a flag even larger, more
majestic, and more powerful than America's: the Christian church!
As Christians, each of us represents heaven in a very powerful way.
We are the standard of God's Kingdom, an emblem of His love and
justice here on a foreign and fallen planet. We must follow the flag
code! When we don't love our neighbors as ourselves, when we
don't turn the other cheek, when we profane God's name, when we
dishonor the Sabbath, and when we disrespect our parents, we might
as well be flying Heaven's flag upside down! As an ambassador from
God's government, an icon to the unbelieving, and a flag representing
freedom on a scale unknown to this planet, what kind of message are
you sending? Will others look at you and see a representation of the
devil's sinister empire, or will they see a peace and joy that can only
come from being a citizen of God's kingdom?

~ Michael Jensen

Thanks, But No Thanks

And the King shall answer and say unto them, Verily I say unto you, Inasmuch as ye have done it unto one of the least of these my brethren, ye have done it unto me. - Matthew 25:40 KJV

When I was a little boy, I had a friend who lived close to my house. We were good friends and spent a lot of time playing together. One day, he invited me to his birthday party, so I went with my mother to the store to buy a toy car for his birthday. I carefully wrapped the gift I had purchased, and then placed it on the dining room table until it was time for the birthday party.

A few days later, the time came for my friend's birthday party. As I walked closer to his house, I saw other guests coming, all with their own gifts in their hands. My heart beat with excitement as I approached the house with the gift in hand. I knocked on the door, and his mother opened it.

"Oh, you brought a gift for my son. I'll take it for him," she said as she took the gift out of my hands. "We never invited you to the party, but thanks for the gift." With that, she slammed the door in my face, leaving me outside, speechless.

I felt hurt and sad as I trudged slowly home. When I arrived home, I told my mom what had happened. I was very discouraged. I had wanted to give the gift myself and spend time with my friend; instead my gift was taken from me, and I was turned away.

Jesus wants to bless us in hundreds of ways each day. But some people want to take Jesus' blessings without receiving Him. They want to take the gifts He offers, but slam the door in His face. More than anything else, He wants a personal relationship with us. To know the Giver is infinitely better than to receive the gift. How many times do we receive gifts without acknowledging the giver? How many times will we slam the door of our hearts in Jesus' face?

~ Esra Eliasson

A Reckless Moment, Part 1

Wherefore, my beloved … work out your own salvation with fear and trembling. - Philippians 2:12 KJV

We wiggled and squeezed past each other, trying to get out of the busses. Finally—freedom! I was on the annual California music tour with Fountainview Academy. After being stuck in a stuffy, cramped bus, I welcomed the opportunity to get some fresh air and exercise before our concert that evening.

The sun was shining beautifully that Friday afternoon as I joined fellow students playing soccer on a nearby hilly lawn. We were flitting around like birds just released from their dusty old cages. It was exhilarating! But after a vigorous hour and a half, my friend, Ashley, and I decided to change activities and work on gymnastics. We chose some nearby trees to conceal us from potential onlookers. After spotting each other on a few practice jumps, I went first to do the actual back tuck. Putting my arms up and stretching straight and tall, I suddenly felt a cold chill run through my body. Should I actually do this? Oh, whatever… I've done it before. I wouldn't think long and hard about it; I would just do it. I jumped into the air, and brought my knees up and over my head for the rotation of the flip—or so I thought. I didn't tuck enough. Suddenly, my head impacted the ground, followed by an audible crunch. Stunned and gasping for breath, I sat up out of the heap I had dived into. Wiggling my fingers and toes, relief washed over me. I felt no tingling in my limbs, had no headache, could move my head from side to side, and I did not have any dizziness—no symptoms of a broken neck.

This experience made me realize how easy it is to lose that which is precious through carelessness. One small moment of recklessness could have ruined my life forever. This doesn't just apply to our life here on this earth—the decisions we make every day affect our eternal destiny. Don't let one thoughtless moment jeopardize your eternal reward.

~ Esther Ferraz

A Reckless Moment, Part 2

For he shall give his angels charge over thee, to keep thee in all thy ways. - Psalm 91:11 KJV

A few hours after my miscalculated dive, the planned concert for that evening took place. By God's grace, and thanks to some Advil, I was still able to participate. That evening I went to bed with a very stiff and aching neck. Any movements that forced me out of my now very straight posture—such as slouching—sent shocks of pain down my spine.

In the morning, the pain from my back had concentrated at the base of my neck. Deciding it would be best to have it examined, the deans and my parents wanted me to go to the hospital. In the middle of Sabbath school, I slipped away to the nearest hospital in downtown Sacramento. All of the x-ray images showed no signs of a fracture, so I was released from the hospital in time for the afternoon concert.

At the end of our California tour, I returned home, and my neck was still very tender to the touch. Wanting to be sure that nothing too serious had happened, my family and I talked to a chiropractor. He found that the swelling was on the outside of the spine, rather than the inside where it would have compressed my spinal cord. The tenderness was from an inflammation caused by the impact—hence the "crunch." But had I fallen with my head turned sideways, I would have undoubtedly broken my neck and been paralyzed from the neck down.

Looking back at that close call, I am very grateful that God protected me. The concept of being paralyzed from the neck down is hard to wrap my mind around. But God, in His great mercy, had given His angels charge over me, to keep me in all my ways. Oh, how my Father loves me, and how I want to love Him more!

~ Esther Ferraz

Giving It Up

… my Lord, for whom I have suffered the loss of all things, and do count them but dung, that I may win Christ… - Philippians 3:8

Give it up.

"Please, Lord, no! How could you ask me to give it up? Please, I want to follow you, but isn't there another way? I am changing in so many areas already…"

I had grown up doing power tumbling: a specific type of gymnastics, made up of strength, speed, technique, and flipping. When I did it, I was intense. I did not want to be just good at the sport I loved—I wanted to be great at it! I wanted to be the top of my tumbling class. I wanted to look strong and be strong.

My presumption claimed that gymnastics was indispensible. The sport provided me with many great benefits: joy, exercise, stress relief, and an outlet for witnessing to non-Christians. I thought that I would forever be craving it if I quit, and that would be torture. Still, I knew giving up tumbling was so right for so many reasons. The music played at the gym was worldly and… appealing. The shorts and tank tops that I wore sharply contrasted Christian modesty, and my competitiveness while doing the sport was not a good thing either. But, the bottom line was that gymnastics absorbed my mind. It was my idol.

As I drew nearer to Christ, I began to see very clearly the chains that held me to this world. He pointed out to me that I needed to let go of my idol, and I saw that this chain was strong—too strong for me to break. Jesus is the only one who could break it. I had to make the choice to trust Him and let go of something that was really important to me, in order to receive something better. To follow Jesus I had to give up all; He gave up all for me.

I gave it up.

~ Ashley Wilkens

The Big Picture

For My thoughts are not your thoughts, neither are your ways My ways, saith the Lord. - Isaiah 55:8 KJV

Tears streamed down my face as I walked towards the front door of my home. Behind me the headlights of a van slowly faded down my driveway. I had just said goodbye to my best friend. She had recently graduated from high school and was now off to college. Sadly, this college was located in another province, which meant that she would be moving about sixteen hours away. Saying goodbye to her had been really hard; ever since I could remember, she had always been there for me. I stood in the front yard of my home, recalling all the many memories of our friendship, and glanced up at the sky, wishing that the answers to all my questions would be written there. But all I saw were the stars, twinkling silently back at me. As I stood there, gazing up at the sky, I began to realize how I'd neglected to realize just how much God leads in each of our lives. When I looked at the night sky, all I was seeing was a small bit of the infinite expanse of cosmic wonder. Yet my God was the very Creator of this universe, and He knew every star, every galaxy, and every planet. He had placed each star in the universe and had orchestrated their every movement.

That night I realized that, when I look at my life, I see only a small frame of options in what really is a panorama of opportunities. I become too secure in my little picture of what I think life should look like. When my best friend left, I felt really sad and confused. I didn't understand why God would allow someone who I loved so much to move away. Too often, I forget that God can see the panoramic view of my future. I need to remember that God knows much better than I do what is good and necessary for me as His daughter.

~ Sierra Buhler

Family Time

… The Sabbath was made for man, and not man for the Sabbath.
- Mark 2:27 KJV

"He's coming! Run!" Flying around a corner in our house, I meet my mom coming the other way. I barely escape from colliding with her and run straight into my dad, who is "it." He tags me, and I yell, "I'm it! Here I come!" The shout echoes through the house as I chase my prey.

Family time is a common occurrence in our home, and it is the best part of our day. It's time to enjoy having Dad home and time to have fun together. Dad and Mom lay aside everything else just to be with us. As I think back on the family times we have had, whether we played tag, scrabble, or just sat and read a book together, I feel this is the biggest factor that has made my family inseparable. It's the perfect time to get to know each other better and to become close friends. It also shows my parents' love and commitment to me, because they are willing to take time from their busy schedules to make our home happy. The great thing is that they don't just take time once in a blue moon—they set that time aside every evening.

Did you know that God has set aside some "family time" to be with His children, too? God set apart a whole day every week so that He could show His children how much He loves them. This day is the Sabbath. On the Sabbath, God's children get to spend time with Him. They get to know Him better, and they see His love for them in a deeper way. Do you long for a father who would spend this kind of time with you? In Galatians 3:26, the Bible says: "For ye are all the children of God by faith in Christ Jesus" (KJV). Therefore, God has set this family time aside to be with you. You can choose to skip your time with God if you want to, just as I could skip my time with my parents. But once you experience God's love first hand, you'll never want to miss out again.

~ Bethany Corrigan

"Will You Be A Fire Lookout For Me?"

But the Lord said unto me, Say not, I am a child: for thou shalt go to all that I shall send thee, and whatsoever I command thee thou shalt speak. - Jeremiah 1:7 KJV

As my cousins and I rounded the bend, a small cabin set on tall stilts appeared straight ahead. I had seen glimpses of this lookout through the evergreens, but I had not been expecting it to be a full six stories tall. As we trudged up the five never-ending flights of stairs, I craned my neck in every direction, trying to see the whole 360° view at once. I struggled to listen as the ranger gave us a tour—I was too captivated by the catwalk's view. Pine, spruce, and fir forests stretched on rolling hills for miles in every direction while little creeks and waterfalls dotted and crisscrossed the landscape. As I looked straight down at the bare, rocky mountaintop, my ten-year-old brain tried to imagine how scary it would be to live up in that tall tower, all alone, for the whole summer. Shuddering, I imagined a windy thunderstorm whipping around the supports and shaking the cabin. I looked at the brave ranger talking with new admiration, and wondered how he could stay in this exposed fire lookout, weathering storms and watching for fires all summer!

As I got older and more outdoorsy, I decided it would actually be fun to be a fire lookout, even if it meant weathering some bad storms alone. While I have never been asked to be an actual forest fire lookout, I have been asked to stand as a fire lookout amid the storms of life, the raging infernos that threaten to burn up my faith. Promising to provide the strength I need, Christ asks me to trust completely in Him and be brave. He begs me not to worry about what other people think of me or about what struggles are coming my way. He wants me to be a beacon of light shining out over the mountains, pointing everyone I meet to Him. He is calling a lookout who will stand firm for Him. He asks, "Will you be a fire lookout for Me?"

~ Katie Sloop

Go. God Will Supply.

… Go into all the world and preach the gospel to every creature.
- Mark 16:15 NKJV

Sharing Jesus is not the easiest task. I have often wished that I would just bubble over with the joy and words of Jesus. I have also wished that as a result of my relationship with God, I would find myself automatically sharing Him with others. However, I have not found this to be the case. It takes conscious effort for me to talk of Jesus to others. Am I just not connected with God? Is that the problem?

My friendship with God is not perfect, but I am convinced of another problem. I have been depending upon my desires instead of moving forward in obedience to God. I have been waiting for more desire to share Jesus, instead of actually sharing Him. In a way, I have been saying that God has not given me what I need in order to witness for Him. Jesus wants me to ask Him for His Holy Spirit and for the desire to share Him, but He has also called me to go and make disciples. Jesus does not have in mind that I spend all my time asking Him to help me. He has promised to answer my prayer and supply God's power to me through His Holy Spirit. I can trust Him to come through on His promise as I seek to fulfill His commission.

Now, God commands me to move forward and share my Redeemer. He will supply me with power and a genuine desire to bring others into His family. He will provide exactly what I need in order to be His witness. As I step out and share Jesus, the Holy Spirit will keep working in me. My desire to testify for my Master will grow and grow, and repeating Jesus' words to others will become more spontaneous and natural.

But, God is not calling me to wait until I am more properly suited to be His messenger. As I faithfully go and do the work, He supplies all that I need in order to spread His message of Salvation. For now, He asks that I trustingly share my Redeemer in whatever circumstance He puts me. Could He now be calling you to go and share your Redeemer?

~ Andrew Sharley

To Know, or Not to Know

And this is life eternal, that they might know thee the only true God, and Jesus Christ, whom thou hast sent. - John 17:3 KJV

Paul once said: "I know whom I have believed" (2 Timothy 1:12 NKJV). Job exclaimed in his trials: "I know that my redeemer liveth" (Job 19:25 KJV). At these declarations, I am inspired to ask: what does it mean to know—to really know someone?

Johann Navratil, my German great-grandfather, was a new convert to Adventism when he was drafted into the chaos of WWII and forced to leave his home and newly married bride behind in Czechoslovakia. Now in Germany, and wanting to stay true to his convictions, he took up the loathsome position of a conscientious objector. This, combined with trying to keep Sabbath, provided him with many challenges. But because he was a very kind man and faithful in all he did, he soon gained the respect and trust of many of his fellow soldiers and supervisors. Later on, however, he and many others were taken as prisoners to Luxemburg. When he was released from prison, but still not allowed to go home, he shared his faith with a fellow prisoner who ended up becoming a firm believer in Christ. Through these twenty-plus years of hardship and the painful knowledge that his girls had grown up without a father, Opa Navratil remained faithful to the God he had come to know and love. Near the end of his life, one of Great-Grandpa's last wishes was to have this verse written as his epitaph: "For I know that my redeemer liveth..." (Job 19:25 KJV).

Grandpa knew that his redeemer lived. But once again: what does that mean—he knew that his redeemer lived? The dictionary definition is: to understand from experience or attainment. My grandpa's life was a testimony to the fact that he did know and understand God. He had experienced God in his life, and understood just like Job that despite all the trials he had been through, despite the traumas life brings, God is a loving God who still lives. He has this world under control. It is my desire to know God like that also.

~ Esther Ferraz

Why Child

"For My thoughts are not your thoughts, nor are your ways My ways," says the Lord. "For as the heavens are higher than the earth, so are My ways higher than your ways, and My thoughts than your thoughts." - Isaiah 55:8–9 NKJV

I've always been a curious kid. I have a never-ending stream of questions and a need to understand things for myself. In pre-school, my teachers called me the "why-child." Personally, I was constantly amazed at their seemingly infinite supply of answers. But sometimes, it seemed to me that the adults in my life had all conspired together to deflect my queries and give me as little information as possible.

"Just trust me. You'll understand when you're older," they would say.

But I never did trust. Grown-ups only used the "when you're older" line when I was asking about something I shouldn't know. But forbidden knowledge only further piqued my interest. I would pester everyone I knew until I finally got the information I wanted. Once I got my long-hoped-for answer, however, I always felt so disappointed. Instead of the empowering knowledge I'd wanted, I found my parents and teachers were protecting me from things that I really shouldn't know.

Often, God doesn't answer my prayers the way I'd want Him to. Sometimes He tells me that I'm asking for something I shouldn't have, or that I need to wait on His timing. He knows what is good for me, even when I don't. But I know that eventually, I'll be able to look back and see the wisdom in His plans. Instead of becoming impatient for His answer, I can wait for His timing, and rest in the knowledge that He is more trustworthy than anything or anyone else.

~ Saraiah Turnbull

A Day to Rest

And he said unto them, Come ye yourselves apart, and rest a while.
- Mark 6:31a KJV

"We're here!" Dad announced as we pulled into the parking spot in front of our campsite. Flinging open the car door, my ten-year-old sister and I raced each other to the top of a large sand dune. As we reached the summit and gulped in the fresh, salty air, a beautiful panorama of the Atlantic Ocean greeted us. Ever since I was a little girl, my family's annual trip to Assateague Island, Maryland, has been one of our most anticipated vacations. Throughout the summer, we push ourselves to work our hardest until we are able to take this break. The reason this vacation means so much to us is because we know that, regardless of how busy our summer is or how many people are in our house, there's a special time that's set apart to rest and reconnect with just our family.

There is another day that my family looks forward to: Sabbath. Life on our farm is busy during the week, but we're able to work together and pull through it because we know we'll be able to rest on Sabbath. When God created the Sabbath, He had you and me in mind. He knew that, without a special day to rest and reconnect, our relationship with Him would fall apart. Whenever my family is at Assateague, the stress from the summer slowly ebbs away with the falling tide. The quiet noise of waves rolling over the wet sand, squabbling seagulls, and the soft wind fills us with peace until we are rejuvenated and once again become a family unit. It is the same on Sabbath. On this special day of rest, God desires to wash away all of our cares so we'll be able to refocus, rejuvenate, and reconnect in our walk with Him. He wants for you to go away feeling refreshed and stronger. Won't you take this day out of your busy week to spend just with Him?

~ Sarah Miller

Lost and Found

Wherefore, if God so clothe the grass of the field, which today is, and to morrow is cast into the oven, shall he not much more clothe you, O ye of little faith? - Matthew 6:30 KJV

I have a hard time keeping track of my stuff. Because I am at a school that travels frequently, it becomes quite easy to lose your belongings, especially when you are exhausted after being in a bus for hours on end. You get so tired that when you reach the destination, your only mission becomes to hit the hay.

One morning I woke up and realized that I was going to sing in a concert that morning. As I got dressed in my uniform, I was unpleasantly surprised when I couldn't find my suit jacket anywhere in my closet. I checked lost and found, but to my dismay I found nothing. Then I remembered that I left it at a previous concert location. This was not good, since I had to perform that morning. I went to breakfast, and while I ate, I prayed to God that if it was His will, I would find my jacket. I put my full trust in Him because I knew that if it was His will, He would solve my problem at the right time. When I went to put my plate away, something impressed me to ask a girl who was standing by the table where my jacket was; but I thought to myself, "That is ridiculous; what is the likelihood that she would have come across my jacket? After all, it has been three weeks since I lost it." But sure enough, when I asked her, she lit up and started running. I followed her into an office and up into the attic. After scrambling around for a bit, she pulled up a dusty suit jacket—I could not believe my eyes: God answered my prayer!

Often it is easy to think that God is so great that He only cares about the big things; but I have found through my experience that it doesn't matter how small the petition is, God cares, and He will still—if it is His will—honor your request.

~ Esra Eliasson

The GPS

Thy word is a lamp unto my feet, and a light unto my path.
- Psalm 119:105 KJV

For the past four years, my parents have wanted to get a GPS. Usually Mommy + map = GPS, but it was decided that they needed this device for work. When visiting people at unfamiliar addresses without a navigator and with hands glued to the wheel, it proved too difficult to consult a map. With the help of a talking GPS and its colorful display, finding the right way should be much easier. This gadget has been very useful so far. Now, instead of juggling ten different maps when we go on vacation, and Mommy having to awaken from her slumber to point out every other exit we must take, we can comfortably enjoy our rides without having to worry about navigational difficulties. Thanks to satellites, we are now able to enjoy this luxury. A GPS can locate our exact position anywhere with the help of these satellites. However, one satellite is not enough—three satellites are needed to pinpoint our location, allowing the GPS unit to analyze hundreds of thousands of roads in a matter of seconds and determine the best route to our destination. Then all that Daddy has to do is follow every direction of the GPS, and we will arrive at our destination.

So it is in our life. We need someone from above to tell us where we are, where to go, and how to get to our destination. And if we go in the wrong direction, that Someone can recalculate our route and get us on the right track again—if we let Him and don't keep driving in the wrong direction on purpose. But even then, He'll keep recalculating to lead us back whenever we're ready to turn around. Psalm 119:105 says that God's Word is a lamp unto my feet and a light unto my path—a lamp to show me where I am and a light to lead me to where I need to go. God will show me those things through his Word. With that kind of a GPS, arrival at my destination is certain!

~ Esther Ferraz

Correction

A fool despises his father's instruction, but he who receives correction is prudent. - Proverbs 15:5 NKJV

My younger sister, Kari, and I both play the cello, so we enjoy practicing music together. Since I am older and have played longer, I often show her what she is doing wrong and how to fix it.

One evening, we were preparing a piece to play for church. After we had played the music a couple of times, Kari attempted to show me how to change something that I was doing wrong. Because I am more experienced, I wasn't willing to listen to anything she had to say. That built a wall between us, and we started to argue. I knew that she was right, but because of my stubbornness and selfish absorption, I didn't want to admit my fault.

Like me, the religious leaders in Jesus' time were not willing to admit that they were wrong. They disliked John the Baptist because his growing popularity was causing them to lose control over the people. The Pharisees went to John with a false air of penitence, thinking to regain their influence on the multitudes, but John saw their real motives. When he accused them of being insincere, they rejected him and his message of repentance.

The religious leaders rejected Jesus as well because His mission was not what they had so eagerly anticipated. They knew He was the Messiah, but did not want to admit that their idea of the Savior was wrong. Their desires to exalt "self" contradicted Jesus' example of self-denial, and they wouldn't give up "self" and change.

If I had been willing to listen to Kari, and not let my pride get in the way, I would have become a better cellist. In the same way, the religious leaders missed out on salvation because they let their selfish pride get in the way. When the Holy Spirit convicts me of something that I know is wrong, I need to be willing to change. The only correct course is to always keep your heart open to the Holy Spirit's correction.

~ Kami Rose

Hungry?

Like newborn babies, crave pure spiritual milk, so that by it you may grow up in your salvation... - 1 Peter 2:2 NIV

"Ksh, ksh, ksh" the bottle grunted as the newborn baby calf ferociously tore into the tepid milk.

"Stop that!" I said, smacking the older bull on the nose as it came in for some of the baby's milk. As I stood feeding the heifer, my thoughts began to wander back to what had happened earlier that morning. Waking up late, I had rushed outside with an apology still tumbling off my lips for missing my date with God. Although I'd had good intentions of reading my Bible a little when I came in for breakfast, I knew that I wouldn't be able to find time to read it, due to the fast pace of a day at the farm.

Guiltily, I remembered that this hadn't been the only time that I'd skipped out on my devotions. Although I wanted to apologize to Him, I just couldn't. Feeling uncomfortable, I tried to think about something else. But slowly, the still, small voice pushed its way through the mental wall that I'd built up against it.

Finally, I gave in and listened.

Just like the calves are dependent on me for their food, so I am dependent on Jesus for my spiritual food. If I don't go to Him, then I won't be able to grow up into the person He wants me to be. Every morning, Jesus invites you out for a breakfast date with Him. Will you go?

~ Sarah Miller

Later, God! I'll Do it Later!

And now, Lord, what wait I for? My hope is in Thee. - Psalms 39:7 KJV

As a 15-year-old girl, I had felt God tugging at my heart several times. I had given it to Him; what more did He want? I knew what He wanted, but didn't want to give in. I was afraid to be in front of people!

As I sat in the auditorium one night listening to the speaker's appeal for baptism, my heart burned. I didn't want to say yes to baptism—not because I didn't want to follow God, but because I was terrified to speak in front of people. I didn't want them to notice me. As excuses flew through my head, I could hear God speaking to me: "Do you want to follow Me?"

"Yes, but I have already given my heart to you!"

Somehow, I knew that I hadn't totally given myself to Him. I was not willing to do what He was asking me to do.

I nervously raised my hand, so low that I was sure nobody could see it. But the speaker saw, and he smiled reassuringly. He knew it was difficult for me, and he was happy that I had made the decision. That look gave me peace. I knew God would stand by my side.

As I talked to God about it, He helped me to realize that I had a sickness—a sickness called selfishness! I was choosing to allow what I feared people would think of me to determine how I would live life. Now, as I look back, I can see that my fears were ridiculous. As I came out of the water after my baptism, I was full to overflowing with joy! God enabled me to overcome my fear, and now I can rejoice in His freedom!

Will you give God your all now? He will help you surrender completely, and save you by His grace.

~ Bethany Corrigan

The Marshmallow Study

Rest in the Lord, and wait patiently for Him… - Psalm 37:7a NKJV

In the 1960's there was a study done by Stanford University called The Marshmallow Study. This is what happened:

A teacher walked into his classroom and placed one marshmallow on each of his students' desks. The teacher then told the children they could do one of two things with their marshmallow: either eat it immediately, or wait fifteen minutes. If they chose to wait fifteen minutes, they would receive one more marshmallow. If they didn't, then that would be the only marshmallow they received. Many of the students ate their marshmallow before the fifteen minutes were up; however, there were a small number of them that waited and received a second one. Many years after the experiment was finished, Stanford contacted the kids, now adults, who had been in the study. Stanford discovered that those who had waited for the second marshmallow were much more successful individuals than those who ate theirs right away. This test was done to see if the children would act on impulse, or realize that if they waited they could have something better.

Often times I pray, asking God to show me what to do and where to go, or to help me in whatever I'm struggling with. Instead of waiting for His answer, I do what I think is best and it ends up not turning out how I thought it would. When I look at the mistakes I have made, I see that most of the time it's because I did something before thinking about the end result. God's plan and timing is always best; next time you have to make a decision, try waiting to see what God has in store for you.

~ Raina Walker

The Holes in His Hands

*And one shall say unto Him, What are these wounds in thine hands?
Then he shall answer, Those with which I was wounded in the house of
my friends. - Zechariah 13:6 KJV*

There was a young man who was always happy, kind, and bright.
He had such a great family that he had nothing to fear. But then his
dad passed away, and everything changed. He and his mom lost
almost everything. Quitting school, he had to work so the family could
survive. Life started to get better, but not by much. Before his dad
died, he had been carefree; but now everything around him was falling
apart, and that caused a change in him. He became violent, began to
steal, and acted disrespectfully to his mom. Of course, she reminded
him not to do these things, but he wouldn't even listen to his mother.
She didn't know how to correct his behaviour; so she decided to
hammer a nail into her wall each time he did something bad. BANG,
BANG!! Every day, clanging, clattering sounds were heard from her
home, and her hammering didn't stop until the wall was full of nails.

One afternoon as the young man was passing by the wall, he
realized it was different. Wondering why, he asked his mom about
it and she told him that the nails each represented one of his many
misdeeds. He was shocked at the number of his sins, and realized
how sinful he really was. He decided to change and pull out the nails
by doing good things. Even though it was hard for him to change, he
succeeded and became a new person. He was so happy that all the
nails were gone now, but one thing made him very sad. He had tried
to undo what he had done in the past, but he couldn't remove all the
holes that reminded him of his past.

Jesus has holes in His hands. These holes are a reminder to us of
our past. Although God will one day "make all things new" (Revelation
21:5 KJV), including all of our defects and scars, the holes in His Son's
hands can never be removed and will remain for eternity.

~ Hannah Lee

Monster Dog

Yea, though I walk through the valley of the shadow of death, I will
fear no evil: for thou art with me; Thy rod and Thy staff they comfort
me. - Psalm 23:4 KJV

Nine years ago, on a bright sweltering afternoon in Brazil, I was on my way home from school with my brother when he suggested we take a shorter route. As we passed by a farm, a huge, terrifying creature suddenly charged towards us with razor sharp teeth, cold, evil eyes, and a growl like that of a Tyrannosaurs Rex. It was... a Chihuahua! I was so frightened that I jumped on my brother's back and shrieked at him to run. Even though he wasn't really afraid, he had sympathy for my fears and ran all the way down the street to escape the "monster dog." It was a close call, but we got away and reached our car just in time.

Now that I am older, I can see a lesson in this experience. For me, this Chihuahua was a big, terrifying creature; for my brother, it was only a little, crazy dog. He wasn't afraid of it because he knew that it couldn't do anything to hurt us. When I ran to him for help, he saw how scared I was, picked me up, and ran away with me from that "monster." Once we were far away from the Chihuahua, he put me down but continued to walk beside me so that I would know, should I need help again, that he was right there for me.

In my walk of life, I can call God my brother and Satan a little, crazy Chihuahua. For me, Satan is so big and terrifying; but to God, he is only a little Chihuahua who is trying to hurt His children. When I run to God for help in the trying periods of my life, He picks me up and carries me until everything is safe. He is always walking right there beside me, ready to help whenever trials come. If you want, you can walk beside Him, too. Then you can be sure that regardless of the trials that come your way, He is big enough to carry you through them.

~ Diane Carvalho

Carrot Trials

And not only that, but we also glory in tribulations, knowing that tribulation produces perseverance; and perseverance, character; and character, hope. - Romans 5:3–4 NKJV

There is a diverse assortment of jobs that can be done at Fountainview's farm: driving the forklift, bagging carrots, and putting bags into bundles. The normal routine for bagging carrots is quite simple. We first pick all the finest carrots off the conveyor belt. Next, we weigh the carrots, then tip the scale, causing the carrots to slide into the bag that is waiting to be filled. Taping the bag closed is almost the last step. Then the bag can be dropped into a bin, and the next bag started.

Several times, when I have tipped the scale, sliding the carrots into the bag, the momentum of the carrots has made a hole in the bottom of the bag, revealing its weak points. I then have to put the carrots into a new bag.

These bags are like a person's character. When the bags were new in the box, I couldn't see any problems with them. When life is easy and going well, an individual's character often appears strong. However, it is when trials and tribulations come that one's true character is revealed. The carrots are like hard times. When the carrots fell into the bag, holes were made. The weak points weren't exposed without pressure.

I want God to build my character into something that will glorify Him. Through the trials that come my way because of the sinful choices that I make, my sinful character is revealed. I can ask the Lord for help with my weak points, and He will give me the strength to overcome them. Then when additional trying times come, my weak points will be strengthened.

~ Kami Rose

Weed Wipeout

For a righteous man may fall seven times and rise again, but the wicked shall fall by calamity. - Proverbs 24:16 NKJV

As the younger of two children, I usually end up with the lousier chores: picking up after the dog, scrubbing bear dung off the dog, weeding the garden, burying the cat's latest victim, and the list continues. One of the chores I do like, though, is mowing the lawn. I love the smell of cut grass, mixed with the fresh air that blows down from the treetops. But one thing ruins this joyful experience: dandelions. No matter how many times I pull them up, stomp them down, or mow them over, they always come back—along with three of their friends. I even thought of coloring them with a green sharpie so they would blend in, but that would take too long. I could have eaten them on salads, but grass grew well in that area for a reason—the dog lives there.

In a last ditch effort to evict those yellow speckles of evil, I armed myself with a bottle of vinegar and sprayed them all generously. For other weeds, this works well; but a week later those squatting monstrosities were still growing strong. Nothing I did could rid the yard of them! Finally, I embraced the fact that my yard had yellow polka dots.

In a weird sort of way, I have to admire the determination of the dandelions. I was trying to eradicate them from the vicinity only because I didn't like them. Day after day, they were still there, spreading their cheery yellow color. These little flowers made me think of our Christian experience. Constantly we are being hammered, slashed, squished, and pulled apart by temptations and the evils of this world. Every trial that comes our way is aimed at destroying us, but with the deep roots of study and prayer, we can withstand the devil's attacks. But we need to have deeper roots than our own. We need to be joined to Jesus, the "Tap Root" of life. It is only through Him, as a community, that we can flourish and grow. Together, we can spread the seeds of the gospel to all the world.

~ Morgan Metcalf

Yucky, Dirty Insides

My soul shall make its boast in the Lord; the humble shall hear of it and be glad. - Psalm 34:2 NKJV

I love being praised. Without praise, a deep muddled mess of feelings forms in the pit of my stomach, sloshing around and building up to my heart. When praise and admiration pass me by, the feelings come.

On what my pride calls "a good day," when the praise flows, I feel "better," but inwardly my pride looks oh so ugly. Pride fills the space where the muddled mess once was, and it looks even more horrible.

The feeling is what counts to me. I am addicted to the ecstasy of pride. It is a drug outlawed by God, for He is the one who sees what is hidden in my heart. "Why does the truth not speak to my heart?" I start to wonder. God knows. He sees the yucky, dirty insides of His daughter.

The Great Controversy tells us, "When Christ came to speak the words of life, the common people heard Him gladly; and many, even of the priests and rulers, believed on Him. But the chief of the priesthood and the leading men of the nation were determined to condemn and repudiate His teachings" (pg. 595). The pride of the chief priests who were determined to condemn our Savior is the same pride that entangles me.

How does pride begin? It begins the same way meekness begins. You see, both meekness and pride come by "seeking." As Jesus talked, they sought the truth He was teaching, and God was allowed to work in their lives.

I have been seeking after myself, but God will honor my longing and seeking after Him. Then He can work and heal me by His power.

~ Ashley Wilkens

A Nightmare

… If ye have faith as a grain of mustard seed, ye shall say unto this mountain, remove hence to yonder place; and it shall remove; and nothing shall be impossible unto you. - Matthew 17:20 KJV

I woke up and just wanted to cry. I felt so terrible. And this was not for the first time, nor the second; it had happened every single night that week. This had to stop. A terrifying image kept coming up in my mind. I was scared and kept asking myself why this was happening to me. Was it something that I was doing wrong that made it happen? I was only six or seven years old, and I had this same nightmare over and over again, night after night.

Only one person could help me, and that was God. None of us decide what kind of dreams we dream, but God can prevent us from dreaming something if we ask Him to. So in our family morning worship I asked my family to pray for me, and, although it may sound ridiculous to pray for something like that, God answered our prayer and I never had that nightmare again!

This is something that, through the years, I haven't forgotten because it showed me how much God cares about and loves me. Life throws many nightmares at us, but God is always there to help us through them, no matter how big or small they are.

It does not really matter how small the things we ask God for are; He always listens to us. Jesus promises us that if we have faith as a mustard seed, nothing shall be impossible for us.

~ Diane Carvalho

A Tuna Fish Character

Therefore if any man be in Christ, he is a new creature: old things are
passed away; behold, all things are become new.
- 2 Corinthians 5:17 KJV

I'm somewhat of a perfectionist. If I'm going to do something, I
want it to be done right. Lately, I have been agonizing over the fact
that I don't feel as though I've grown at all spiritually. Every time I try
to help myself become a better person, I fail and reinforce in my mind
how horrible I really am. Just last week, as I was chopping lettuce in
the cafeteria, the reason finally hit me: I can't remember a single time
when I have asked God for help! I have been trying to mold myself into
what I know He wants me to be instead of simply asking Him to perfect
me.

I remember wanting to do things by myself as a child. One day,
my mom consented to let me make my own meal. I innocently tried
to make ice cream out of tuna fish, milk, applesauce, and barbecue
sauce. As you can imagine, it turned out disgusting! Fascinatingly
enough though, after it froze, it turned out looking pretty good, with
nice red swirls. However, frozen tuna fish is still tuna fish. This reminds
me of what I am trying to do in my relationship with God. I can make
myself beautiful and seemingly good on the outside, but on the inside
I have a repulsive, dirty heart that only Jesus can clean. If I had only
given my whole heart to Christ in the beginning, it would be beautiful
already.

So many times we rely on our own strength to get things done,
when if we would only give our problems to God, He would save us
so much confusion and heartache. I tried so hard to be the person I
knew God wanted me to be, but in the end, I failed, because only God
knows the recipe required to change my heart.

~ Moriah Mays

Dragging Feet

*If they had been thinking of the country they had left, they would have
had opportunity to return. - Hebrews 11:15 NIV*

"We're moving!" my parents told us. "We are going to Canada. It's a
beautiful country and you will really like our new neighbors." However,
I determinedly fussed about moving. I dug in my heels and dragged
my feet. In my five-year-old mind, I didn't think I would enjoy a place if
it didn't have lizards and tree frogs like we had in California. And what
about leaving our friends?

Dad and Mom knew God was calling us to move, and so, despite
my fears, I had to go along. As we drove, my parents talked about
the beauty, but I didn't think it was beautiful at all. All there was to
see was sagebrush and ugly mountains. When we finally rolled in to
our new home, I was exhausted from traveling and didn't even think
of complaining; I was happy to have a house to live in and a place to
sleep.

I didn't know what was best for me. I didn't think it would be
enjoyable to move, and therefore, I had decided not to like it. My
parents, on the other hand, had a better view of what was ahead.
They knew that Dad would have more time for us, and the peaceful
environment would be just what we needed. I am so glad God showed
my parents this place. We have lived in Canada for over eleven years,
and I love it here. I now see the beauty in the sagebrush, the high,
rocky mountains, and the roaring, splashing river that flows below our
home. And yes—we have an abundance of wonderful friends here.

Jesus is coming to take us to our new home very soon! He has
prepared a place for you that is exceedingly better than anything you
can imagine. He's invited you and all your friends to come home with
Him. Are you excited or are you dragging your feet?

~ Bethany Corrigan

Plywood Instruments

I am the vine, ye are the branches: He that abideth in me, and I in him, the same bringeth forth much fruit: for without me ye can do nothing.
- John 15:5 KJV

As the final chord of our last song hung in the air, we were confronted by a tremendous wall of wild applause. We had just finished a concert in a large concert hall on the island of Kauai, and it had gone startlingly well. Since Fountainview was in Hawaii on a filmmaking trip, we had not risked our valuable instruments by bringing them to Hawaii's hot and humid climate. Instead, we purchased scores of cheap, trashy instruments that we used to film our production. However, our trip to Hawaii also included two live concerts that we would have to play using these "fake" instruments. But despite the exceptionally adverse circumstances confronting our final concert, it is generally believed to have been one of our finest ever.

There can be but one explanation for the unexpected and undeserved success of our last concert on Kauai: God worked through our wretched instruments, sending angels to sing and play with us, and using the resulting music as a channel for His Holy Spirit. If not for His extreme help, that concert would undoubtedly have been one of the worst concerts in Fountainview history. But because God substituted His perfection for our imperfection, it was one of our best.

When it comes to being a Christian, humans are all a bunch of filming instruments. On our own, we are merely out-of-tune, squeaky, failing shadows of something that should produce beautiful music. However, God can work through us just as He worked through the terrible instruments during that concert in Kauai. When we allow Him to come into our heart, selfless actions of inexplicable beauty will flow from our lives, replacing the piercing squeaks that powerless filming instruments like us should be producing. Won't you open your heart to God, and let Him shine through your imperfection?

~ Michael Jensen

God's Windex

For now we see through a glass, darkly; but then face to face: now I know in part; but then shall I know even as I am known.
- 1 Corinthians 13:12 KJV

Mike and Cathy had been recently married and were eating their first breakfast in their new home. As Cathy reached across the table for some more syrup to put on her waffles, she noticed her new neighbor, Martha, stringing her laundry out to dry. "Mike," Cathy said, interrupting his concentration on the morning newspaper, "the laundry Martha is putting out is filthy. I bet her soap isn't working." Mike looked out the window but didn't say anything. Every morning, the same thing happened: Cathy would comment on how dirty Martha's laundry was while Mike continued to read his paper in silence.

About a month later, Cathy happened to glance out the window while she was washing the dishes, and, to her surprise, saw that Martha's laundry was sparkling clean. "Look, Mike! Someone must have taught Martha how to wash her clothes properly. I wonder who helped her?"

Lifting his head momentarily, Mike sweetly replied, "No one taught her, Dear; I just got up early this morning and washed our windows."

Often I find that the windows through which I see God are dirty. Let me explain. Once, I really wanted my friend to come to my school with me. When things didn't work out, I became frustrated at God. "Why aren't You doing things my way?" I fussed. Later, I saw that she would grow much better where God put her than she would have where I had wanted her. How can I clean the dirty window through which I see God? Thankfully, you and I are given Windex: the Bible. Every day we can go to Christ and ask for our windows to be cleaned. Once He's cleaned them, you'll be able see how pure His so-called "dirty laundry" really is.

~ Sarah Miller

Thirsty?

*Jesus answered and said to her, "Whoever drinks of this water will
thirst again, but whoever drinks of the water that I shall give him will
never thirst. But the water that I shall give him will become in him a
fountain of water springing up into everlasting life."*
- John 4:13–14 NKJV

I own a red stainless steel water bottle, and it is very handy when
I get thirsty. During English class a couple of days ago, when I went
to get a drink of water, I found that my water bottle was empty. *Oh,
I don't have time right now. I'll have to fill it up later,* I decided. In
math class, a few hours later, I got thirsty again. *But we just finished
P.E. class, and I'm too tired to go fill up my water bottle right now,* I
reasoned. Throughout that whole day, I became increasingly thirsty.
Nevertheless, I kept coming up with trivial excuses why I couldn't go
fill up my water bottle. There was no logical reason why I couldn't, yet I
didn't. I was only hurting myself and dehydrating my body.

Did you know that we are given a similar choice every day? We
are given the choice to "fill up our water bottles" with living water:
Jesus. He is the only one who can satisfy the longings of our thirsty
hearts. We can choose to "fill up" our spiritual water bottles from the
fountain of Christ, or we can choose to remain thirsty all day. "He in
whom Christ dwells has within himself the fountain of blessing – 'a well
of water springing up into everlasting life.' From this source he may
draw strength and grace sufficient for all his needs" (*Desire of Ages*,
pg. 187). Jesus is longing to fill us so we may never thirst again. He
is longing to be our source of strength for all our daily needs. Are you
thirsty enough to take the time to drink from the fountain that will lead
you to eternal life?

~ Kami Rose

Freedom of Choice

And if it seems evil to you to serve the Lord, choose for yourselves this day whom you will serve... But as for me and my house, we will serve the Lord. - Joshua 24:15 NKJV

I was about to move on to junior high when all my friends started to care about fashion and how they looked more than anything else. I had grown up in an Adventist home and learned about Christian modesty. I had also learned that beauty on the outside is not everything. But when I saw my friends wearing makeup, I really wanted to start wearing it too. My mom never forbade me to wear it, but I knew she would disapprove of me wearing makeup, since she was the one who had taught me how God's children should act.

One day, my mom asked me to go shopping with her. She took me to the beauty shop, where they sell makeup. I was a little confused at first, but I was soon having fun looking around. In fact, I found myself enjoying it. I saw my mom picking up mascara, powder, base cream, blush, eye liner, lipstick—all the makeup that I would need to do my whole face. Even more surprising, she bought everything. She added the earrings, necklace, and rings that I always wanted to wear too. I wasn't sure what she was going to do with it all. That day ended with lots of questions about the mysterious things that happened. The next morning, I got a present from my mom. I knew what it was, but I wasn't sure if I should take it or not. While I was thinking, I found a little note in the bag. The note said, "There is a huge difference between you not doing something because you don't have it, and you not doing it because you choose not to do it. I hope you make the right decision for yourself. Love you, Mom." My mom actually knew everything I was struggling with, and she allowed me to exercise the freedom to choose.

Jesus also gives us the freedom of choice. He loves us enough to give us rules, but allows us to choose whether we will follow Him or not. Will you choose Jesus today?

~ Hannah Lee

214

Your SIM Card for Today

A good man out of the good treasure of the heart bringeth forth good things: and an evil man out of the evil treasure bringeth forth evil things. - Matthew 12:35 KJV

Last summer, I acquired a new cell phone. It was supposed to be my mom's, but she didn't like the style, so she decided to keep her old one, and I got the new one. I really enjoyed using it, but unfortunately it didn't last long. My mom accidently took her cell phone into the shower and ruined it. I didn't mind sharing my cell phone with her, but both of us wanted to keep our own phone number. After a lot of research, we found out how to have two numbers on one cell phone. It was the SIM card! (Every cell phone has a SIM card that stores all the information.) My mom took her SIM card out of her old cell phone and put it in my cell phone. Guess what? It displayed her screen and features. She could find all her contacts, pictures, memos, and messages; she could even use her own phone number. Whenever I put my SIM card in, it would change all the settings back to mine. After discovering this, we made a schedule and decided when each of us would use the cell phone.

Just like those little SIM cards changed the settings of that cell phone, the first thing that we do at the beginning of each day can change our whole outlook. When we start the day talking with God and reading His Word, our whole mindset will be focused on Him. It's like putting God's SIM card into our life. However, if we begin without spending time with God in prayer and in His Word, Satan will try to put his SIM card into us so that we will be receiving his messages, and thus, He will keep us away from displaying God's "features."

Whatever I put into my mind will produce fruit, reflecting what I have put in. A tomato seed will not produce a potato. Satan's seed will produce evil things, but the seed of God's Word will produce a Christ-like character. We have a choice between God's SIM-card and Satan's SIM-card. What is your decision for today?

~ Hannah Lee

Fireflies

For since the creation of the world His invisible attributes are clearly seen, being understood by the things that are made, even His eternal power and Godhead, so that they are without excuse...
- Romans 1:20 NKJV

One evening, just as the sun was sneaking over the tops of the trees, my dad and I took a walk in our backyard. As we started out along the fence line, I just barely caught a glimpse of an incredible sight: the sky seemed as though someone had painted it a beautiful shade of pink with a slight hint of orange. My attention then turned to the field behind our house; there were hundreds of tiny, white lights blinking on and off. It was absolutely breathtaking! The forest beyond the field seemed to be lit up by the continuous sparkling. I was blown away by the incredible sight.

As I think about that magical moment, it gives me a clearer picture of what our Creator is truly like. Those tiny bugs were not powered by any man-made device. God Himself was the one turning them on and off; He made them to be such magical, beautiful creatures.

Imagine with me the Creator going to work at designing our world. Each tree, each flower, every person He thought out and then knit together. When we see little creatures or pretty scenery, we need to remember the care that was put into the creation of that very scene. There is so much love put into each blade of grass and every body of water, but sometimes we are just too busy to notice. God wanted to show us His love in a way that no one else could, and that is why His love can be clearly seen all throughout nature—even in every firefly.

~ Elizabeth King

Quality Harvest

I am the vine; you are the branches. If a man remains in me and I in him, he will bear much fruit; apart from me you can do nothing.
- John 15:5 NIV

When we lived in New Zealand, we owned a 40-acre vineyard. Our vineyard had many different varieties of vines which produced delicious grapes. During the growing season, the vines would produce lots of branches which would be covered in large leaves and bountiful bunches of juicy red grapes. I would ride my quad through the grapes and see how they were progressing. As I was going through the vineyard one day, I noticed that there was a small clump of vines that were especially big. They had lots more leaves than all the others, and there were so many branches that you could hardly get between the rows. I thought to myself, *These vines will grow some pretty impressive grapes.* So, as the weeks went by, I kept my eye on this clump of bushy vines to see what they would produce.

When it came time to harvest the grapes, I went off to my little clump of vines ready to feast on the amazing, big juicy grapes I was sure I would find. To my amazement and disgust, the grapes were only little tiny grapes that tasted disgusting. It was a bitter disappointment. I couldn't understand why these grapes hadn't produced the fruit I had expected, so I asked my dad why this was. He told me that those vines were root stock and that in order to produce good fruit they needed to have a better vine grafted onto them. They weren't able to produce the good fruit by themselves.

This experience made me think how at times I am like the grape root stock. I may be growing and putting out lots of leaves, looking like I am a vibrant Christian. However, when it comes to the harvest, am I producing anything of real value or am I just all show? In order for my efforts to be as productive as possible, I need to be attached to Christ—the good vine. Without Him my efforts are in vain.

~ Kyle Smith

Still Watching You

He hath said, I will never leave thee, nor forsake thee.
- Hebrews 13:5 KJV

When I was ten, my dad took me to the pool every morning to teach me how to swim. Each day, I got better and better, and in three months I had mastered the basics.

Then one day when Dad and I went swimming as usual, Dad asked me to do something new: to swim in the bigger pool, that was two meters deep, instead of the kiddie pool. I was too scared to go into the deep, dark pool by myself. But Dad told me not to worry because if something happened, he would be right there. I trusted him and started playing in the bigger pool. At first it was hard, but with lots of Daddy's help I was able to swim freely.

The next day, I was playing in the deep pool again. After making sure my dad was watching me, I went to the deepest part. I had fun doing back flips, handstands, spins, and pretending I was a water dancer. When I started to get tired, I looked around for my dad. He wasn't there! I started freaking out. I was getting too tired and started to sink. Just then I felt someone grab and push me back to the surface. It was my dad! He asked why I was afraid to swim—he had been under the water watching me the whole time. Because I couldn't see him, I forgot he promised he would always be right there.

Similarly, God sometimes puts me into a bigger pool by asking me to do things outside of my comfort zone. It can be really scary because I can't always see God or what He is doing, but just as my dad never stopped watching me, I know that God will never leave me nor forsake me.

~ Hannah Lee

What Can You Do with Thirty Dollars?

*Learn to do good. Seek justice. Help the oppressed. Defend the cause
of orphans. Fight for the rights of widows. - Isaiah 1:17 NLT*

I have two brothers. One is my biological brother and the other is a
boy that my family sponsors. My 'adopted' brother lives in Bangladesh.
Even though I have never seen him face to face or even talked to him,
he is still a part of my family.

My mom and I saw a program on television about UNICEF, an
organization that helps orphans and the impoverished. We saw that
many children are dying every day due to a lack of food and water.
After watching this program, my family decided to adopt one of these
children. That's when Rafiqul became my younger brother.

Because his father can't work to support his family due to illness,
Rafiqul is supposed to earn the money for his family's living. But if my
family supported him, he could go to school instead of working all day.
So we started supporting him financially and sending thirty dollars
every month. For us, thirty dollars will buy one t-shirt or a large pizza,
but for Rafiqul's family, thirty dollars can keep them alive. It always
made our day when he sent us letters with pictures. One day, he
sent us a Christmas card. Inside, he had written, "Hope God always
blessing your family." At that time, we could see God's glory working to
influence him and our family. Truly, the Lord was blessing me through
him.

As Christians, the Bible tells us it is our duty to help others. When
we take the focus off ourselves and become more concerned about
people, we can help others—all the other little Rafiquls. There are
143 million children suffering from malnutrition. With a tender heart,
you can help them with a prayer! You can pray specifically for those
organizations whose mission it is to help the orphans. Trust God to
impress upon your heart what you might do or give.

~ Ellen Yoon

No Swimming!

Judge not, that ye be not judged. - Matthew 7:1 KJV

My extended family lives in the eastern United States, which means that we don't get to see them very often. One summer, we went to visit my dad's parents in Massachusetts. His three sisters and their families joined us there as well. On the Fourth of July, we decided that we would spend some quiet family time at a lake near my grandparents' house. When we got to the lake, there were lots of other people there swimming; but finally we found a quiet, private place to play. After a delicious picnic lunch and a relaxing afternoon of swimming, kayaking, and canoeing, we were just packing up to leave when a park ranger pulled up. "You are not allowed to swim here." he told us. "This is the boat launch, so you need to move over to the beach."

We replied, "We're actually leaving, but we're very sorry. We didn't know we weren't allowed to play here." The ranger looked at us with a funny expression and then left. We quickly finished packing up and got in our cars. As we pulled out of the parking lot, we were shocked to see what was written on the large sign we had been sitting behind all afternoon. It clearly stated: "No swimming at boat launch. Swim only at designated beach area." We had never even gone around to read it!

Sometimes, we see others doing things that we think are wrong. It may seem obvious to us, but they may not have considered it could be wrong—just like it was clear to the ranger that we were disobeying the sign, but we had never even seen it! One reason this happens is because God does not reveal everything to us at once, and He may have seen fit to show us something that He has not shown someone else. Because of this, we can never judge others; but should remember that God is working with us all, and He will show them the truth in His time.

~ Aileen Corrigan

Trapped!

Like as a father pitieth his children, so the Lord pitieth them that fear Him. - Psalm 103:13 KJV

One morning, my brother and sister and I decided to play house on our back porch with an old refrigerator. After a while we got tired of our game and started looking for something else to do. Someone had the great idea of seeing if we could all fit inside the refrigerator. So we pushed and squeezed until we could pull the door shut. We were delighted until we realized that we couldn't get the door open from the inside. We started banging on it, hoping that Mom would come to the rescue, but she couldn't hear us. My sister and I started screaming and crying, but my brother firmly told us, "Don't talk or make noise, it will only make things worse." I wasn't old enough to understand why crying would make any difference, but I did as I was told. After what seemed like hours, Mom popped open the door and freed us. She had been cleaning the house, and suddenly noticed that there wasn't any chatter coming from the back porch. After several minutes of searching the yard and calling for us, God impressed her to look in the refrigerator. As she opened the door, to her surprise, we tumbled out.

We were too young to know that we could have suffocated inside that refrigerator, but God had His hand over it all. He gave my brother the knowledge that the more we talked, the more air we used. God also helped my mom to notice the absence of noise and to look for us right away, and then He prompted her to check in the refrigerator.

Sometimes we as humans aren't smart enough to know that something will hurt us. But God, in His great pity, puts His hand over us and saves us. Praise the Lord today for His protection and care!

~ Bethany Corrigan

The Dull-Witted Cow

Behold, I stand at the door and knock. If anyone hears my voice and opens the door, I will come in to him and eat with him, and he with me.
- Revelation 3:20 ESV

"Stand still and don't move. You're not helping the situation!" I yelled at the cow. I was trying to get a cow to accept her newly born calf so that it could drink from her. For some unknown reason the cow had disowned her calf and didn't want to have anything to do with it. Unfortunately, when this happens, it takes a lot of time and effort to convince the cow to allow the calf to suck from her. When the cow doesn't want to know the calf, it really doesn't want to know the calf. She was kicking, jumping and running all round the pen trying to get away from her baby. The poor little calf was getting hurt, and wasn't able to latch onto its mother to drink. As a result of the cow not allowing the calf to drink, her udder had filled up with so much milk that she was in a lot of pain. Because of the cow's stupidity, every morning and every evening, I had to go and force the cow to stand still so her calf could drink from her. Some days it seemed like I would make a little progress, but then the next day I would be back at square one again.

This frustrating situation caused me to think about how I am like that stubborn cow, and how God is like her persistent calf trying to get closer. Just like the cow, I am often kicking, jumping, and running all around and not letting God come into my life. If I would only stop and realize that if I allowed God to come near me, He could help relieve the pain and anguish I am causing myself. Just as I had to stand there trying to convince the cow to take her calf, God is knocking on the door of my heart, longing to come in and change my life.

I am grateful for a God who perseveres with me. When I allow Him to come into my heart, my life is so much better. He has come very near and helped me learn to trust Him in all things. So if you find yourself kicking and running away from God, stop and think about how much better off you would be if you allowed Him to come closer.

~ Kyle Smith

The Selfless Sacrifice

Greater love hath no man than this, that a man lay down his life for his friends. - John 15:13 KJV

Everybody who has studied anything about World War II knows that Adolf Hitler was an evil man. At first, his government seemed like a good idea to the German people, but once they saw him for what he really was, many turned against it. One of these people was a Christian man who had joined a group that was trying to assassinate Hitler. This fact made me wonder. Since he was a Christian, how could he break the Ten Commandments by killing deliberately? When he was asked how he could purposely kill and still consider himself to be in line with the Law of God, he said that if he were to kill Hitler, he was not sure that he would go to heaven. But it was his mission to kill Hitler anyway. He reasoned that he had to stop Hitler from killing more innocent people—people who might not have had the chance yet to learn of Christ. If in the process of killing Hitler he lost his salvation, he felt it would be worth it to have thousands of others saved instead.

I believe that what this man did was wrong. On the other hand, he believed what he was doing was right and was willing to go so far as to give up his own salvation for other people he had never even met. To him, it was more important to save others than himself. That is extreme selflessness. Philippians 2:3–4 says, "Do nothing out of selfish ambition or vain conceit. Rather, in humility value others above yourselves, not looking to your own interests but each of you to the interests of the others" (NIV). Today, most people consider first, "How will this benefit me?" But instead, we should want to give of ourselves to help and bless others, no matter what the cost. Sometimes we really won't want to be unselfish; our inner mind screams at us to just do what we want, but the Holy Spirit working in our life gives us the power to put others first. Jesus manifested this perfect connection with God throughout all His life and death. In His final hours, Jesus said, "Not my will but Thine be done." He gave everything, but yet He was so peaceful. That is because He gave knowing of the rewards—our lives. He died for us. What are you willing to give for others?

~ Morgan Metcalf

Piercing Words

Even so the tongue is a little member, and boasteth great things.
Behold, how great a matter a little fire kindleth! - James 3:5 KJV

"Oh, no!" My dad exclaimed as he looked outside one Saturday afternoon. "A woodpecker is on the grapevine again!" Shooing us kids outside, he instructed us to grab a bow and arrow, and shoot at the bird in hopes of scaring it away. He thought, of course, that we had no aim and the arrow would miss, alarming the bird enough to scare it away. Well, he was wrong. Taking position a distance from the vine so as not to scare the bird, my brother took aim and shot. Unfortunately, the arrow went in between the bird's feet, and he didn't notice. However, the next shot struck true, and with an arrow in its side, the bird took flight right over the heads of a pair of alarmed guests who were visiting that Saturday afternoon. The impression we made was not a good one. The bloodied arrow fell out as the bird was flying, and the unfortunate bird wasn't seen again.

Now, picture arrows flying through the air, not made of carbon fiber but of words. These arrows pierce the inmost heart of the person the words are aimed at. I must admit that there have been many times when I have used my words to wound rather than to heal. The Bible warns that the tongue is a deadly evil that no one can contain. It can make a person's life a living hell, or it can be the help that gets them through the day. Every day we use this powerful weapon, but we can choose how we use it. That's why it is important for us to think before we speak: because we are in danger of losing control of our tongues. Have you thought recently about what you've said and how it could have affected the person you spoke to? Did it encourage them and lead them closer to God, or has it discouraged and darkened their life? Let's think carefully before we say anything. It may make an eternal difference.

~ Chris Donatelli

Who Will Open the Door?

*Submit yourselves therefore to God. Resist the devil, and he will flee
from you. Draw nigh to God, and he will draw nigh to you.*
- James 4:7–8a KJV

Once there was a little girl who was questioned about how she
triumphs over Satan. "Well," replied the little girl, "when Satan comes
and knocks on the door of my heart, I let God answer the door. When
Satan sees God, he says, 'Oops, I must have the wrong place,' and he
goes away."

I love this story because it illustrates how we can have victory over
Satan. To have that victory, we must have a personal connection with
Jesus, because only through a relationship with Christ are we able to
receive the power we need to resist the Devil. It is necessary for us to
daily submit ourselves to Christ, so He can answer our heart's door for
us.

Ellen White wrote: "The tempter can never compel us to do evil.
He cannot control minds unless they are yielded to his control. The
will must consent, faith must let go its hold upon Christ, before Satan
can exercise his power upon us. … Every point in which we fail of
meeting the divine standard is an open door by which he can enter
to tempt and destroy us" (*Desire of Ages*, pg. 125). We must totally
submit ourselves to God if we are to be out of Satan's grasp. If we do
not do this, our door is left open, and Satan is able to come in without
knocking.

For the little girl to defeat Satan, she had to have God in her heart.
Jesus says, "Behold I stand at the door and knock. If anyone hears
My voice and opens the door, I will come in to him and dine with him,
and he with Me" (Revelation 3:20 NKJV). The little girl had opened her
door and let Jesus in. When we let Jesus into our hearts, we become
His. It makes me so happy to know that I belong to such a loving
heavenly Father who gives me the power to gain the victory over
Satan. "But thanks be to God, who gives us the victory through our
Lord Jesus Christ" (1 Corinthians 15:57 NKJV).

~ Kami Rose

Buddy

… I have put my trust in the Lord God… - Psalms 73:28 KJV

"Come get in the car!" Mom called with a twinkle in her eyes. My three siblings and I raced to the van and jumped in.

"Where are we going?" I asked.

"You'll have to wait and see!" she answered. We drove to Dad's office and picked him up. *What's going on?* I thought as we drove into a neighbor's driveway. It didn't take long to find out. Soon we were following the neighbor out to his shed to see his kittens. I was elated! I had always wanted a kitten, but I knew that Dad didn't like them, so I didn't think I would ever get one. After watching the kittens, I chose a little gray and white one with blue eyes for my own.

There was one small problem: "Buddy" wasn't really used to people handling him, and so he was quite a challenge to manage. He scratched and bit me, doing everything he could to get away from me. Sometimes when I tried to hold him, he would take off and hide, and I had to call and beg and wait until he decided to come back. I persevered, however, holding him, petting him, and doing everything I could to get him to love and trust me. Eventually, he learned to reach out his paws for me to hold him, and when I picked him up, he "hugged" me around my neck. Although he learned to love me, he was still a wild cat, and sometimes when he hugged me, he would suddenly bite my ear or scratch my neck.

As humans, we have hearts that are wild and untamed. When we first learn of God, we are wary of trusting Him. Sometimes we run and hide and He has to woo us back to His arms. When we don't like our training, we scratch and bite with our words and actions. Eventually, because He doesn't give up, we can learn to trust His love; and unlike Buddy, our characters can be completely transformed into the likeness of Christ.

~ Aileen Corrigan

Claustrophobia

I press toward the mark for the prize of the high calling of God in Christ Jesus. - Philippians 3:14 KJV

I can't believe I'm doing this! I thought to myself as I pulled my body through a jagged, narrow cave. Here I was, 15 feet from the sight of daylight, crawling like a caterpillar through a cave. The light from my headlamp seemed as bright as the sun as it beamed out the features of the dark rock walls. The rocks jabbed painfully into my stomach as I inched my way through the cave, and my throat constricted with worry as the hole ahead of me started to shrink. I began to visualize the huge boulders around me shifting and trapping me beneath them. Suddenly, I heard the voices of the people up ahead of me. They had made it through to the very end of the tunnel. *I can do this!* I thought to myself. *With God by my side, what is stopping me?* Ignoring my discomfort, I determinedly pushed my body forward through the tunnel. When I reached the larger room at the end, I felt victorious. I had done it! I thought that I wouldn't be able to make it this far, yet I had not given in to my fears and had pushed myself forward. By placing my mind on a goal, I had done what I thought I could never have accomplished without having a heart attack.

God will sometimes call each one of us to do things that are out of our comfort zone. He has a special purpose for each one of us, and that purpose may be far from what we expect. We will sometimes feel like what we are called to do is like crawling through a tunnel that is getting smaller and smaller. Panic will build up in our throats as we look ahead. We will feel that to press forward is absolutely crazy. But we must remember that God will not place us in a situation that we can't handle if we rely upon His strength.

~ Sierra Buhler

Look Up

I will lift up mine eyes unto the hills, from whence cometh my help.
- Psalm 121:1 KJV

I walked slowly in the park, looking at the ground. I felt very bored and alone. I could not find my best friend; she had gone with some of the other kids. So I looked at the sidewalk; it was worn and dirty, covered with leaves and bird messes. It was a disgusting sight, and it didn't lift my spirits. This went on for a while, and my view didn't get any better.

Then I looked up, and suddenly it was a gorgeous day. The sun was shining down, warming my skin. There was a pond with a fountain and lots of birds. My friends were over in the field playing a game, and I could hear their laughter. Right then my outlook did a complete about-face—everything at that moment was right with the world.

When I was looking down, all I could see was the dirt, pavement, and filth. I did not see the light from the sun or the lovely birds. I could not see the happiness of my friends or hear the music of their voices. All that was visible to me was gloom and despair, there was no reason to look up, and I did not know there was something different and more pleasant to see. When I did look up, though, everything was so much better. Even though the sidewalk and filth was still there, and I had to step carefully to not get my shoes dirty, I felt cheerful and happy.

I look down a lot, and see only the trials in my life; and so I complain of the difficulties. I cannot, or am not, willing to see the sunshine and hope that comes from Jesus and His salvation. If I but look up, my life could be filled with joy, despite the troubles that still surround me. I can rejoice in the hope of a risen Saviour and look forward to His soon coming, and so can you. So look up, friend, and be glad!

~ Sarah Wahlman

The Link

Immediately Jesus reached out his hand and caught him. "You of little faith," he said, "why did you doubt?" - Matthew 14:31 NIV

I was standing on the tarmac of a little jungle airport. The air was hot and steamy and seemed to begin suffocating me as soon as I left the chilly airplane. I could tell that I was in for a once-in-a-lifetime adventure. My family felt that God had called us there, to a bustling, dirty town in the jungles of Peru. I was excited. But before long, reality sunk in, and I found myself miserable. Endless heat, scary food, and frustrating cultural differences took their toll on my "happiness" (or so I thought). My attitude took a turn for the worst, and I started to get bothered by almost anything. My brother and sister seemed to be my enemies more often than they were my friends. Things weren't going so well, but I blamed it all on my circumstances.

That experience as a missionary proved to me that my faith was largely circumstantial. I could appear loving and friendly, and even Godly, back at home where there was air conditioning, healthy food, and people who spoke my language. But when things got tough, what was left? My true character. Ironically, I was supposed to be a missionary; I was supposed to set an example of a Christlike life. I was supposed to show those around me a bit of God's love. But I didn't. I failed the mission.

Since my time in Peru, I have begun to learn that circumstances should have absolutely no bearing on true faith in God. While difficult situations or trying times may test that faith, God will never let us go. We only fail because our link to our Heavenly Father is weak. As Christians, we are all called to be missionaries. Whether in Africa, Asia, or America, God has trusted each of us to spread the message of His love. To successfully complete that mission, we need a strong link between us and our Heavenly Father. If we are lacking in this respect, we will fail.

How strong is your link?

~ Michael Jensen

He Longs for That Day

… Grace be unto you, and peace, from God… - Colossians 1:2 KJV

I was elated to find out that a close friend, whom I consider my brother, and his wife were going to have a baby. I had always wanted to have a niece or nephew, and now I would finally have one. Months before the baby was born, my sisters and I began dreaming about what things would be like when it came. Finally one night, we got the long-awaited phone call—the baby was here! It was a girl, and I loved her from day one. She was, naturally, the very cutest and most special baby ever! We made cards, got gifts for her, and eagerly awaited the scattered times when we would be able to see her.

My "niece" is now fourteen months old, and my love for her is even stronger than when she first came. I enjoy watching her grow, toddling around making funny little talking noises. Her delight in the smallest things is a continual source of pleasure to me.

This is the way it was for God when He created the world. I picture Him spending weeks planning a beautiful and perfect home for the people He was going to create. Finally, the blueprints were finished. Then came the exciting part: the actual creation. Jesus created tall, green trees, delicately tinted flowers, agile birds, screaming monkeys, and rushing rivers. Now, He came to the best part of all: stooping down, He carefully formed Adam from the dust of the ground, breathing into his nostrils the breath of life. Then Jesus waited with intense excitement. What would Adam think of His wonderful gift? "…He watches with a Father's joy the delight of His children in the beautiful things around them" (*The Youth's Instructor*, March 24, 1898).

Just like my love for my niece, God loved us even before He created us. He delights to watch us enjoy the simple things in life, and He longs for the day when we will be able to live with Him eternally.

~ Aileen Corrigan

Where is Your Focus?

My eyes are always on the Lord, for He rescues me from the traps of my enemies. - Psalm 25:15 NLT

Most everyone appreciates words of affirmation, including myself. I feel good inside when people tell me I have done an excellent job on an assignment or that I'm very good at something. Several times, when I am practicing my cello, somebody will walk by and say, "You're doing a fantastic job," or "You are a skilled cellist." I know that these people are being encouraging, and we all need encouragement; but far too often these comments cause me to concentrate on myself. I lose focus because I'm thinking about how accomplished I am. It's when I focus on their words of praise instead of my practice that I start to make mistakes.

One night, Jesus walked on the sea to His disciples' boat. When they saw Him coming, they were terrified. They were certain that they were seeing a ghost. At that moment, Jesus soothed their fears by saying, "Be of good cheer! It is I. Don't be afraid."
"If it's really you, let me walk out to you on the water," called Peter.
"Come," responded Jesus.

Peter got out of the boat and started to walk towards Jesus. As Peter walked on the water, he glanced back towards the boat hoping that the other disciples were watching him. Immediately, he began to sink.

"Help me, Lord!" he cried out. At once, Jesus reached out His hand and pulled Peter out of the water.

When my focus shifted from practice to praise and I lost my concentration, I couldn't play the piece anymore. I had to start over. The same was true with Peter. "When he turned his eyes from Jesus, his footing was lost, and he sank amid the waves" (*Desire of Ages*, pg. 358). We often focus on the praise of men instead of focusing on God. However, it is so critical that we keep our concentration on Him. Our eternal lives depend on it.

~ Kami Rose

It Only Takes a Spark

… to You, O Lord, I lift up my soul. For You, Lord, are good, and ready to forgive, and abundant in mercy to all those who call upon You.
- Psalm 86:4–5 NKJV

My dad once told me a story about a summer camp director who was new at his job at Camp Conejo in California. He wanted to add something fun to the activities at the camp, so he decided to start a model rocketry program. There was only one small problem: he forgot to check with the authorities about the legal aspects and fire hazards of firing off model rockets into the sky. Launch day came, and the campers fired off their rockets one by one. Suddenly, a rocket's parachute burst into flames. It was a very hot day, and the grass field was extremely dry, so all it took was one spark, and the field was ablaze. The fire that burned for the next hour or two caused thousands of dollars of damage, and it also landed the summer camp director in jail. Sitting alone in that jail cell, he was very stressed about the consequences of his mistake, and particularly worried about what his father would think. He expected that he would be furious when he came to bail him out of jail. Then he heard footsteps echoing down the long hallway… his father's footsteps. But wait—his father was whistling. What was that tune? Suddenly he recognized it, and tears stung his eyes. The tune was *It Only Takes a Spark.* He knew his father had forgiven him (and that he also had a sense of humor).

I have repeatedly called to God to come and bail me out of my life of sin. Satan thrusts my many sins into my remembrance wanting to bend me, crush me, and forever lock me in his prison of sin. But wait! God's footsteps are quick and light, eager for a reunion. Suddenly He is there, and I can say with the psalmist, "To You, O Lord, I lift up my soul. For You, Lord are good and ready to forgive…"

~ Derek Glatts

Mud Puddles!

You shall be My people, and I will be your God.
- Jeremiah 30:22 NKJV

"HELP! HELP US! DADDY, HELP!" My four year-old brother's scream threw my heart into my throat as I whirled in the direction of his voice. He had been running ahead with his friend, wanting to hike without us. What had happened? Then I saw them, chest deep in a huge mud puddle and sinking deeper and deeper as they flailed their arms! I ran to help them, only to turn and backtrack as I started sinking in myself. Cautiously, my dad crept around the rim of the soft mud. Stretching out his arm, he grabbed my brother's friend and then my brother. Once they were safely out of the danger zone, we looked back at the now perfectly flat, shallow looking mud puddle and realized that it must be quicksand-like mud filling a very deep hole. Now subdued, my brother and his friend hiked with us for the rest of the way.

A few weeks ago, I was hiking with my dad and came across another little boy with his dad. This little boy had the same "do it myself" attitude that my brother had that day years before. This little guy was jumping down the steps on the trail, all by himself, ignoring his dad's outstretched hand. I knew a fall was coming as he jumped down the next step. His dad was there for him though, and he caught him before he face-planted. My dad and I smiled as we saw this dad trying to protect his little independent munchkin from hurting himself.

While I may now be at boarding school hours away from my parents, I still have a Dad looking after me, wanting to protect me. Christ desperately wants the best for me. He wants to guide me, but He won't force me to let Him. I have to choose to let Him, the Master Guide, lead me. If I I do, He will lead me away from the mud puddles, towards His heavenly kingdom.

~ Katie Sloop

Reflection

In the same way, let your light shine before others, that they may see your good deeds and glorify your Father in heaven.
- Matthew 5:16 NIV

It is 250,000 miles from the earth, but it is still the brightest object in the night sky. Every day the moon makes a journey of over 2,000 miles, but still we see it every night. Even though it has no light of its own, it reflects light from the sun bright enough to read by.

For thousands of years, great men and women have been inspired by this "small" light in the sky. It has prompted them to learn more about our universe and to discover new theories of math and science. The moon is something that we have all taken for granted, but even though it may seem to have little to do with our daily lives, it can affect us greatly. One of the greatest contributions the moon has had on science occurs during a solar eclipse. This is when the moon in orbit passes between the earth and the sun. Ordinarily we cannot look directly at the sun; it is too bright. But in the few moments when the moon is blocking most of the intensity of the sun, scientists can catch a view of the solar corona—the outer atmosphere of the sun, where solar flares take place. This has allowed us to study the sun and get a better understanding of how it gives us heat and light. These occurrences have shown philosophers and scientists throughout the ages how our solar system works and how the moon and the sun interact. Because of the regular path of the moon, and because it reflects the light of the sun, we are able to learn so much more.

Just like the solar eclipse, others can look at me and get a better understanding of God. Sometimes I feel insignificant, especially when I am far away from home at school. I am not close to lots of people or a big city. However, as I think about the impact of the moon, I realize that, though I seem insignificant and small, God can use me to give light to others, as long as I am reflecting Him.

~ Derek Glatts

Good News

As cold water to a thirsty soul, so is good news from a far country.
- Proverbs 25:25 NKJV

Last California tour, when I had just finished tossing my clothes into the Laundromat washers, I stood outside, impatiently waiting. A group of us were ready to hit the beach, but one girl was hindering us from leaving right away. She was inside helping staff lay our concert uniforms out to dry. Her helpfulness was nice, but I wanted to run in the sand and stick my feet in the frigid Pacific Ocean without further delay. My impatience took hold of me, and I marched in to collect our preoccupied friend. She was just ready to join my group, but as we started out the door, an announcement was made. A fellow staff or student thought serenading the Laundromat workers would be a perfect opportunity to be a Christian influence and say, "Thank you."

Ugh! Reluctantly, I joined the gathering group of young people. As we sang *Sweet, Sweet Spirit*, tears instantly began to stream down the manager's face, and in a moment my attitude flipped upside down. The lady smiled and thanked us, saying fervently, "That made my day!"

It made mine, too. I had been so impatient to do something fun and thrilling, but God had something much deeper and more meaningful in mind. So many times I jump to do something that offers momentary happiness, rather than being patient and consulting God about His will, which is ever more filling than short-lived pleasure.

I asked God to forgive me for my selfish impatience and proceeded to hug the lady. Really, what was playing in the sand worth compared to this? I was able to be a part of bringing "good news from a far country."

~ Ashley Wilkens

Finding Fulfillment

… be content with such things as ye have… - Hebrews 13:5 KJV

Have you ever wished that you could have chosen your family or other things in your life? When I was younger I used to do a lot of daydreaming. I would spend hours thinking about and talking with my "family," which, of course, was only composed of imaginary characters who spoke, thought, and acted just the way I wanted them to. I chose how many brothers and sisters I had, what my parents were like, where we would live, and many other aspects of our lives. I even decided what I would look like, my name, and my personality.

Then one day I made a startling discovery. I recognized that the reason I was daydreaming was that I was not satisfied with the life God had given me. I thought that my parents were too strict, that I would be happier with different siblings, and that the way we lived was not the best for me. I wanted to be more beautiful, more popular, better at school—the perfect girl. Because I couldn't change these things, I tried to live the life I wanted in my thoughts. I realized that I needed to learn to be content with the person God made me to be.

After I made this discovery, I decided that I would give up my daydreaming for good. It wasn't easy, and many times I forgot and went back to it for a while; but God helped me to gain the complete victory. Now, as soon as I find myself starting to fantasize, I pray and ask Jesus to help me to give these thoughts to Him and to be happy with the life He has given me. I have found that when I choose His way, I have a peace and joy that I never had when I was dissatisfied. Are you content with the person God made you, the life that He chose for you, and the people that He put in it? If not, go to Him right now and ask Him to help you find fulfillment in the life He's planned for you.

~ Aileen Corrigan

Sharpen Your Saw

If the ax is dull, and one does not sharpen the edge, then he must use more strength; but wisdom brings success. - Ecclesiastes 10:10 NKJV

In every community there is a wide variety of people—each one with a different reputation, and each with a different skill set to be used to benefit his community. My grandfather had the reputation for having lots of firewood. If there was a tree that needed to be cut down, he was the man to ask. Often, people in his town would ask him to remove a tree, and he would be there with his chainsaw ready.

One day, the town hall needed him to remove a tree from their grounds. My grandfather grabbed his chainsaw and his four boys and jumped in his truck. The easy part was cutting down the tree, but the real work started when he had to cut it into rounds so that it could be split into firewood. My grandfather would rapidly cut small sections, then my father and his three brothers would roll them into the trailer. Suddenly, my father noticed that another man had arrived and started to cut up the other end of the tree. At first my father was upset. He sidled up to his dad and said, "Dad, look! That man is trying to take our firewood. They asked us to take down this tree. It's ours, not his!" My grandfather just looked at his son and said, "Tommy, don't worry. He won't get more than two rounds of wood. Look, he did not sharpen his chainsaw." Sure enough, my dad watched as the other man struggled with his saw as it jerked and rebelled at the hard oak wood. Turning, he watched his dad's sharp saw slice though the wood as if it were a completely different tree.

Sharpening a chainsaw is not an easy task, and my grandfather spent hours making his saw as sharp as he could so that when the time came for him to use it, he was well prepared. So often I have expected that when the time came, I would be able to arise and seize the opportunity to share the Lord's message. However, if my saw has not been sharpened by daily spending time in God's word, then when it comes to cut some wood, I will not be effective in achieving what the Lord calls me to do.

~ Derek Glatts

Liberty Gained, Liberty Given

*He has sent Me to heal the brokenhearted, to proclaim liberty to the
captives and recovery of sight to the blind, to set at liberty those who
are oppressed... - Luke 3:18b NKJV*

While in Italy this summer, I visited the Waldensian Alps. As I hiked
up into the mountains, I thought of how they had provided shelter for
escaping Waldenses. I remembered how the Waldensian Christians
had been hunted by the offical church, and I tried to envision the
emotional turmoil of running from persecution. Little families fled while
carrying tiny babies. Tears poured from the eyes of children whose
parents had been captured. They could have avoided tears and
homelessness; however, they had chosen to obey only the Bible. It
was their treasure. Each Waldensian student memorized the books of
Matthew and John, and other Bible passages. During school, students
copied down Bible texts, and in this way, God's truth was kept alive.

What was the life focus that drove these people to sacrifice
everything in upholding the Bible? It was to share God's Word with
trapped people. The Waldenses had found the joy of complete
salvation through Jesus, and they yearned to share this truth with
the sincere masses trapped in a counterfeit religion. The Waldensian
mission was to share the gospel that had freed their own minds from
a religion of works and human traditions. With this goal, Waldensian
missionaries and college students would go into the world. They
secretly gave copied Bible texts away, baffling the receivers of these
treasures. The fact that they could not work to gain their own salvation
was too good to be true! I can imagine myself, unable to hold back
tears of relief upon hearing the news: "The blood of Jesus Christ His
Son cleanses us from all sin" (1 John 1:7b NKJV). Captives were set
free by Jesus. Sharing this truth of God's free salvation was the life
mission of the Waldenses.

We can have the same life focus. We can share Jesus with those
enslaved by a religion of works and traditions. We can share the
news that Jesus is our only Savior. He wants to proclaim liberty to the
captives through us.

~ Andrew Sharley

What I Really Want

Come to Me, all who are weary and heavy-laden, and I will give you rest. - Matthew 11:28 NASB

I tossed and turned, unable to sleep. I couldn't stop the train of thoughts rushing through my head at a hundred miles per hour. My family moving, our upcoming music tour, seeing my sister and her baby, schoolwork—I was worried about almost everything I could think of. As my stomach re-knotted itself, I glared at the 9:40 P.M. displayed on my clock. I had been in bed for almost two hours without sleeping a single wink! I just wanted to sleep; why couldn't I doze off and stop worrying about everything?

As my mind rushed back in time, I remembered, two weeks earlier, standing on the crest of a hill gazing at the beautiful mountains across the powerful Fraser River. The setting sun was reflecting off the snow, painting the peak a light, rosy pink. Bright little stars began twinkling their way through the thickening darkness, foreshadowing the round, glowing moon that soon peaked over the shadowy ridge. Struck with the beauty that surrounded me, I couldn't help but remember the Master Sculptor who had formed and painted that brilliant landscape.

Car lights shone in my window, interrupting my thoughts. That evening, I realized that the Sculptor of the surrounding mountains is my Maker. He knows me better than I know myself, and He will work out every situation in my life. I finally understood He was there with me in my dorm room, promising to take care of me. Peace filled me as I surrendered to Him.

If the Sculptor of the lofty peaks unfailingly carpets the field below my dorm with wildflowers, how much more will He care for me, a creature created in His own likeness! My Maker cares; my Maker loves; my Maker offers peace. I want His peace.

~ Katie Sloop

Losing Control

For in many things we offend all. If any man offend not in word, the same is a perfect man, and able also to bridle the whole body.
- James 3:2 KJV

Finally, after a long evening of intense studying and homework, the time for rest came! I imagined the blissful silence that awaited me in my cozy room—outside the reach of all the havoc around me.

I entered and took it all in for a moment. *Strange,* I thought, *I never leave my iPod dock playing music that loud.* A slight breeze blew in my window. Walking over there, I listened and realized that the music wasn't coming from my room, but it came from the person a floor below—Michael Jensen. Suddenly, with a weird awareness, I realized that if I couldn't make him turn the music down, I would suffer all night waiting for it to end. Storming downstairs, I entered the culprit's room and demanded, "Turn the music down, or I will put my fist through your speakers." Simple. He hesitated for a bit, until our dean walked in and told him that it was way above volume limits.

As I reflected, I realized that I had not asked as kindly as I could have. If I had asked him nicely, he probably would have turned his music down without hesitation. Inside, I felt guilty for being so rude and blunt, yet I couldn't bring myself to actually say sorry. I had failed in one of the most common areas of temptation—self-control.

God wants us to be able to control ourselves so we can present an accurate picture of Him to the world. Jesus would not have rudely yelled at or threatened anyone, yet I did. God can give me strength to control my temper if I will only ask Him and yield my will to Him. If I lose my temper, I am totally failing to represent His true character to others. What about you? Do you want to portray a Christlike character or blow up when faced with a difficult situation? Jesus can give us victory over anything in our lives, if we will commit it to Him.

~ Chris Donatelli

Did He Leave Me?

As a shepherd seeketh out his flock in the day that He is among His sheep that are scattered; so will I seek out my sheep, and will deliver them out of all places where they have been scattered in the cloudy and dark day. - Ezekiel 34:12 KJV

One day, my dad asked me if I wanted to come with him to a hardware store. Excited for an opportunity to go somewhere, I quickly agreed. We got ready and jumped in the car. As we walked into the store, something caught my eye and I ran over to look at it, unaware that I had just run away from my dad. A couple of minutes later, when I got bored, I looked around and noticed that my dad wasn't anywhere near me. So, I went to look for him. I checked the first aisle: no Dad. I checked the second aisle: no Dad. I checked all the aisles in the store, and still, no Dad. Now I was starting to get scared. *Did he leave me? Did he forget that I was here? Where is he? Maybe I didn't look thoroughly enough.* So, I checked the store a second time, and a third. I was just about to give up when I turned around and saw my dad standing there. I ran to him and asked where he had been, and he said that he had been right behind me the second and third time I had looked for him, and had I just turned around, I would have found him. Relieved, I took my daddy's hand and we went home.

In the same way, distractions in life sometimes catch our eyes, and we run towards them, totally oblivious to the fact that we just ran away from our Heavenly Father. Suddenly, we notice that He isn't there anymore, and we go looking for Him. We get frustrated when we don't find Him in the places we think he would be, and we get scared that He just might have forgotten about us or left us. But if we just turn around, we'll see that He is right there next to us, watching to make sure that we're okay.

~ Agnes Grétarsdóttir

Laundry Detergent

In my Father's house are many mansions: if it were not so, I would have told you… - John 14:2 KJV

I love laundry detergent. It makes life so much better. At my house we use a specific brand of laundry detergent and dryer sheets, giving our clean laundry a unique scent. When I moved into the dorm and started doing my own laundry, I made sure I used the exact same brands. I wanted my laundry to smell the same as home. Every morning when I put on a fresh pair of school clothes, the smell of home fills my nose. I can't help but smile as I think of when I would sit on our green shag carpet watching my mom and cat fight over the laundry: Mom wanting to wash it, the cat wanting to sleep on it.

One year I went to my grandparents house for Thanksgiving break instead of going all the way home. While I was staying with them, I did a couple loads of laundry. About a week after I returned to school, I slipped on a shirt I hadn't worn since break. As the smell of my grandparents' laundry detergent filled my nose, a soft tear rolled down my cheek, and I began to cry. It wasn't a sad cry, almost a happy cry: a cry for times gone by, memories made, and conversations had. It gave me hope as I carried the memories with me throughout the day.

I can let the smell of my grandparents' laundry detergent make me sad, or I can associate the smell with good times gone by. On this planet, we can sense signs of Christ's coming in the air. When we see the signs of sin and decay, we can either let them ruin our day, or we can think of the days ahead of us, when we will forever be with our heavenly Father. How will you respond to the "laundry detergent" in your life?

~ Mason Neil

Apple of His Eye

Nor height, nor depth, nor any other creature, shall be able to separate us from the love of God, which is in Christ Jesus our Lord.
- Romans 8:39 KJV

My dad and I share a very special bond. Ever since I can remember, I have always felt as if I were the apple of his eye. He loves me so much, and I have always known that he would do anything for me. He never tells me that my dreams are impossible. He always encourages me and tells me to do my best. He is always patient and loving towards me, even if I am not towards him. When I wanted to build a three-story tree house, my dad was the one who patiently helped me construct it. Whenever I cook a meal at home and set the fire alarm off in the process, my dad never complains. He always calmly eats the burnt food I cook and makes no comment on the sorry charcoal remnants of food emblazoned on the bottom of the kettle. When I was little, my dad was the one who came to my tea parties. Even if the tea was imaginary and the cookies were plastic, he still acted as if he was having the time of his life. Those days of pink bows in Dad's hair, and playing dress-up together are over now. And even though we don't spend as much time together anymore, I know that my dad loves me just as much, and that his love for me will never change. No matter what I do, who I become, or where I go in life, I can always trust in his love.

We all have a very special Dad. We may not all have an earthly dad, but we each have a loving and devoted Father in Heaven. Just like my dad's love for me, our heavenly Father's love for us is unchangeable, immeasurable, and infinite. Even when we let go of His hand and try to push Him away, His arms are always open, and His voice is pleading with us, reassuring us of His love. No matter how far we run or where we hide, our Father's love is still with us. We are the apple of His eye, and His love will never lose sight of us.

~ Sierra Buhler

Stryne

I can do all things through Christ who strengthens me.
- Philippians 4:13 NKJV

Some of the students from Fountainview Academy were backpacking in a nearby valley called Stryne. I was really looking forward to the campout, especially since my friends had told me awesome stories about the cabin and the river.

When we arrived at the trailhead and unloaded the backpacks, everyone heaved on their packs, and our leader prayed for our safety and for a good time; then off we went on our adventure. There was one problem though: my water bottle was empty, and I needed water for the hike. So I stopped to fill it from a larger water container at the back of the bus. When I finished, I was already behind, so I walked faster, trying to keep up; but it was difficult because my pack was so heavy and the path went uphill. I slowly progressed up the mountain, sometimes tripping, trying to focus on breathing and stepping. I was so glad when I caught up with some other people who were also having trouble walking up the mountain with their heavy packs. The rest of the hike we encouraged each other on. We were in no hurry, so we figured "we'd get there when we got there."

The hike got harder and harder, and I was having trouble thinking positively. I felt like complaining and giving up, so I prayed, "Jesus, please give me strength to make it and help me have a positive attitude." And I claimed Philippians 4:13, "I can do all things through Christ who strengthens me." God did give me strength, and by His grace we did make it!

When I got to the top and rounded the last corner, I saw the tents that the other hikers had set up already. I was so excited to see everyone, and I felt so accomplished! I felt like I was coming home! Everything that I had gone through to get there was so worth it. Just as Jesus gave me the strength I needed to make it to the top of the mountain, so He will help you with every step along the narrow way to heaven. Won't you join me in the climb?

~ Anna Ford

Downpour

*And all things, whatsoever ye shall ask in prayer, believing, ye shall
receive. - Matthew 21:22 KJV*

Tears rolled down Lander's cheeks, adding to the downpour around
him. He sat down on a moss-covered rock, not caring if it was wet.
Frent, his dog, laid down beside him. Lander rubbed his eyes, trying
to see through the woods that engulfed him. He knew the trail couldn't
be far away, but in the midst of the rain he had lost his way. He stroked
his dog's fur, softly talking to him. "What have we gotten ourselves
into? I don't think I've ever been this lost before. What if we never
find our way back home?" With that last thought, Lander broke down
into tears again. What could he do? He felt helpless, lost in a sea of
hopelessness with no one to hear his cries for help. Then it dawned on
him. There was Someone who would listen to him.

"Dear Jesus, You see my situation. Frent and I are lost. We're cold,
hungry, and it's almost bedtime. Please, help us to find our way home."

Lander stood up, brushed himself off, and began walking. "Come
on, Frent, the trail has to be somewhere." They walked around a large
maple tree, over a rotting log, and finally scaled a small knoll. As the
two neared the top, they saw a most welcome sign. There, before
them, was the trail. They trudged down the knoll and before long were
back on the trail, heading for home.

I too have been lost so many times. I feel the cold rain around me,
ushering in darkness. I know I've wandered off the trail. No matter how
hard I try, I know I cannot get back on the trail by myself. I have to call
out to God. I know He will help me find my way back to the straight
and narrow path.

Let Him guide you out of the downpour today.

~ Mason Neil

Harmonious Harmonics

… there are many parts, but one body. - 1 Corinthians 12:20 NIV

With a last sweep of the bows and a glorious note from the choir, the final majestic chord rang out, shaking the chapel. Bows in the air, the choir standing motionless, and Craig's hands still dramatically poised, the adrenaline of having played well and hard pumped through our veins. Slowly, Craig lowered the baton and everyone relaxed. "Did you hear that? Did you hear those harmonics?" he excitedly exclaimed. From the amazed look on his face we could tell that we had just managed to accomplish the goal, and we all could breathe again. We had been working hard to get the tuning exactly right, so when we heard the harmonics, we knew we were victorious! You see, harmonics are multiples of the base sound frequency that are only heard when everyone is in tune. The violinists had to have their fingers in just the right position on their fingerboards; the operatic sopranos and booming basses had to sing just the right vowel at just the right pitch; the brass and woodwind sections had to have their lips at perfect tension; and everything had to be perfectly in time with the ictus of Craig's flying baton. Only when this happened could the beauty of the harmonics be heard.

We all play an important part in the orchestra. If one makes a mistake, we all have; and if someone does well, we all should rejoice—for then the whole group has done well as one orchestra, one instrument, under one conductor. But if I, in my pride, don't work together with my stand partner or with my section or with the whole orchestra, then of what value am I to the orchestra? We all play an important part in making music. It is only when we are all in tune with Christ, following His baton, that we truly experience unity—whether it is in our spiritual lives or in making the harmonics ring.

~ Esther Ferraz

Knowing for Yourself

And this is life eternal, that they might know Thee the only true God, and Jesus Christ, whom Thou hast sent. - John 17:3 KJV

As I sleepily shuffled into my parents' room, I noticed my mom's red eyes and heard her sniffles. *What is going on? Why is she crying? What has happened?* As thoughts flew through my mind, my mom sobbed out the answer to my unexpressed question.

"Papa died yesterday."

I didn't really comprehend it at first. I knew my grandpa had been sick, but since we were living overseas, we hadn't known how sick. As I robotically turned and left the room, a question hit me: Will I see Papa and Grandy at Christ's Second Coming? I mentally answered the question yes; I didn't dare to think of any other answer. But, as I started thinking over my grandparents' lives, I became more scared.

My grandparents were educated professionals living in a well-known church college town. When my mom was in high school, my grandparents became friends with a skeptical theology professor. This professor had so great an influence on my mom's family that by the time she graduated from college, my grandpa was the only one of her family going to any part of the weekly church service. To this day, it hasn't really changed; all four of my mom's siblings have left their childhood church, and only my mom's youngest sister is going to any church at all. The eternal destiny of my mom's family was most probably altered as a result of the influence of that skeptical professor.

What would have happened if my grandparents had searched for God themselves, making a personal relationship with Christ a higher priority? Would my mom's family be different today? Would their eternal destiny be different? It makes me wonder what my eternal destiny is. Do I have that personal relationship with Christ, or am I following another's opinions? My desire is to search to know God for myself.

~ Katie Sloop

Our Sandcastles

See then that ye walk circumspectly, not as fools, but as wise,
redeeming the time, because the days are evil.
- Ephesians 5:15–16 KJV

Ken Karpman had it all. A large house situated on a Florida golf course, a salary of $750,000 a year, and the girl of his dreams. He had no idea the prices of things in the store, because it didn't matter to him. Money existed in abundance, and it seemed like this fairy tale of a life would continue forever. Ken was living the "American dream."

After enjoying such a lavish life, confidence mounted. Ken quit his job so he could start a hedge fund. But it wasn't long before $500,000 of his personal savings evaporated in an endeavor to keep this new business afloat while maintaining his family's extravagant standard of living. Unable to attract enough investors, he was forced to dissolve the fund. In a tremendous reversal of fortune, Ken was now left with hundreds of thousands of dollars of debt, a home in foreclosure, and a desperate need for quick money. So he took a job as a pizza delivery man, pulling in only $7.29 an hour.

How often do you occupy your days with sandcastle building? How many hours of your life have been spent planning a lofty future that might not even exist? It's not bad to plan ahead, but where is your real focus? Is your time, money, and energy invested here on Earth? Do you realize that where your treasure is, there your heart will be also. Ken's future as he imagined it was destroyed with one wave, just like a sandcastle. It didn't matter how big it was or how securely it was built. A sandcastle is made of sand. No matter how big your house, or how much life insurance you have, your future is as fragile as a sandcastle if it is not grounded on the enduring truths of Christ's word. So where will you invest your treasure and your heart: in sand, or in gold that can never depreciate, get stolen, or be destroyed?

~ Michael Jensen

A Rich Life

There is one who makes himself rich, yet has nothing; And one who makes himself poor, yet has great riches. - Proverbs 13:7 NKJV

What makes a person poor? The dictionary defines poor as a state of being without money, food, or other material things. But is this an accurate definition? There are many wealthy people who have everything they could ever want and are still very much poor. Does being "poor" actually mean having little money, clothes, or food, and a rundown house?

In 2007, we moved to South Carolina. My family is not wealthy, but we are most definitely not poor. My mom, inspired by home makeover shows she'd seen on TV, decided to buy a run-down old house, fix it up, and sell it. This house was terrible! The paint was faded and peeling, the siding had holes, the floors were splintered, and there was a broken chimney in the middle of the living room.

The people we met at our new church thought we were very poor because we lived in such an awful house. They thought we were so poor, in fact, that a group of kind-hearted members got together at Christmas time to give us gifts they thought we could not afford. For me, it was a little embarrassing having people think we were so poor we could not buy presents for ourselves. Now though, I realize how blessed we were to have friends who cared so much for us, even though they misunderstood our situation.

You see, I think my family is rich, very rich, in fact. I have parents who love God. They love me and want the best for me. I have six siblings who love me as well. I have friends who enjoy spending time with me and who encourage me in my spiritual walk. I have more material possessions than I need. Best of all, I have a loving Father God who longs to save me from sin and take me to heaven to live with Him, where I will be an heir to riches untold.

~ Sarah Wahlman

Scarred for Life

*I will give you a new heart and put a new spirit in you; I will remove
from you your heart of stone and give you a heart of flesh.*
- Ezekiel 36:26 NIV

When I was young, noodles were my favorite dish. Although the
Korean staple food is rice, I always craved noodles. One day I begged
my mother to let me eat ramen instead of rice. Of course, she said
no at first, but because I bothered her hundreds of times, she finally
gave in. I was four years old at the time, and I didn't know how to cook
ramen. So my mom poured some hot water into an instant ramen
cup and placed it on the dining table. She ordered me to wait three
minutes until the noodles were cooked. However, for my four-year-old
self, those three minutes felt like thirty hours; I had no patience. As
soon as my mother left the table, I snuck towards the bowl and tried to
see if it was cooked yet. But I had a problem: I was too short. Since I
could barely see over the table, I grabbed the bowl of ramen and tilted
it toward me. The hot water spilled all over the front of my body, and
I was burned badly. I screamed, and my mom sprinted from the other
room. Realizing what had happened, she threw me into the bath tub
and poured ice cold water all over me. Fortunately, my face wasn't
burned at all, but the skin on my stomach was red and blistered. I was
taken to the hospital right away, but I had huge, hideous scars on my
tummy for a long time afterwards.

Our sins also leave scars—scars on our character. When we
make a wrong decision, it affects our character, leaving ugly marks.
These scars will stay with us until Christ cleanses us and gives us a
new, perfect character. But before He can do that, we must make the
decision to allow Christ to come into our hearts and get rid of our ugly,
scarred hearts. I know I didn't like to look at my scars and be reminded
of the pain that I suffered. I also don't want to look inside my heart and
see the ugliness of the scars of all the bad choices that I have made. I
want to have the pure, beautiful heart that only Christ can give me.

~ Ellen Yoon

Don't Hesitate to Obey

… Listen, please. Listen to God's voice. I'm telling you this for your own good so that you'll live. - Jeremiah 38:20 MSG

"Wheee! I can fly!" I squealed in my happiness. I was having so much fun jumping from the back of our couch and landing on a foam pad, which was only about 2½ inches thick. My mom had warned me not to do it since I could get hurt, but in my five-year-old mind, I thought I was smart enough to know what to do and what not to do. So I just kept jumping and trying to go as high and as far as I could. Then I had a great idea: I should jump and land on my belly! Unfortunately, I did that and ended up losing my breath. I panicked, because I was really scared that I might be hurt.

Even though I didn't deserve it, my mom comforted me and helped me to catch my breath again. If I had only listened to her warnings, that wouldn't have happened; but I didn't know why she told me not to do it, and so I didn't trust her. Because my mom gave me the freedom of choice to listen to her or not, I learned a very important lesson: when my mom warns me, it is for my own good. She is wiser than I am and can see the unavoidable consequence of disobedience, and she doesn't want me to have the pain that would come with it.

God gave Adam and Eve the choice to listen to Him and not eat the fruit of the tree of the knowledge of good and evil, or to go their own way and disobey Him. He knew the results of both: if they obeyed Him they would live a perfect life without death, sadness, and sin; if they disobeyed, they would reap the inevitable consequences and pain. Unfortunately, they chose to not listen to God and instead brought sin into this world. This pain is not like losing your breath and hurting for a little while. It is like losing your breath forever. We shouldn't hesitate to trust our own Creator who loves us so much that everything He wants us to do will be for our own good.

~ Diane Carvalho

"Hi, Sweet Girl"

Fear not, little flock; for it is your Father's good pleasure to give you the kingdom. - Luke 12:32 KJV

"Ashley, you have mail!"

Yes! I thought as I bounded over to the smiling letter-bearer. Sure enough, it was from Mema and Poppop, my grandparents, and it was sent all the way from Tennessee. Without fail, I received a letter from them each month, and I always looked forward to each one. My grandma was the designated letter writer, and she had neat, pretty handwriting. I enjoyed reading her favorite introductory phrase, "Hi, sweet girl…" This first line made me picture her smiling expression, sweet voice, and the warm hug that she would give me whenever I visited their house. The rest of the letter would help me catch up on recent family events and activities that my immediate family and relatives were enjoying at home.

My joy grew more and more as each letter came. What love! I did not expect the cards; I did not deserve the money my grandparents sent in them, and the strength that came with each enclosed miniature memory verse card surprised me.

Their wonderful monthly letter is only one of innumerable blessings they give to me. They love me, and it is their joy to sacrifice on my behalf because I am more important to them than their earthly possessions.

But Christ loves me even more than my own grandparents. He has already given me so much more than they ever could. Do you realize how important you are to God? Did you know that it is His good pleasure to give you His kingdom? He delights in giving you good gifts—that's how strong His love is.

~ Ashley Wilkens

Weeds of Sin

*The labour of the righteous tendeth to life: the fruit of the wicked to
sin. - Proverbs 10:16 KJV*

When I was a kid, I had a rather low-salary job. I pulled weeds for
one dollar an hour. Despite the simple salary, I held down the job and
pulled weed after weed, hour after hour, earning my scanty supply
of spending money. Weeds constantly grew in the flowerbeds, fields,
and occasionally broke through cracks in the concrete—meaning
that I never lacked a job. These weeds always puzzled me, because
they didn't seem to need any cultivation while useful crops, like corn,
needed plenty of nutrients and care.

The same idea applies to sin. Because every human has a sinful
nature, the weeds of evil will pop up in our lives constantly. Whether in
the form of temptations or sinful thoughts and actions, they don't seem
to require cultivation. This is not only because of our sinful nature, but
because it's so easy to "go with the flow" in a world that has fallen into
the pit of sin.

Despite our sinful tendencies, we can go to battle against the
growing weeds with the help of Jesus, our weed-puller. Often we think
we can build ourselves a concrete wall to keep out the weeds, but
reality reveals that they can still pop through that seemingly invincible
barrier. The only way to truly exterminate them is by letting Jesus
come in to uproot the sin. When we cultivate a relationship with Him,
He'll get rid of the weeds and help us grow useful crops: a better
character and a relationship with Him.

~ Christian Welch

A Day of Remembrance

"For I know the plans I have for you," declares the Lord, "plans to prosper you and not to harm you, plans to give you hope and a future." - Jeremiah 29:11 NIV

September 11, 2001 started out as any other day. I wasn't old enough to be in school yet, and I can still remember waking up super early. Because my mom and dad got divorced when I was still young, Mom and I shared the same room and slept in the same bed. I would always shoot up in the bed and ask my mom, "Mom, can I watch TV if I put it really, really low?" It was nearing 9:00 A.M. as the morning cartoons rolled across the television screen. The cartoons finished and I woke my mother up and asked her to play with me. My mom is so awesome that she actually did. After our playtime, when I got bored, I turned on the TV again and flipped through the channels. Then something drew my attention. On one channel I saw a plane hitting a building. I thought I should ask my mom to come because I knew this did not usually happen on TV, and it looked important. She reluctantly came to the bedroom, and as soon as she recognized what was happening, her faced turned to horror. I, on the other hand, as most little kids would do when parents don't respond, lost interest.

My mother had resigned from being an EMT one week before 9/11. God had a plan for me, to give me a future. God knew that I needed my mother in my life to train and guide me. He knew that I would be parentless if she still worked as an EMT. Her EMT base got called to go into the twin towers, and she lost a lot of good co-workers. I thank God every day that she wasn't among them. By the grace of God, she is still in my life today to train me up to be the man who He wants me to be. Remember that no matter what's happening in your life, good or bad, God has a future for you. God wants to guide and train you up to be the child He wants you to be!

~ Daniel Tentea

The Scars Tell the Story

For God so loved the world, that He gave His only begotten Son, that whosoever believeth in Him should not perish, but have everlasting life. - John 3:16 KJV

It was September 12, 2001: the day after the twin towers fell. My sisters and I were sitting in a small room with a big window. We had been having lots of fun, singing and playing song games. On this specific sunny September day I had chosen to sit by the window and let the sun shine on my back while a slow but steady breeze blew by the window, rustling the bushes outside. We were sitting there singing when the old window made a strange creak and suddenly came crashing down onto my head. The frame came to a rest on my shoulders like a wreath. The window frame had become loose in its sliding track because it was an old building that had settled, resulting in a distorted window frame. When that slight breeze came, it gave it just enough pressure to push the window frame out of the wall and onto me, causing severe cuts to my forehead and face. I went to the hospital and got stitches on my forehead. Ever since that day, people have asked me questions about the four long scars on my forehead. My scars have become a part of me over time.

I soon realized that I could become overly self-conscious about them; but instead, I chose to let them remind me every time I look in the mirror, that I have a Heavenly Saviour who has scars on His hands like I do on my face. Every time He looks at His scars, He thinks of me; just like when I look at mine, I choose to think of Him. I choose to remember that God sent His Son to die on the cross for me, and because of that, I can choose to have eternal life.

~ Rebecca Hall

Ready or Not

Take heed, watch and pray; for you do not know when the time is.
- Mark 13:33 NKJV

Wow! I love this song! It's so beautiful! Those were my thoughts as I sat on stage with the orchestra, waiting for the part where I should play. *It's almost there… all right, now it's probably time to raise our violins. Wait, none of the third violins are getting ready to play! But I'm sure we are supposed to play now… What should I do? Play all by myself and look awkward, or just wait to see when they will play?* I chose to go with the second option, and by the time the rest of my section was ready to play, we realized that our part was finished. I was depending on them to bring me in at the right time, but by doing that, we all missed our part.

One thing is for sure: the orchestra will never stop and wait for the third violins to realize that they should play. We had time to practice and should have known when to come in. But we missed our chance to play our part because we weren't watching carefully.

There are so many things that we have to be ready for in our lives. If we're not ready, we miss out on all sorts of opportunities that we can never get back. Sometimes we get a second chance, but not always. Jesus' second coming will not have a "second-chance offer"—He's only coming for us once. The sad thing is that when Jesus came the first time, only a few people were ready. We don't want that to happen again, do we? Satan is trying his very best to prevent us from being ready, and the only way we can resist his attempts is if we watch and pray.

~ Diane Carvalho

Giving to Live

A generous person will prosper; whoever refreshes others will be refreshed. - Proverbs 11:25 NIV

My eye caught the cluster of honey-brown pine cones nestled beside me in my gently swaying evergreen. From my perch, I could see light blue berries peering out of branches of juniper and, a little farther away, yellowing Saskatoon leaves. Farther down the tree-filled valley, bordering the rapid Fraser River, sat Fountainview's campus, with the school building sandwiched between apple and apricot orchards. "Everything lives to give." My Bible teacher's words floated into mind. *Everything lives to give… everything lives to give.*

Beaming sunflowers, thick green apple leaves, pine trees, and rippling fields of tall grass—all live to give. Nature not only clothes this world with its beauty, but also continually gives oxygen, food, and love. Through it God pours out His love. If nature didn't give, it would be unable to live.

Selfishness doesn't naturally exist in nature. All of God's creation is happy with giving. That is, all of creation except humanity; selfishness is a result of man's sin. We look at humanity around us and see incredible selfishness: Hitler, Stalin, Gaddafi, Mugabe, Kim Jong-Il. We condemn them and their cruelty, but which one of us doesn't secretly wish for their power and riches? We hate the sinner, but love the sin. In striking contrast, Christ hates the sin, but loves the sinner. While He abhors our selfishness, He loves us. His pardoning and transforming grace is a manifestation of His unselfishness, a manifestation of His love.

Selfishness can only bring suffering and unhappiness, but there is hope—Christ can make us unselfish, and only as He does this can we be happy. To be happy, to live, we have to give.

~ Katie Sloop

God Is Always Watching Out For You

And how bold and free we then become in his presence, freely asking according to his will, sure that he's listening. And if we're confident that he's listening, we know that what we've asked for is as good as ours. - 1 John 5:14–15 MSG

I had just enjoyed a fun weekend camping with my friends. Now, we were packing up for the trip down the mountain and the bus ride back to school. We swept the campsite for trash and then put out the campfires. My dean Jay told us to head down.

We were about ten minutes into our hike back when someone radioed over and said, "You have a group of guys on ATVs with three vicious hunting dogs heading your way." Jay instantly took action, and we stepped off the trail and spent a few minutes asking God for protection. After we finished, he told us to carry a good sized rock and our fixed-blade knives. We thought we should stay out of sight to gain the advantage. We sat for a while and waited for them. Since they didn't show up, we kept moving. About fifteen minutes later, Jay heard them and told us to get ready. He saw the dogs come less than thirty feet from him, but they turned right around as if we were not there.

I believe that God put a guardian angel there to turn the dogs around. Our prayer made a difference, because God always hears our cries. God will hear your prayers and answer them according to His will.

~ Daniel Tentea

Waiting for Daddy

Here is the patience of the saints: here are they that keep the commandments of God, and the faith of Jesus. - Revelation 14:12 KJV

The little white picket fence started resembling prison walls. The monkey bars and slide sitting on the wood chips didn't look as inviting as they had before. I wanted to cry. Why wasn't Daddy here? It was a warm summer day at the South England Conference Camp Meeting that my family and I were attending. I had been walking the grounds with my father when I saw some kids playing in a little playground and wanted to join them. Daddy was on an errand and couldn't watch me, so I was allowed to stay and play. Looking up into his dark brown eyes, I promised to stay inside the playground until he came back for me. Waving bye-bye, I joined the other children. I enjoyed myself tremendously, and time passed quickly until one by one, all my new friends were picked up by their parents until I was left alone with the wood chips and monkey bars.

More time passed and now I was worried. Daddy still wasn't back. *Why wasn't he here? Had he forgotten me? Surely not! Maybe he got lost—I should go look for him... But he told me to stay here! What should I do?* My five-year-old conscience knew that to be obedient I would have to stay here and wait until Daddy came back. But it was so tempting—all I had to do was open the white gate and walk out. No one would stop me. But no, Daddy had told me to wait, and wait I would. It seemed like ages, but finally I spotted Daddy coming down the dusty road. I ran towards him and threw my plump little arms around his neck while squealing, "I knew you would come, Daddy! I knew it!"

This memory reminds me of the promise of my heavenly Father to come back and get me. As long as I faithfully obey Him and His directions in the Bible, I can trust that He will fulfill His promise and take me with Him on that day.

~ Esther Ferraz

Lifting the Fallen

Rejoice in the Lord always. - Philippians 4:4 NKJV

"I booked your ticket," my mom commented absent-mindedly as we wove our way up the yellow and red tree-covered hill. As she continued, "You're flying out of Cincinnati on Sunday," my eyes locked on the double yellow line dividing the black ribbon in half. I had wanted to look at Southern Adventist University for a whole weekend, but that wouldn't be possible now. On top of this disappointment, I was sick. As my cold worsened and I felt as though I was on the count down to cranial explosion, my heart sank lower and lower. When we got to our destination, a lookout point, I stumbled out of the car, staring at the gravel and road-side weeds, trying hard not to cry. *Why did she book it—Oh, my throat, ugh.* I was in a depressed state of mind.

"Let's take a picture!" my mom exclaimed. *What is there to take a picture of?* I inwardly grumbled as I glared at the crude gray pebbles below me. Glancing up, I froze—before me stretched brilliant red, deep pumpkin orange, and rich yellow-covered mountains as far as my eye could see. "Oh, wow! Incredible!" I gasped. What had I been doing staring at dead road-side thistles when this vivid collage of fall colors was cascading up and down the valleys before me? As we climbed up the lookout tower, a 360-degree watercolor with mist at its horizons spread out below us, testifying of a Master Artist being at work. With this breath-taking panorama encircling me, how could I focus on my discouragements and pains?

When I looked away from myself and my discouragements to the Master Artist's work, I realized my situation wasn't nearly as bad as I had imagined. Christ knows best, and every trial that comes my way is for my good. I needed to focus on His goodness, His love, His power, and not my pain. Like the deep fall-colored leaves about me, around every discouragement there are promises of Christ's love. Why focus on our pain when brilliant depictions of His care surround us?

~ Katie Sloop

Saved by a Prayer

For He shall give His angels charge over you, to keep you in all your ways. - Psalm 91:11 NKJV

I lurched to a halt. My heart stopped. A bear! I was twelve years old, running through a field of ferns at dusk. I had just left my neighbor's house and was headed for home when I saw that my uncle's lights were on. I decided that instead of going straight home, I would stop for a quick visit. I was all alone among ferns as high as my waist when suddenly, eight feet in front of me, a black bear sprang up in the middle of the ferns and stared into my eyes.

"Lord, I claim your promise that you will never leave me nor forsake me. Please save me!" I helplessly prayed. Just as I finished praying, my dog, Sacha, ran up from behind, barking ferociously. The bear was startled and immediately ran away with my border collie close at its heels.

I know that God heard my prayer even before I prayed, and He sent my dog to save me that night. I knew that He would deliver me if I just asked. Jeremiah 33:3 says, "Call to Me, and I will answer you, and show you great and mighty things, which you do not know" (NKJV). God asks us to hide His Word in our hearts, so that in our time of trouble it is easily accessible. Whenever we are in danger or need His help, we can call on Him. We do this so that He will send His angels to protect us, just as He heard my cry for help and saved me from the bear that summer night.

~ Raina Walker

Wild Ride!

I have set the Lord always before me: because he is at my right hand, I shall not be moved. - Psalm 16:8 KJV

My siblings and I used to give each other rides in our little red wagon. The wagon wasn't really big enough to hold my older brother, but one day he consented to let me give him a ride. He hopped in, and I pulled him to the top of a hill in our yard. I began pulling him down the hill, but he got going too fast; so I let go and jumped out of the way. He was headed straight for the manhole at the bottom of the hill. I yelled, "Watch out for the manhole, Kevin!" but he was going too fast to get out, and he hit the manhole. The wheel cracked off, and he flew out of the wagon.

Sometimes life feels a little bit like an out of control wagon ride. With the recent financial crisis in the United States, the nuclear fiasco in Japan, and the earthquakes and storms all over the planet, people are beginning to feel that they are on a ride without a driver. They are afraid to think about what might happen next because they are realizing that they don't have control over their own lives. Any moment might be their last, but they are not prepared to face the afterlife.

I have realized that I don't need to fear an uncertain future. I can trust in my all powerful Driver to see me through the ride of life. During the past few weeks, traumatic things have happened to several people I know. Looking back at each experience and the circumstances surrounding them, I can clearly see the Lord's hand guiding in each situation. I need not worry or doubt His wisdom. Instead, I can have perfect peace knowing that He is in control. The next time you feel like your life is getting out of hand, rest yourself in God and remember that even if He sees fit to allow you to have great trials, He will be with you and help you to trust His perfect wisdom.

~ Aileen Corrigan

Virtuoso

Thou art worthy, O Lord, to receive glory and honour and power: for Thou hast created all things, and for Thy pleasure they are and were created. - Revelation 4:11 KJV

It all started with a worthless glob of clay. A torso was then shaped, then the arms, legs, fingers, toes, and a head. But it was still a worthless, hopeless, and lifeless piece of clay. Then the craftsman took a deep breath, leaned down, and blew into the sculpture. Like a butterfly from its cocoon, the clay became a living creature. It wasn't just a worthless glob anymore. It could now talk, walk, think, and love. That piece of clay became what we are today—alive!

Who could breathe into a piece of clay and make it come alive, other than our Creator? Everything He touches turns into something breathtaking. Everything truly beautiful that we see and hear comes from our God—the ultimate virtuoso.

This world is a symphony, and God, the conductor. But so many times in our lives we can't hear the piece of music He wants us to hear. We fill our hearing with "bad notes" that clash with His orchestration. When you're in harmony with Him, there won't be one note of mediocrity. I think this song by David Phelps puts it best:

A timeless melody of beauty and emotion
Perfect harmony, inspiring true devotion
No one else can play its chords so graceful yet so strong
You made the instrument and wrote the song.

To me, this describes our virtuoso God. Our God is so perfect in designing and orchestrating that it would be impossible to find fault with His work. The only way we're going to hear this song is if we give our hearts as His instruments and our lives as His orchestrations. Then others will truly be able to see through us our virtuoso God.

~ Julie Kelly

Little Things

He who is faithful in what is least is faithful also in much...
- Luke 16:10 NKJV

This morning, as I was sitting in the lobby, I saw two boys walk by with big work boots on. One of them glanced behind him and saw a chunk of dirt on the floor. They both picked up their feet to check their boots to see if it was from them—it wasn't. But one boy bent down anyway to pick up the dirt and throw it away. I'm sure he didn't think anyone was watching him—but I was.

We often tend to think that life is about the big things: your job, marriage, education, etc. But what makes up the big things are little things. To most people it might not seem like a big thing to pick up a chunk of dirt from the floor, but to me that simple act showed his true character. I know that if he were to carry a bigger responsibility, he would do a good job because he pays attention to details. Little things are what make up life. They are the things that prepare us for greater things. They really do matter, whether it's picking up a chunk of dirt off the ground or doing our homework to the best of our ability, it all matters in the long run. The only way we can truly let God use us is to give our utmost effort for His cause. God needs people who will go the second mile—people who will give every ounce of their energy for Him.

When I get to heaven I want to hear God say, "Well done, thou good and faithful servant!" And I know that the only way to hear that is to be faithful to God even in the littlest things.

~ Moriah Mays

Bye Biplanes!

*If you turn away your foot from the Sabbath, from doing your pleasure
on My holy day… Then you shall delight yourself in the Lord; and I
will cause you to ride on the high hills of the earth, and feed you with
the heritage of Jacob your father. The mouth of the Lord has spoken.
- Isaiah 58:13–14 NKJV*

"Jacob, you wanna see this movie?" My oldest cousin held up a
movie with biplanes flying across the English Channel on the front.

My brother's eyes lit up as he exclaimed, "Yeah! Can we?"

As my cousin pushed play, my brother and I plopped down in front
of their TV. Soon monoplanes, biplanes, and their pilots had our full
attention—we forgot everything else, and barely noticed when my
mom came into the room with my aunt to see what we were up to. I
don't know what their conversation was like, but I certainly remember
my conversation with my mom that night. My brother and I knew
our parents don't want us to watch movies, but we had; and I was
expecting punishment. Shockingly, my mom didn't scold or punish us:
she told us that she wasn't going to punish us because we were at
our cousins' house. But she did remind us that we had lost something
special: a Sabbath blessing. It was Sabbath, and my brother and I had
done something we knew our parents didn't approve of, something
I don't believe God approves of on His holy day, and something that
drives Christ away. My brother and I lost the peace that comes from
spending time with God on the day He has sanctified—a loss I felt
throughout the whole week.

God doesn't force us to spend time with Him on Sabbath, but He
can't give us His blessing, His peace, if we don't. If I really love Him
and desire the blessing He longs to give me, I will choose to spend
time with Him.

~ Katie Sloop

Contributor or Cumberer?

... A certain man ... said to the keeper of his vineyard, "Look, for three years I have come seeking fruit on this fig tree and find none. Cut it down; why does it use up the ground?" - Luke 13:6–7 NKJV

Before my family moved to Canada last year, we lived in New Zealand. We owned a 35-acre vineyard, from which we would harvest the grapes to make pure fruit juice. People tend to think that vineyards are romantic, but let me tell you first hand that they are not; they are simply a lot of hard work.

To get the maximum crop from the vines, we had to tend them all year round. This meant pruning them each winter and making sure their branches were laid in the right place. We would mow between the rows and make sure the vines were doing well. To ensure that the vineyard was as productive as possible, we sometimes had to replace vines. Throughout the vineyard we would find vines that were dead or not producing fruit like they should. These vines were ripped out and replaced with new healthy vines.

In His parable about the fig tree, Jesus talks about trees that don't bear fruit. He tells us that a fruitless fruit tree is worthless. His message is aimed at people who "are trees in the garden of God." "It is not enough that they are trees in the garden of God. They are to answer His expectation by bearing fruit. He holds them accountable for their failure to accomplish all the good which they could have done, through His grace strengthening them. In the books of heaven they are registered as cumberers of the ground" (*Lift Him Up*, pg. 354). Jesus expects us to bear fruit by living His gospel. It is not enough that we are vines in the vineyard, we actually need to contribute to the harvest—we need to produce fruit. As one of Jesus' followers, it is my duty to do all I can to further His work so that I will not be held accountable for missed opportunities and be called a cumberer of the ground.

~ Kyle Smith

Real or Fake?

*Beware of false prophets, who come to you in sheep's clothing, but
inwardly they are ravenous wolves. - Matthew 7:15 NKJV*

As a little girl, I was very fascinated by the fact that the security
men at the airport could tell the difference between what was fake and
what was real.

My fascination began after a friend of my family phoned to tell us
about her experience at the Frankfurt airport on her journey home.
During her trip she had bought many cheap counterfeit clothes.
However, the airport had hired a couple of counterfeit detectives
who would point out fakes and confiscate them. This was my first
introduction to illegal products from third world countries. Everything
looked the same to me, and I couldn't understand how the men at the
airport knew right from wrong.

Many of us don't know the difference between what is fake and
what is real. Often times it seems to be the best decision to buy the
fakes. After all, they are cheap and they look the same.

However, this summer, on my trip to Turkey, I saw a pair of fake
All-Star shoes. I had a hard time understanding how anyone could
possibly buy these, or even worse, wear them. Now I understood. I
knew the All-Stars on the table were fake because I knew what real
ones looked like: how the brand logo is put on, what kind of materials
they're made of, and what kind of shoelaces they have.

Multitudes today don't know if what they are following is right.
They attend church every week, listen to the pastor, but never search
their Bible to find the truth. How can we know what is fake? How can
we know what is real? Satan is a student of the human mind, and he
knows exactly how to get you to believe whatever he says. He can
make anything look good, and he will try to sell you as many fake
"All-Stars" as he can. Often I wonder if I would be able to tell one of
Satan's All-Star lies apart from God's real promises. I need to study
the "label" of God's real All-Star truth so that I can tell the difference.

~ Agnes Grétarsdóttir

Feeling the Pain of Sin

In all their affliction He was afflicted… - Isaiah 63:9 KJV

Brazil has lots of big trees, and most are perfect for climbing. When I was a little kid, I used to climb up trees with my brother a lot. One day, my brother and I were waiting for my mother to come and get us after school. We decided to climb up a big tree that was there in front of the school building. We clambered up the tree just like we were two little monkeys, then waited there for our mother. When she finally arrived, my brother decided to go down first. He went to the lowest branch of the tree and jumped, but unfortunately his foot got stuck in a crook of the tree, making him go straight down and… CRACK! My mom went running to see if he was all right as I, still up in the tree, anxiously waited to see her reaction. His wrist was broken! Carefully I went down, and when I saw my brother's wrist, I could tell it was broken. It looked so painful! He wasn't crying, but I could see that he was in pain. Sitting in the car on our way to the hospital, I started to cry; just by looking at his wrist I could feel his pain.

I know someone who loves us so much, that every time someone rejects the truth, He feels the pain with them. The heart of the infinite Father is pained in sympathy. He wants everyone to know the truth, to know Him, for He is the truth. "Few give thought to the suffering that sin has caused our Creator … The cross is a revelation to our dull senses of the pain that, from its very inception, sin has brought to the heart of God. Every departure from the right, every deed of cruelty, every failure of humanity to reach His ideal, brings grief to Him" (*Education*, pg. 263). He loves us so much, and He doesn't want us to feel the pain of sin. He cannot take it away yet, but one day He will if we choose to let Him. Until then, we can at least do one thing to make our Father happy: repent, for when sinners repent, heaven rejoices.

~ Diane Carvalho

Undying Beauty

*And out of the ground made the Lord God to grow every tree that is
pleasant to the sight, and good for food... - Genesis 2:9 KJV*

Fall is the season when the trees are set aflame with the glorious
colors of burnt gold and ruddy red. Every year, I love watching the
aspen and birch begin their glorious metamorphosis. To me, the hills
and valleys around me are like a painter's canvas. When Fall first
begins, I see the first tentative strokes of yellow brush the aspen trees.
A day later, I may see some dabbles of red and brown scattered about
the forests. The next day, streaks of vibrant gold may be emblazoned
down the mountainsides. As time moves on, more and more color is
added to the forests until it seems as if the hills are on fire. But then,
the winds of fall begin to chill and the color fades from leaves. Soon,
the leaves begin to fall from the trees, fluttering down and quietly
blanketing the forest floor.

Each time I witness the changing of the fall colors, I am reminded
of the Creator's love of beauty. I often wonder what the Garden of
Eden must have looked like. The trees were laden with fruit that was
tasteful and vibrant in color; the whole earth was delightfully arranged
with fragrant flowers of every variety and hue, and trees cloaked in
luxuriant leaves. The most beautiful thing to imagine for me is how,
before sin entered the earth, this garden never knew death. To us, it
is a passing theme to watch the leaves of the trees die and fall to the
ground. But just like our Savior's love for us, the natural beauty of the
new earth will never die. How beautiful it is to know that our Father's
love for us is just as enduring as the never-fading trees and flowers of
Heaven! I know I want to be in Heaven with my Savior. Don't you?

~ Sierra Buhler

Exquisite Beauty

And we know that all things work together for good to them that love God... - Romans 8:28 KJV

The scenery outside my window is beautiful this morning. Fall has come and the leaves on our trees are fiery red intermixed with gold and orange. The sun still shines brightly, but the breeze has a hint of ice on its breath. As the wind blows through the leaves, making them ripple and spin, my mind turns to God. This lovely scene, believe it or not, is the result of sin. Sin brings death, but God painted the dying leaves with fantastic color to assure us of His pledge to make all things work together for good.

In the home that God prepared for our first parents there was no sin, and therefore no death. It's hard to imagine what it would be like with no sin, because this world has lived in sin for longer than we can remember. For the first couple, however, sin was not a part of their life—until they chose to disobey God. "As they witnessed in drooping flower and falling leaf the first signs of decay, Adam and his companion mourned more deeply than men now mourn over their dead. The death of the frail, delicate flowers was indeed a cause of sorrow; but when the goodly trees cast off their leaves, the scene brought vividly to mind the stern fact that death is the portion of every living thing" (*Patriarchs and Prophets*, pg. 62). Just as the leaves fell from the trees, so all of the people in the world would have to die because of their sin. But God loved us too much to let us perish. He decided to let His only Son come down and die for our sins, so we could regain eternity. Now as we see the falling leaves, instead of thinking of the fact that we will all have to die, we can let their exquisite beauty remind us that even though sin brings death, God has made a way of escape.

~ Bethany Corrigan

Transformation

*But Jesus looked at them and said to them, "With men this is
impossible, but with God all things are possible."*
- Matthew 19:26 NKJV

Not good enough—this was the essence of my life. I was always
thinking that I was too ugly, too dumb, too fat, and never good enough.
Everything pointed to this one phrase—never good enough. I would try
my best and end up falling, not wanting to get back up. As I went on in
life, the thought became more and more prominent. I spent time with
God and people who thought that I was doing well, but when I was
alone, all I could think of were the shortcomings in my life. I pleaded
with God to help me, but I could not stop thinking about how I was
failing.

One day it all came together. I was in PE class and was trying
my hardest to get to the front of the class. I was almost there when
it struck me: I always try my hardest only to fall short of what I think I
need to do. I never tried to do what was pleasing to God; I just wanted
to be good enough for myself so that people could be proud of me.

God wants us to do our best—with Him guiding our steps. No
matter how hard we strive to be good enough, we will always fall
short; but if we accept God's love into our lives, we will not have to
worry about being good enough. Sometimes our eyes focus on the
shortcomings, and we lose sight of the things God has in store for us.
I need to let God have my whole life. I need to realize that the Lord
loves me the way that I am, and give Him permission to work in my
life. That is the only thing I can do to be the one God wants me to be.
Once you surrender your shortcomings to Him, He can and will start to
transform you. Will you accept His wonderful grace?

~ Raina Walker

Tea

Beware of false prophets, which come to you in sheep's clothing, but inwardly they are ravening wolves. - Matthew 7:15 KJV

I stared at the disaster in front of me. My entire collection of loose leaf tea lay on my table in mass confusion. I felt like crying. I had spent so many hours organizing, dividing, and categorizing my tea. All my work had gone to waste. My loose leaf tea was kept in clear, unlabeled Zip-loc® bags, because they were all kept in their own spot. I only used one at a time, except for on rare occasions when I mixed and matched to attain certain healing attributes. Therefore, I didn't need to label them. Somehow my miscellaneous bags had gotten mixed up, and they now lay in unstructured confusion. The dried herbs and leaves all looked the same to the untrained eye. For the amateur it would be very hard to identify which tea was which; and at this point, I was an amateur. There was only one way to really tell what kind of tea lay inside each Zip-loc® bag. Brew it.

Slowly and painstakingly, I went through each kind of tea and brewed myself a cup, drinking then labeling. It was slow and monotonous; however, it needed to be done. By the end of the day, I had successfully rehydrated myself and returned my stash to a neat, clean arrangement.

We are all tea bags. People may look one way on the outside, yet we all hold a different flavor within us. Our character is our specific flavor or variety. We may never know the true character of those around us until the trials come, and we get brewed in the hot water of life. Each and every day we can ask our Heavenly Father to send us trials to help purify our character and strengthen our relationship with Him.

~ Mason Neil

Void

*Now the God of hope fill you with all joy and peace in believing, that
ye may abound in hope, through the power of the Holy Ghost.*
- Romans 15:13 KJV

A soft tear rolled down my cheek as I realized my desperate
situation. I felt so alone, so cold, so helpless. My one and only friend
had moved away, my dog had died, and I was left with nobody to
talk to. First, I had run to music to fill the gap left inside me, but the
emptiness was still there. I tried books, a desperate attempt at getting
out of the world I had grown to hate. I started with biographies or
memoirs, but slowly I was drawn into fictional books, depicting sorcery
and witchcraft. The only result from my desperate attempts was a
growing pit inside me.

I would see people at church talk about "surrendering" to God.
They seemed to be so happy when they talked about it. *Weird*, I
thought, *how could giving up to God make you happy?* They seemed
so pleased to let God control everything in their lives. I wasn't too
sure about totally turning over my life to Him. What about all the
crutches I had learned to love? I knew I would have to give them up if
I surrendered to God. Finally I got so frustrated with being seemingly
the only unhappy person around, that I gave in. Right then and there I
fell on my knees and surrendered everything to God.

That day I experienced a true joy that only God could give me. I
wouldn't give it up for anything else. In our lives we face loneliness,
hardship, and depression; however, God has promised to carry the
load for us. As He has done for me, won't you let Him fill the void in
your heart, too?

~ Mason Neil

Perfect Peace

Trust in the Lord with all thine heart; and lean not unto thine own understanding. In all thy ways acknowledge Him, and He shall direct thy paths. - Proverbs 3:5–6 KJV

My family and I were tramping through the woods behind our house one afternoon, when suddenly something crashed off the path right beside us. Jumping, I looked around just in time to see a bear cub scramble up a nearby tree. My first thought was to run, but Dad and Mom whispered to move slowly and to look for the mother. A crash just behind us revealed a second cub shinnying up another tree to safety. Because I knew that mother bears could be quite aggressive if they think their cubs are in danger, my heart raced and I felt fear rising up into my throat. Where, oh where, is their mother? Just then my eyes fell on mama bear, who was standing on a slope below and to the left of where we were. She made no move toward us, but calmly stared in our direction.

"Let's go," I said. As we continued moving down the path, I wished my family would move faster. Why did we have to stay near the bears any longer? Instead of being afraid, they were excited about the tiny cubs and wished they could have reached out and touched their soft fur as they climbed the trees.

Because I wasn't big enough to keep myself safe, I was afraid. If I had put my trust in God, I would have been able to enjoy those precious little cubs and their beautiful, strong mother. Instead, I forgot that God was directing my paths, and that He had promised to keep me safe.

Since then, I've come to realize that there are many situations that I'm too "small" to handle. As I learn to acknowledge God in all of my ways, my trust in Him grows, and I experience the perfect peace He has promised.

~ Bethany Corrigan

Have Faith

Do not let your hearts be troubled. You believe in God; believe also in
me. - John 14:1 NIV

Our faith influences whether we live or die. Let me explain. One
day when I was about twelve, I was out in my backyard on the banks
of our creek where blackberry vines grew. It was my job to cut them
down, and I was using an electric hedge trimmer with very sharp
blades that cut through the vines effortlessly. While I was working, I
went to move the cord and accidentally cut my thumb. I didn't notice
that anything unusual had happened until I glanced down, and,
surprised, saw a slit in my thick leather glove. Ripping off my glove,
I saw the blood gushing out of my thumb; it was then that I began to
panic. As fast as I could go, I ran inside, and my dad calmly sat me on
our kitchen counter. As I sat there, it finally hit me what had happened,
and I began to cry and fainted. My dad cleaned my wound and
bandaged it with his first-aid tape and gauze. Later my dad gave me
some water to drink and tried to get my mind off my pain. When I felt
scared, he patiently comforted me until I realized that I was all right,
and my panic ceased.

This reminds me of a story my teacher told me about a man who
was in the Vietnam War. Having gotten shot in the arm, the man was
sure that he would die. "I'm going to die!" the man moaned to his
friend. The friend tried to convince him that it was only a small bullet
wound and there was no chance that he would die. Yet only a short
time later, the terrified man died. He believed he was going to die, and
he did. I thought, *What if I had overreacted like that man did?* Our faith
plays a huge influence in the outcome of our lives. My sliced thumb,
the soldier's gunshot wound, or your acceptance of Christ's ability to
heal you from the wounds of sin—can make all the difference in the
world. When Jesus healed people, He often said to them, "Your faith
has made you well." If we have faith in Jesus, He will heal our wounds.

~ Elizabeth King

Pepper Spray

For now we see through a glass, darkly; but then face to face: now I know in part; but then shall I know even as also I am known.
- 1 Corinthians 13:12 KJV

I laced my hiking boots and threw on my backpack. Like a flash, I was outside the chalet to where my parents and sister were waiting. "Come on, we need to go or we'll be late for the bus!" my dad said. We sped down the trail towards civilization, not heeding the nature around us. About an hour later, we came to a sign that read: Bus Pick-Up—5 Miles. "Ok, I have a plan. I'll go ahead and catch the bus so I can pick up the car; you guys take your time. We will meet back at the head of the trail. But first, I need to show you how to use the pepper spray," my dad added as he looked at me. Being the only man left, the duty of holding the pepper spray fell on me. He gingerly pulled the can out of his backpack and held it up for me to see. "Just point it in the direction of the bear and pull this little trigger-looking thing..." His voice trailed off as I felt a horrendous burning sensation. The spray hadn't been pointed at me, but the wind had. As the vapor entered the air, it drifted my direction, coating my face.

"Aaaah! It burns!" I yelled.
"Oh no! Did I get it in your eyes? But there's no time to lose. I must be off now."

With that last sentence, my dad ran down the trail in the direction of the bus pick-up spot. I was now laying on the ground, moaning softly to myself. My mom knelt over me, gently splashing water over my face. After thirty minutes, I regained my mental state and began stumbling down the trail, squinting to see what lay ahead. The rest of the day there was a subtle burning sensation across my entire face.

Sometimes in life, we find ourselves blinded. Our sight may be dimmed by discouragement, stress, or anxiety. We may feel that all is lost and our situation is hopeless. However, there is hope. We have a heavenly Father who is in control of everything and can see our situation clearly. Let us trust in Him and let Him guide us on our path.

~ Mason Neil

Cut the Coat-tail

*For He saith, I have heard thee in a time accepted, and in the day of
salvation have I succoured thee: behold, now is the accepted time;
behold, now is the day of salvation. - 2 Corinthians 6:2 KJV*

A man once told me a story about the time he was in school. He
was in college, being trained in the art of filmmaking. As the teacher
was lecturing, he said something that made him stop and think. "It will
only take one of you in this room to make it big; the rest of you will
ride in to the big time on his coat-tail." This reminds me a little bird that
follows herds of cattle to eat the bugs that follow them; so we call it
the cow bird. This bird raises its young different than most. In order to
follow the herd wherever it decides to go, it will find a nest of another
bird and lay her egg in that nest for the other bird to incubate, feed,
nurture, and raise. Since raising young is one of the most important
parts of a creature's life, it seems strange that this bird would leave its
young with another bird to take care of at its extreme inconvenience.

The coat-tail has to be cut. We can't ride into heaven on someone
else's coat-tail or experience. Nor can we leave the most important
thing we possess—our relationship with the Lord—for anyone else
to feed, nurture, and grow. You aren't saved just because you work
with this really nice person, and they happen to be a Christian. Or
just because your brother-in-law's cousin's uncle's friend's nephew
twice removed is a Christian person and you go over to his house
on weekends to work on the car together, doesn't make you saved.
Even if you go to church on the right day; that doesn't make you
saved either. Paul says to "work out your own salvation with fear
and trembling" (Philippians 2:12). It is up to me to take the time each
morning to cultivate that relationship with Christ—nobody else can do
it for me.

~ Nolan Knuppel

God's Antibiotics

… we have redemption through His blood, even the forgiveness of sins… - Colossians 1:14 KJV

My finger bled profusely. As the blood poured out, I sought help and a rag to apply pressure. Fortunately, although the hatchet I had been using was sharp and sunk cleanly to the bone, it went no further. Unfortunately, we were camping in the wilderness, far away from any medical facilities. I would have to wait for a couple of days to see the doctor. Until then, I taped the cut to at least diminish the rapidity of my blood loss.

More than a week after the incident, I was back at the dorm with the finger bandaged, hoping for a quick recovery. I looked down and noticed the swollen bulge of my finger and hand. Something wasn't right. I showed some of the deans and they promptly took me to the hospital. Upon arrival, the nurses and doctor immediately identified my problem as a serious infection stretching from my fingertip to my shoulder, close enough to my heart to cause worry. If something wasn't done quickly, I could go into cardiac arrest or come down with a deadly disease called gangrene. To zap the infection, the doctor inserted an IV needle and started to pump intravenous antibiotics into my system. It wasn't an easy or short process. Every six hours, night or day, I had to drive 30 minutes to the hospital to receive my cleansing dose. After five days of treatment, the antibiotic had purified my system of the nasty infection.

When we swing the hatchet of life, we often cut ourselves and become infected with sin. Although we can cause this infection, we cannot cure it. The only way to get rid of this infection is by running to Jesus, our heavenly Doctor, and receiving a dose of His "antibiotics." If we surrender everything and exercise complete trust in Him, He will cover our sins with His blood of forgiveness and love.

~ Christian Welch

Sacrifice of Love

"Yet not as I will, but as You will." - Matthew 26:39b NIV

Every summer my family used to go on a trip to the Oregon coast. I always looked forward to flying my kite, playing at the beach, and eating ice cream. One year my older sister, my younger brother, and I decided to secretly save all the money we could for the trip. We found a loose baseboard by our door, and decided that that's where we would stash our cash. Eventually we saved up around three hundred dollars. We were so excited to show our mom, and immediately we started planning our trip.

Aspen, our golden retriever, was my dad's pride and joy. To us though, she was very obnoxious. She had the bad habit of chasing cars. We were always afraid she would get hurt. A few days later, we came home from town only to find one of our dogs missing and a note in our mailbox saying that she had been hit by a car. Our other dog, Lady, led us right to the side of the road where Aspen lay in the grass whining and moaning. My mom told us that we had a choice: either to go on our trip and let the dog be put down, or stay and take Aspen to the vet. Taking her to the vet would cost a lot of money, and we weren't sure she would live even if we did. We were not so hard-hearted that we would go away and leave her to die! Dad loved that dog. So we took her to the vet and found that with surgery—which would use all of our money for the trip—she could walk again. It was a real sacrifice for the three of us children to give up the trip that we had saved up for and that meant so much to us, but we did it because we loved our dad and his dog.

Doing the right thing is not always easy. Even Jesus, in Gethsemane, fell with His face to the ground and prayed, "My Father, if it is possible, may this cup be taken from me..." (Matthew 26:39 NIV). He could have left us to die, but He made the ultimate sacrifice of love.

~ Sarah Wahlman

Skin Attack

If you then, being evil, know how to give good gifts to your children, how much more will your Father who is in heaven give good things to those who ask Him! - Matthew 7:11 NKJV

"Hey Morgan, Demon is out of the cage!" my sister called to me from the next room. When the implications of her words sank in, I was suddenly alarmed.

Quickly, I dashed around the corner and screeched, "Megan, run!" Megan was barefoot, and Demon, my gerbil, was on the loose. Normally, that wouldn't have been a problem because all my gerbils were very friendly. But Demon, the female, was a different story. After I had kept her for three weeks, something changed. She was pregnant, but more than that, she became evil. Any time skin-like things were in her vicinity, she would bite them tenaciously. When she spotted Megan's bare feet, Demon scampered forward to attack. Fortunately, Megan was able to dart away just in time.

I love all my pets, and in return they love me back. But I couldn't figure out Demon. I gave her everything! All the food, warmth, and clean bedding she could want weren't enough for her. I tried to change Demon's attitude, but it didn't work. Finally, I was forced to let her brave the elements alone in the woods, where she could use her survival skills to stay alive.

In the same way that I cared for Demon, God has provided everything that we need in life. But God cares so much more for us than I ever did for Demon. So many times, we bite the hand that feeds us. We desire the things that hurt us, and we walk away from God. But even before we were born, God knew all the hurtful things we would do. That is why He gave us His only Son, Jesus, to take away our sins. He risked everything, even though we don't deserve it, to make sure we have every opportunity to turn our lives around. He loves us, but He needs us to love Him back. Until then, God will be patiently waiting to receive us home with open arms.

~ Morgan Metcalf

Spiritual Lizards

Beloved, think it not strange concerning the fiery trial among you,
which cometh upon you to prove you… - 1 Peter 4:12 ASV

"No, you can't hold it! You will just drop it."

"Please!" I begged. "I will hold it real tight!"

"Okay!" my siblings finally agreed. My sister reached over and carefully laid a lizard in my trembling hands. I squealed, instantly pulling my hands away, causing the lizard to dart off to safety.

"Aileen," my brother and sisters complained, "don't ask to hold things if you don't even want to!" The trouble was, I did want to! Well, sort of…

My family lived in central California, home to many lizards and other small reptiles. My siblings delighted in chasing, catching, and holding these slimy creatures, but I simply couldn't handle it. I wanted to enjoy these things like they did, but in my three-year-old mind they were horrible. Every time I tried to hold them, the same thing happened, and my siblings soon tired of allowing me to try.

I often drop my spiritual lizards—God's gifts to me. I pray, "Please, Jesus, help my faith to grow. I want to trust You with my whole heart." In answer to my prayer, He allows me to have trials and temptations. I jump away, crying, "No, Jesus, I just want my faith to grow."

"Yes," He patiently answers, "this is the only way. It is just what you need! Trust me to help you through it and your faith will grow." He could tell me how foolish it is to ask for something I don't really want; but instead He simply continues to work with me, helping me see my weakness and drawing nearer to Him for strength.

~ Aileen Corrigan

His Staff Kids

… I say unto you, there is joy in the presence of the angels of God over one sinner that repenteth. - Luke 15:10 KJV

I'm a staff kid here at Fountainview Academy. This brings some challenges, but it is also filled with lots of joys. Even though I am not a staff member, my family's plans, hopes, and dreams are centered in our ministry at the school. We have the opportunity to make a difference in the lives of the students who live here. It is so fulfilling to see a student whom I have been praying for come to know Christ, or to see that a struggling one has overcome. My heart thrills to see the change He brings to their lives, and I know it thrills His heart too.

Weeks of planning and praying before the students come give way to months of active duty, where their exuberant attitudes carry us through to the end of the year. My work is not noteworthy. I may need to help answer phones or clean guest rooms or pull weeds in the carrot fields; but I know that each task is part of the great work that happens here. I am also given opportunities to encourage others to press towards the mark. As we work with God for the salvation of these precious souls, I can see a little bit of the joy one soul's salvation brings to our Father.

All of those who are working together with God are His staff kids. God and the angels could save all the souls in the world by themselves, but they enlist our help too. There are always humble tasks needing to be done. People need to be listened to, prayed for, and cared about. They need to know how God changed us and that He can change them too. If we choose to be the biggest help that we can be—doing all in our power for His work—the work will go on quickly, and we will share in the joy of seeing souls won for His kingdom.

~ Bethany Corrigan

Protected

I will say of the Lord, He is my refuge and my fortress: my God; in Him will I trust. - Psalm 91:3 KJV

I flew up the swinging rope ladder, my eyes set on my destination twenty-five feet above the ground. When I reached the top, I rested and looked down. It was a long way to fall. My limbs began to shake as I inched my way out onto one of the branches growing out over the lawn. My dad had built my sister and I a tree house when we first moved to Maine, and for the first couple of years of my life there, it was my favorite place on planet Earth.

As I left the safety of the main structure, adrenaline began to flow through my veins. My dad had also built a zip-line, and it was my second favorite place on Earth. It left the tree at an altitude of about thirty feet and traversed across our lawn to a tall oak eighty feet away. I grabbed the handle that was connected to the cable that held my life. It always gave me a thrill. Without thinking, as is typical of my nature, I jumped. The thrill was all I had hoped it to be. In fact it was much more. At first I felt like I was flying, but I quickly realized that what I was experiencing was more like falling. I looked at my hands. My eyes immediately took on the appearance of extra-large pizzas. The handle was not there. I was free falling. At first I tried to imitate a flying squirrel, but I was not designed in quite the same way. Before I could think any further, I landed with a soft thud on the ground. I prepared to feel a piercing pain somewhere in my legs or arms—I had landed on my hands and knees as if I was praying. Slowly I stood up. No pain at all! I brushed myself off and tried again, this time successfully.

The way I acted that day was slightly foolish. But despite my impulsive actions, God still protected me. I did not deserve His mercy or care, yet He was still looking out for me. Aren't you glad you have a Father watching over you?

~ Mason Neil

Flying in Formation

Neither pray I for these alone, but for them also which shall believe on me through their word; that they all may be one; as Thou, Father, art in me, and I in Thee, that they also may be one in Us: that the world may believe that Thou hast sent me. - John 17:20–21 KJV

Scientists discovered why geese fly in a V formation. When the lead goose flaps its wings, it creates lift for the one directly behind it. So by flying in a flock, geese have a 71% greater flying range than if they were each to fly alone. When one gets tired of the full drag at the front, it circulates to the back. It is also thought that the geese in the back honk to give support to the ones in the front. Furthermore, if a goose gets sick or is wounded by a gun shot, two other geese will drop out to stay with it until it gets better and is able to fly, or until it is dead. Then they will set out on their own, or join another formation in order to catch up to their original group.

In the days of the early church, the members made it a practice to take care of their own. "Neither was there any among them that lacked: for as many as were possessors of lands or houses sold them, and brought the prices of the things that were sold, and laid them down at the apostles' feet: and distribution was made unto every man according as he had need" (Acts 4:34–35 KJV).

As members of the church and as Christians on our journey together, do we recognize when leaders are getting tired and help where we can to create lift for fellow members of our flock? When we honk, is it encouraging to the ones in the front? When one drops out because they are wounded, ill, or experiencing a loss of spirituality, are we there for help and support? How would people (newcomers especially) respond to a church like that?

~ Nolan Knuppel

William

… ye are all one in Christ Jesus. - Galatians 3:28 KJV

I don't quite remember the first time I met him. However, I do remember my thoughts. *You're telling me I have to take care of him? Oh, and better yet, we're related?* There he stood. Short, blonde haired, with blue wire-framed glasses that were obviously too big for his head. His blank eyes gazed at me as he absentmindedly chewed on his thumb. His expression seemed to convey a message of apathy and boredom. His name was William, and he had Down syndrome.

I decided to try to bond with him first. I began with a simple conversation starter. "William, do you like to play baseball?" All I got for a reply was a blank stare. "Do you want to read a book?" Still nothing. There's one thing I hate more than someone talking too much, and that is someone not talking to me at all. After two more failed attempts I decided to go to the one who knew it all: his mom.

I discovered that William and I shared a common interest: C.S. Lewis's The Chronicles of Narnia. Here goes conversation attempt number five. "William, do you like Narnia?" Immediately a gear turned. "Narnia? I LOVE Narnia! We play Narnia? Here, you be Susan, I be Lucy." Before I knew it, I was fighting off the "bad guys" while "Lucy," as he insisted on being called, was behind me healing the wounded. It was the best play date ever.

I learned that day that my first impressions can be very wrong. Since then, William and I have grown closer and closer. In fact, the last two summers we have spent a week together at our local Adventist summer camp. Satan uses prejudice and judgmental thoughts as a way to hinder the working of the Holy Spirit. If we have hard feelings or misguided judgments about someone God may be using to deliver an important message to us, it can hinder our ability to listen to and esteem the messenger. Each and every day I have to surrender my feelings to God so that I can hear His will for my life. You'll never know what kind of friends you'll make along the way.

~ Mason Neil

285

Maggot Cookies

Know ye not that a little leaven leaveneth the whole lump?
- 1 Corinthians 5:6 KJV

Last year, I discovered that my friends Julie and Moriah shared my appreciation for raw cookie dough. Because we couldn't buy enough dough to last us more than a day, we pooled our money together and bought massive amounts of baking supplies. Every few days, we would get together and mix up a bowl full of chocolate-chip goodness. It quickly became our tradition. But finally, we used up all of our flour, and our cookie dough parties came to an end. Then one day, as Moriah was rummaging through some old cupboards, she found a bag of flour. She ran to get Julie, and together they mixed up a bowl of cookie dough. But as they ate their treat, they noticed that something didn't quite taste right. In fact, it almost seemed to be *wiggling*. Suddenly, it dawned on them: the dough was crawling with maggots!

Later that day, Moriah came by my room to see if I wanted the cookie dough she'd made. I was wary of her offer; she doesn't usually part with her food. Finally, she explained her generosity by saying, "Oh, I almost forgot to tell you! The flour we used had maggots in it. But there are only a few, and other than that, the cookie dough tastes pretty good! Here, you want to try some?" She joked.

Obviously, I refused her not-so-magnanimous offer. Her logic was clearly flawed; maggots do not cease to be maggots when camouflaged with sugar and chocolate.

But often, I find myself giving in to the same faulty reasoning. Satan knows that if he mixes a little bit of sin into something that is otherwise good, we'll all too often excuse the wrong. I often try to justify my actions because something is "mostly good." But just as the tiny maggots ruined the whole bowl of cookie dough, a seemingly harmless sin can corrupt my entire life.

~ Saraiah Turnbull

The Scavenger Hunt

*Ask, and it shall be given you; seek, and ye shall find; knock, and it
shall be opened unto you - Matthew 7:7 KJV*

Thanksgiving is a special time for my family. Every year we go on a
vacation to the ski resort at Whistler. We often have family friends join
us. We bake, walk, swim, rest and think about what we are thankful
for. After finishing Thanksgiving supper, my mom sets up a game.
When we were little, it was always a variation of hide-and-seek around
the hotel. As we have gotten older, the game has slowly changed into
a scavenger hunt around the ski village.

At the beginning of the game, we split into two groups so that it is
easier to navigate around town. My mom gives each team a list, and
we have to work together to decode the clues or the riddles. While
we walk through town, we pay close attention to details because, if
we don't, we might miss what we are looking for. We take pictures,
collect brochures, locate maps and try to find everything on our list
by a certain time. Everything on our list is very important. Depending
on the clue, a deeper understanding of the town may be needed.
The clue may also be something that stands alone, and no previous
understanding of it is necessary.

Bible study is kind of like our Thanksgiving scavenger hunts. The
Bible itself is like the town; the verses are like clues for life; and our
teammates are the people we study with. We go through the Bible
searching out the answers to the clues. We go over and over it with
our teammates trying to find a deeper meaning. Eventually, after
searching, we find the answers to our questions.

I encourage you today to search the Bible. Ask questions and find
answers. Look through it with others, and contemplate the deeper
thoughts and understanding that inspired it. Then you can be the
winner of your lifelong scavenger hunt.

~ Rebecca Hall

Lasting the Winter

Therefore, my beloved brethren, be steadfast, immovable, always abounding in the work of the Lord, knowing that your labor is not in vain in the Lord. - 1 Corinthians 15:58 NKJV

It's a sunny summer day, and everything seems alive. The grass is green, the birds are happily chirping away, and the trees are laced in a beautiful green covering of leaves. The landscape seems to be a perfect picture of health and vibrancy. But then winter's freezing grasp takes control, establishing a reign of utter frigidity. Nature is an entirely different place. Long days shorten, the air is frosty and cold, and green fades to brown. But even amidst the quiet lethargy of winter, the stately conifers live on.

When there's abundant water, and there's sun, and everything is easy, almost everything is healthy and green. The deciduous and coniferous trees live side by side, both beautiful in their adorning. But when things turn bad, one loses its leaves and is left a ghostly skeleton, while the other continues to flourish. The life of the deciduous tree is circumstantial, but the life of the conifer is steadfast and unmovable.

Spiritual life is very similar. We frequently experience the contrast between warm, sunny bliss, and frigid deadly winter that threatens to stifle our heavenly joy. When things turn bad, and we act unchristian, it's tempting to excuse our bad behaviour by saying, "That was out of character for me. I'm not normally like that." But that makes us like deciduous trees—only flourishing when life is easy. God needs someone He can depend on: a steadfast, immovable Christian. So what would you be: A wilting skeleton of a tree that's trying to stand on its own, or a tall, stately conifer standing strong in the nourishment of the Lord?

~ Michael Jensen

Appearances

… man looketh on the outward appearance, but the Lord looketh on the heart. - 1 Samuel 16:7 KJV

I was on the plane sitting between two men; one was a well-dressed young businessman reading a book. The other was an overweight bald man with tattoos and was playing video games. I struck up a conversation with the businessman, but after about 20 minutes of the flight, he put on his headphones and went to sleep. I kept getting the impression that I should talk to the bald man—but I didn't want to! Finally, I worked up the courage to ask him where he was travelling, and our conversation went from there. When he found out I was an Adventist, he asked me what we believed about the Sabbath. I explained to him from the Bible why we worship on Saturday. He seemed interested, and we talked about the Bible. As we were landing, I got the strong impression to ask him if I could pray with him, but I refused the impulse until it was too late.

I wonder what would have happened if I had begun talking to him earlier. Maybe I could have had more influence; but instead of obeying the Holy Spirit, I put it off because of the way he looked.

One day my friend Eddy came from the shop with his hands covered in black grease, and he asked me to shake his hand. I told him to go wash his hands first. How many times have you done that to someone? You see someone who you know you should help, but you want them to go clean up first because you can't talk to someone who's that "dirty." Maybe it will rub off on you!

Christ calls us to reach people where they are; but I wouldn't touch Eddy because he was dirty, and I wouldn't talk to the man on the plane because he looked scary. But sometimes, you have to get your hands dirty to make someone else's clean. In order to help someone off the ground, you must first bend down to pick them up.

~ Moriah Mays

Carry the Light

No man, when he hath lighted a candle, putteth it in a secret place, neither under a bushel, but on a candlestick, that they which come in may see the light. - Luke 11:33 KJV

For two and a half years, I played percussion in an academy band. True to the story of my life, I was the only girl with four guys. The guys and I got along fine, except for one. It wasn't that we were at odds with each other, but I could never be around him because of his behavior. He was constantly cracking crude jokes, talking about his latest atrocity, and generally stalking any girl that was still breathing. The other guys generally ignored him or laughed, but I couldn't stand by and let him talk that way. I tried several different methods, but none of them worked. Finally, I found that if I was pleasant and kind, his manner towards me improved a little. He wanted attention, and the best method he had found to get it was to be crude, lewd, and to make suggestive comments. Since I had changed him a little, I didn't go any further into helping him. That year I quit band, and I didn't ever see him again. When I heard later that he had been kicked out of the academy, I first thought, "Good riddance," but then it hit me: Where would he go now? Who would give him the attention he needed? I had given him enough to stop his bad behavior, but what he really needed was to know about a God who loved him. Since the entire band was Christian, I never thought that I should be witnessing to him too. I had passed him by without giving him something substantial to live by.

Everyone who professes Christianity desires to have Jesus return in the second coming. But before He can come, every single person has to have made the decision between God or Satan. If nobody ever gives them the message, then how long will we wait? Jesus is waiting for you and I to share what we know. We shouldn't keep it for ourselves, but instead we should share it with everyone. It may be their last chance to receive the seeds of truth.

My chance to help that guy is gone, and now all I can do is pray that someone else shows him the Father's love. So many others are out there now—searching too. Will you tell them?

~ Morgan Metcalf

Home in a Bunker

For our citizenship is in heaven… - Philippians 3:20 NKJV

With a bang, jolt, and screech, the wheels hit the ground. We had landed in Guam. As the engines screamed, pulling us to a stop, I eagerly stared out the window at my new home. I watched old houses and palm trees stop whisking past as we slowed to a stop at the small terminal. Coming out of security a few minutes later, we were greeted with plumeria leis by the other missionaries, then driven to our new house. It looked like a bunker: it was a one story, cement block, flat-roofed rectangle. Every wall, including the interior shower walls, was cement block. "It is so typhoons don't blow it away," we were told. This "bunker" was now my home.

Growing up as a missionary kid, there are two questions I have learned to dread: "Where is home?" and "Where are you from?" *Where is home* seems to be the easier question to answer. "My family is living in Kentucky, though we are moving to California. I currently go to school in British Columbia." There. Answered. *Where are you from* seems to be much harder to answer, though. *Where am I from?* Washington, where I was born and where my grandparents live? Guam? Asia feels like home. Kentucky? It's the last place I went "home" to. California, where my parents are moving to, but somewhere I've never been? *Where am I from? Where is home?*

I have struggled with this ever since going overseas, and it still can bother me. I want a place I can call home. Hebrews 11:16 says, "But now they desire a better *country*, that is, an heavenly: wherefore God is not ashamed to be called their God: for He hath prepared for them a city" (KJV, emphasis supplied). My home isn't Washington, it isn't Guam, it isn't Kentucky, and it isn't even California; my home is a Heavenly City, the New Jerusalem.

~ Katie Sloop

Garbage Day

... the blood of Jesus Christ His Son cleanses us from all sin.
- 1 John 1:7 NKJV

In Korea, there are many apartment buildings. They each have a rule that residents only get to take the garbage out once a week. My family lives in one of these apartment buildings. Since my mom teaches many students at home, we always get piles of garbage from the goodies we buy for them. By the end of the week, there will be plastic bottles, glass shards, and wadded up paper all over the place in our garage. Sometimes it even looks just like a junk yard! Our family always gets busy when Tuesday morning (garbage day) rolls around. We bring loads of garbage from the garage and take it to the place where it is collected. I always feel happy when the garbage is gone because our home is clean once again. But, there is also a time when I feel very uncomfortable. When we bring the trash out too late, the garbage officer will make us take it all back home. When this occurs, we have to wait till the next week, which causes the piles of garbage to grow even larger.

Through this experience, I realized a blessing I have to be thankful for. All the bad things that I have in my mind, all the garbage that I have in my heart, all the sins that I have committed, all this junk, piles up and fills my mind. No one else would want to clean it and take all the junk away for me if I wanted to get rid of it. But Jesus took away all my sins, guilt, and all the other junk that has collected. Romans 6:23 says that "the wages of sin is death." Therefore, since I am a sinner, my penalty is death; but through Jesus' death for me, my sin is taken away and I become clean and pure. However, there will be a time when Jesus can't take away my junk. Just like the garbage officer, Jesus will tell me that He can't take my garbage away because the time of cleansing is over. Right now is the time Jesus is able to remove all the sin that I bring to Him. He wants to take your garbage away too. Won't you let Him take it before it's too late?

~ Hannah Lee

The Faithful Baker

Many are the afflictions of the righteous: but the Lord delivereth him out of them all. - Psalm 34:19 KJV

In an old country town, just outside Portugal's capital, where the bronze-orange soil stains everything red and the almond trees and cacti line the edges of the arid sheep fields, there lived a man named Manuel with his wife Theresa. They had four children—my grandma was one of them. Manuel was the trusty town baker, and everyone loved his delicious bread.

During the 1940's, Portugal was still a strict Roman Catholic country, and it was unheard of to keep any other day besides Sunday. So when Manuel became a Sabbath keeper, the townspeople mocked his courageous decision, and he quickly lost all of his customers. Finances became very strained, and soon all the cupboards were empty. One particular evening, with stomachs growling and no food on their plates, Manuel's family knelt at the table while Manuel bowed his weary head in a simple and fervent prayer: "*Lord, only You can solve this problem. I need food for my children. You can make bread out of stones if You want!*" As soon as the "amen" was spoken, there was a knock at the door. To Manuel's surprise, there stood two highway construction workers who asked if he owned the mound of rocks and boulders on the adjacent plot of land. They wanted to buy them for construction projects. The hungry family had a lovely meal that evening. Truly, the Lord had given them bread from stones.

Some, after making a decision to follow God, are perplexed when trials and tribulations come. But of what use are decisions if they are only on the condition of good times? These testing times are to make us stronger and to prove our faithfulness and loyalty to God. Even in our "fiery furnace" experiences, the Lord promises to walk with us. He says: "The righteous cry, and the Lord heareth, and delivereth them out of all their troubles" (Psalm 34:17 KJV).

~ Esther Ferraz

No! It Isn't Dead!

Ye have not chosen me, but I have chosen you, and ordained you, that ye should go and bring forth fruit, and that your fruit should remain...
- John 15:16 KJV

"Katie, it's dead. Why are you watering it?" My brother's opinion definitely looked true. The baby peach tree I was watering had lost all three of its leaves and looked very pitiful. I didn't believe it was dead, though. What would you expect from a tree that had been put in a U-haul truck to travel from Washington to Kentucky, within weeks of being grafted? But since I saw something promising in it, I kept watering it, waiting for it to bud. As the days turned into weeks and the weeks into months, I got worried, but I still watered it every day. One day, when I went to water it, I found a bud! I ran yelling to find my dad.

"It's alive! It is actually going to make it, Daddy!" Although my baby peach tree hasn't produced any fruit yet, it is taller than I am and still growing.

While this peach tree is just a tree in my backyard, let's use it as an illustration. In our illustration, you and I are like the peach tree and God is the gardener. He sees potential in you and me, and chooses to graft us into His tree. He moves us to where He is and where we can grow best. Even though we don't show any signs of being thankful, of growing, or of even being alive, He faithfully waters us. Day after day, He watches us, until one day, His sacrifice is rewarded by a tiny green bud. When He runs to tell His Father, all of Heaven rejoices.

I really hope I haven't watered my peach tree in vain; I hope it decides to produce peaches. Like my tree, we too have the decision to either grow up in Christ and produce fruit for God, or to stay unfruitful. I don't want His watering to be in vain.

~ Katie Sloop

Harvest in the Depressing Dark

*… and they will see the Son of Man coming on the clouds of the sky
with power and great glory. And He will send forth His angels with
a great trumpet and they will gather together His elect from the four
winds, from one end of the sky to the other. - Matthew 24:30–31 NASB*

The cool, dark morning felt dead. As I walked to the barn to prepare
for carrot harvesting, I wished I had worn a warmer jacket. When I
arrived, we fired up the old, beat-up Czechoslovakian Zetor tractor
with the aid of an ether canister to ready her for harvest. This particular
tractor, riddled with problems, required a driver with enough patience
to endure its shifting struggles and odd-ball failures. I happened to be
this driver. After loading eight bins onto the wagon, I hopped in the cab
and set out on a bouncy journey to the fields.

The morning wore on, still inhabited by the cool, depressing
darkness. While harvesting, I sensed a rapid change in the luminosity
of the skies and looked to the east. Swiftly and without hesitation, the
sun appeared over the snowy hills and greeted our cold and lonely
carrot crew. Immediately, the temperatures warmed and inflicted a
positive change in the overall mood. At last, the darkness and cold of
the night were gone.

Ever since the fall of man, we've been stuck in seemingly perpetual
darkness. When Jesus came to this earth, He left us with the promise
of His second coming to bring His followers to an eternal home of light.
He asks us to prepare for harvest; a harvest not of produce, but of
souls who need Jesus. He is willing to make us ready for this task if
we let him pop the hood and perform maintenance on our fallen lives.
Satan will still throw failures and "shifting problems" at us; but Jesus,
our master mechanic, will help keep us on track. It may be dark, cold,
and dreary, and seem the world is against us; but we must press
forward and tell others of the promise that the Son is coming soon with
glory and light to release us from this dark, cold existence.

~ Christian Welch

My Father's Word

Every word of God is pure; He is a shield to those who put their trust in Him. - Proverbs 30:5 NKJV

"That's not true."
"Yes it is!"
"Oh yeah? Prove it."
"OK, then. My dad told me it was true, and I believe him."
(Silence)

When I was little, this is how arguments with other kids went. We would battle back and forth until someone pulled the "My dad said so" card. That phrase trumped all. Unless, that is, someone else didn't know my dad. Under those circumstances, they wouldn't believe what I said, and the argument would end in a tussle.

Because I loved and trusted my dad, I was willing to fight against the crowd. If I got hurt, it was worth it. I wore my bruises proudly because I had received them while fighting for what I believed in. Nothing else mattered because I had stood up for Dad.

As a Christian, I have another Dad. I trust His Word: the Bible. Every word written on its pages is the truth. Inconceivable concepts of science, physics, math, and love are written in it. Even though they are explained precisely, the concepts are so profound that my depleted mind hardly scratches the surface of their meanings. To help me understand, "… He, the Spirit of truth … will guide [me] into all the truth" (John 16:13 NIV). But like any school subject, I don't understand everything immediately. It takes time. But when I do, God's word will be a "lamp to my feet and a light to my path" (Psalms 119:105 NKJV).

Since God is my Father, I will stand for what He has told me in His Word. The going will not always be easy, and I anticipate getting multiple bruises, but I believe what He has said. No matter who I talk to or what I'm told, my Father's words are what ultimately sway my choices.

~ Morgan Metcalf

Scribbles

For if the willingness is there, the gift is acceptable according to what one has, not according to what one does not have.
- 2 Corinthians 8:12 NIV

When I was home this past break, my five-year-old brother wrote me a note and made me promise that I wouldn't read it until I was back at Fountainview. Of course I was curious to see what he said, but I honored his request to wait. Once I was back at school, I opened it at the very first chance I got. Standing by my desk, I reached down to pick up the worn envelope. Inside the small, Hot Wheels thank-you card were lopsided, heartfelt, baby letters that scrawled across the page this message of love: "Dear sarah. You are my faborit sisTer in the worlb. I love you. CaboT." Tears came to my eyes as I thought about the small child at home, intently laboring over this valued piece of paper to express his love for me. In a stranger's eyes, this note would probably be small and insignificant; but to me, it meant so much.

God sees me in the same way. When I share with others the blessings that God has given me, try in my feeble way to obey His will, or give my time to help someone else, these are not even a fraction of the infinite lessons that He has for me to learn. Although in His estimation my attempted acts of unselfishness are but a child's scribble on His page of love, it is my sincerity that makes them so valuable to Him.

Do you ever feel as though you are trying so hard to come up to God's expectations, but you keep falling short? Don't stop writing! Even though in your eyes your attempts may seem small and measly, in Jesus' eyes your sincerity means so much. All He wants is for you to be willing and sincere. Aren't you so glad that He loves our scribbles?

~ Sarah Miller

In The Open

Faithful are the wounds of a friend; but the kisses of an enemy are deceitful. - Proverbs 27:6 KJV

"Yes, Bryan!" I shouted as my brother and I finally convinced my friend to play airsoft. Our game would begin shortly as we had to suit up and load our guns. The three of us went over the rules one more time to make sure we understood them, and the game began. The teams were Bryan and I versus my brother Cam.

Cam had the advantage, not with experience, but with his gun (a fully automatic machine gun) compared to ours (a spring pistol and shotgun). As Bryan and I split off, I warned him of a few things: be quiet, stay low, and if possible, have cover nearby. We reached opposite sides of our playing field and shouted, "Ready!" Unfortunately, our first encounter with Cam was in the open and, as men say, we had to "retreat" for the time being with a few injuries. However, as Bryan and I were running along a road, we saw our target in the open. An opportunity to strike had arisen. We approached our target stealthily, like a hurricane on a forewarned town. He heard us coming and waited till we got close enough (since our guns are short range) and turned around and welcomed us with a hail of BB's. Jumping back, we planted our feet and held our ground, forcing him to run into a nearby shed. Shots were fired on both sides until eventually he charged us and the game ended. There were smiles and soreness on both sides.

When a BB hits, you have a sensational sting where the impact was. You also realize that you must get out of the way before more come. They can be, in a sense, reminders telling you that the closer you get, the more it will hurt. Satan, however, doesn't like to play fair. Instead of warning you like your friends would, he asks you to come closer. Once he knows that you're as close as you'll get, he lets a hail of BB's out on you, inflicting much more damage than you would have gotten from a friend. So, what will you do about it when a friend tries to correct you? Will you accept the correction, though it may be painful, or will you find out too late and learn the hard way?

~ Chris Donatelli

Dangerous Doggie

And all things, whatsoever ye shall ask in prayer, believing, ye shall receive. - Matthew 21:22 KJV

"Hey Josiah! Look at the dog. Isn't he so cute?"
"I dunno, man... He looks kinda mean."
"Yeah, your right, he does kinda have that—"

Suddenly the huge, fluffy golden retriever ran straight at us. His eyes were like windows into a wood stove with hot coals inside. His body flew forward, leaving fur balls suspended in the air behind him. Faster and faster he flew through the air until he looked unstoppable. He definitely had a one-track mind, and his eyes were locked on me. My friend and I turned and stared at each other in fright. "Let's pray!" I said. I shot up a quick prayer for protection. We both looked back. Our eyes met the dog's as he continued hurtling toward us. "Oh no! My eyes weren't closed and the prayer must not have worked!" I quickly prayed again, this time more earnestly. We slowly looked back, not knowing if we wanted to see what was waiting for us. To my surprise the dog was standing stock still, although still glaring at us. I didn't mind, as long as he stayed where he was. What a relief! After a prayer of thanksgiving, my friend and I continued around the block, canvasing each door we passed.

As our day of selling books came to a close, we decided to head back to our leader's van. When we rounded the bend, we stopped in disbelief. There in the van was the dog, slobbering all over my leader's face. My stomach lurched. I was not in the mood to peel a savage dog off my dead leader's body. However, when I looked closer I noticed the dog was being friendly. There had not only been an answer to prayer, but a complete character transformation.

Sometimes I don't believe God will listen to my prayer or answer it. However, by faith I can know that He has heard my prayer and will answer it. The answer may not be what I expect or want, but I can trust that God knows what's best for me.

~ Mason Neil

"Why Did You Do It Three Times?"

But God shows His love for us in that while we were still sinners,
Christ died for us. - Romans 5:8 ESV

A friend of mine once told the story of a young man who was showing off his driving skills. "Watch this, Mom—I can drive a standard with my legs crossed!" He drove off with his mother in the passenger seat. Everything went well until he came to a stoplight at the top of a hill, with a car already stopped in front of him. He pressed down the clutch with one foot, and reached for the brake with the other—but stepped on the gas instead. When his car slammed into the rear end of the car in front of him, he quickly lifted his foot off the pedal and stomped on… the gas again! It took several tries before he managed to stop the car. He got out and sheepishly approached the lady driving the other vehicle. "I'm really sorry, Ma'am. I didn't mean to run into your car."

"It's okay," she replied, "but why did you do it three times?"

Whether it's a little child's antics, a youth risking his life with extreme sports, or an adult vying for the highest position, people try to find their value by impressing others with their performance. With this mindset, when people outdo us, we lose our worth and find ourselves hurt and humiliated. God calls us instead to find our value in the fact that we are children of a King who loves us so much that He sent His Son to die for us! When we accept this way of thinking, our lives will be transformed. Instead of a constant battle to impress, we can rest assured, knowing that we have a Father who loves us just the way we are.

~ Aileen Corrigan

Sacrifice of Love

For God so loved the world that He gave His one and only Son, that whoever believes in Him shall not perish but have eternal life.
- John 3:16 NIV

As I waited in the airport for my plane to board, I noticed a mother and her son sitting a few seats away from me. The boy looked to be about seven or eight years old, and he was trying to comfort his sobbing mother. Soon a flight attendant announced that the plane was leaving, and after several tearful hugs, the mom watched her son walk onto the plane. Until his plane left, she stood at the window, waving and blowing kisses to her son. Finally, the plane took off and the mother returned to her seat to pick up her purse.

We started talking, and she told me that she was sending her only son to go visit his grandparents for a couple weeks. He had never been away from her for more than a day, and so the thought of sending him to fly across the country by himself really scared her. She kept saying, "You're not a parent, so you couldn't understand. It's the hardest thing in the world to send your child so far away!"

After she left, I realized that I had never really considered how painful it must have been for God the Father to part with His own precious Son. The mother I met in the airport was sending her son through an airplane, with a flight attendant to make sure he would be safe. However, God was sending His Son into a world of sinners who wanted to kill Him. But God had a reason to send His Son: He loved this world full of sinners. He wanted each person on this planet to be able to experience eternal life with Him.

God loves us more than any parent ever could. His love is unfathomable, unconditional, and never-ending. His love is the reason for living.

~ Saraiah Turnbull

Washing Our Minds

And the peace of God, which passeth all understanding, shall keep your hearts and minds through Christ Jesus. - Philippians 4:7 KJV

A long time ago, a young boy travelled to Tennessee to visit his grandparents. After a few mornings he noticed that his grandpa had an interesting habit. Every morning he would get up early, take the Bible from the shelf, and sit at the table to read. The boy asked his grandpa one morning why he did that, since it was so hard to understand. The grandfather replied, "Some things in the Word are easier to understand, some things are harder. It's like…" he paused, and told the boy to come outside with him. Grandfather took the coal basket and told the boy to run to the stream, fill the basket with water, and bring it back. The boy earnestly attempted to transport water in the basket, but all the water had drained by the time he got back to his grandpa. This occurred two more times. Grandpa asked the boy to go one last time. He was quite peeved, but agreed to do it once more. Grandpa then asked him what he had accomplished. The boy answered that he had only dumped a bunch of water on the ground. Grandpa told him to look at the basket closely, but the boy saw nothing. Then he pointed out what the water had done.

When he started out, the basket was very dirty from all the coal dust on it. But as he had let the water run through the basket, it had become clean, almost like new. That's similar to what happens when we read something in the scriptures that we don't quite understand. The grandpa went on to say, "It's washing you through and through, just like that basket, even though you might not be able to tell. It may seem like it's just leaking out, but it's making you a lot wiser. Just pray that the Lord will give you the answers when He sees best." When we pray, God will make His word clear to our minds so that we can fully trust His word. "And the peace of God, which passeth all understanding, shall keep your hearts and minds through Christ Jesus" (Philippians 4:7 KJV).

~ Nolan Knuppel

Faith Like a Five Year Old

Assuredly, I say unto you, whoever does not receive the kingdom of God as a little child will by no means enter it. - Mark 10:15 NKJV

"I'll kill you crazy Christians! If it's the last thing I do, I'll kill you!" The screams echoed in my five-year-old ears as my Mom pulled me away from where our neighbor was shouting threats and obscenities at us. I didn't know much about our crazy neighbor except that he had just been released from prison, and he hated Christians with every ounce of his being. I decided right there on the front porch that this man needed Jesus and that I was going to introduce him.

A few weeks later, my sister was watching me while my parents were down the street for a few minutes. I hurriedly convinced my eight-year-old sister that now was the ideal moment to save our "heathen" neighbor. We quickly formed an elaborate scheme and scampered outside to accomplish it. Climbing on the swings in the front yard, we began to sing hymns at the top of our little lungs. Just as we expected, our neighbor came out of his house to see what the ruckus was about. When he saw what we were doing, he quickly swung off his porch and began running towards us; but this didn't dampen our excitement one bit. We kept right on swinging and singing *Onward Christian Soldiers* as loud as our tiny voices would go. About this time he arrived at our gate, and putting one leg over, he began to climb toward us. Suddenly he let out a terrible yell. Staring into the sky with eyes filled with terror, he leaped off the gate and raced into the orange grove near our house. We were left bewildered by this display. A few days later, his father came over to offer an explanation. He spoke with a kind of awe that I can't explain.

"My son was going to kill you," he said, "but there was a big shining man with a sword standing over your gate, and he wouldn't let him come in." God protected my family that day, just as he does every day. But this time we were able to witness God's love with our own eyes. What would happen if we all had the faith of a child? We would live without fear and know that whatever happens, God is with us and will protect us.

~ Moriah Mays

Caught or Free?

I have been crucified with Christ; it is no longer I who live, but Christ lives in me… - Galatians 2:20a NKJV

Nature is the best place to draw near to God; this is where we can learn some amazing things about our great Creator. Mum loves spending time with God by our creek, and it is here that He speaks to her. Often she comes home and tells us about the spiritual lessons that God taught her. Here is an application that stands out in my mind.

In the midst of the creek, there was a rock jutting out of the water with a small object caught on it. The object was bobbing up and down to the rhythm of the water. This object was a long, skinny leaf. Mum, intrigued by the dead leaf, went over to where this leaf was stuck with the intention of freeing it and seeing it go down stream on its merry way. Upon releasing it, however, the leaf disappeared and was no longer seen.

We are like this leaf, caught on a rock. We enjoy heading down the pathway God is leading us on, but something or someone gets in our way, and we find ourselves marooned, going nowhere. The cares of this world stop us, and we struggle to let go and let God take full control of our lives. Then when we choose to face our trials with joy and singing, it is no longer us who is seen, but God. God is glorified when we joyfully abandon our will and face whatever obstacles He allows to be placed in front of us.

It is my desire and it is my prayer that I will be like that dead leaf; where I will not be seen, but God will be seen in my life. What about you? Will you cling and cry out, "No, no, Lord, I don't want to face this trial!" or will you sing praises and rejoice in whatever situation you find yourself?

~ Nateesha Dorrington

Take No Offense

With the tongue we praise our Lord and Father, and with it we curse human beings, who have been made in God's likeness. Out of the same mouth come praise and cursing. My brothers and sisters, this should not be. - James 3:9–10 NIV

It was a cold, rainy day in Gettysburg, Pennsylvania, that Thursday in 1863. His speech began: "Four score and seven years ago our fathers brought forth on this continent, a new nation, conceived in Liberty, and dedicated to the proposition that all men are created equal…" Over the next few minutes, President Abraham Lincoln delivered one of the most famous speeches in American history.

After the battle of Gettysburg, there were thousands of dead upon the battlefield. A nearby field became an instant cemetery. At the dedication of this cemetery, important people from all over the United States were invited. Surprisingly, President Lincoln was not originally asked to speak. He was not even given a special invitation and only received a general notice about the event. It was not until seventeen days before the ceremony that he received an official letter inviting him to give a few appropriate remarks after the main speaker had given the dedication speech. It was only as an afterthought that the committee had decided that President Lincoln should have a brief moment to say something in honor of the dead.

Lincoln could have taken offense, but he decided not to. He chose to not be critical or discouraged. Instead, he gave his few remarks with humility and simplicity. Although the main address by the famous orator, Edward Everett, was elaborate and extravagant, no one remembers it. Lincoln's speech was short and to the point, but his words have never been forgotten. How often we need to overlook situations that could cause us to be offended or discouraged. Instead, let us use our tongues to praise God and encourage others.

~ Derek Glatts

A Kind Deed

The Lord will destroy the house of the proud: but He will establish the border of the widow. - Proverbs 15:25 KJV

It was a cold, crisp evening—the kind that turns your nose into a cherry and makes your lungs burn. The pale full moon made the thick layer of snow almost glow. The boys who had gathered thought it was a great opportunity for sledding, snowballing, or anything fun. One chap informed the group that he overheard Widow Morse confiding that she would be staying up with a sick child that night and would be there at eight o'clock. He lobbied for building a huge snowman in front of her door so that when she returned, she wouldn't be able to get in without first knocking the giant down. Immediately a chorus of voices agreed. But one lad who was famous for good ideas among the group spoke up: "I'll tell you where the most fun is." He instantly seized their attention, and he began. "Have any one of you got a wood saw or an axe?" he inquired. Several of them did, and they were encouraged to get them. They wasted no time. When they all returned, he explained the plan. He knew a man had hauled a load of wood to the widow"s house. She was out of wood and couldn't use it as it sat. So she would have nothing to make a fire when she returned. He turned to the pile of wood, and declared, "We can saw and split that wood as easy as we could make a big snowman. She will be just as surprised and appreciate it much more." Most of the boys were in favor of the idea, and so they began, some of them sawing, others splitting. One fellow slipped though the window, unlocked the door, and carried in wood. The rest busied themselves shovelling a nice wide path.

"God bless the boys," gasped Mrs. Morse when she was later told by a neighbor.

"Pure religion and undefiled before God and the Father is this, to visit the fatherless and widows in their affliction, and to keep himself unspotted from the world" (James 1:27 KJV). For the boys it may have seemed a very small thing, but it meant a lot to widow Morse. Little is much when God is in it.

~ Nolan Knuppel

Homesick for Heaven!

… I go to prepare a place for you. And if I go and prepare a place for you, I will come again, and receive you unto myself; that where I am, there ye may be also. - John 14:2–3 KJV

The feeling of getting back home after being away for a long time is indescribable! Coming home makes me appreciate being there even more than I did before. I remember lying on a pad in my friend's house crying silently; I didn't want to wake anyone up, but I just couldn't hold it inside anymore. I wasn't feeling well, and my mom was not there to comfort me, which made it even worse. Although that was only my second night sleeping over at her house, I was already homesick.

Now that I am a couple of years older, I don't get homesick as easily, at least not in the same way I did then. Now I get homesick in a different way. I get homesick for heaven. What makes me homesick is not that I don't have my mom to comfort me, but seeing lost people getting hurt, killed, and running further and further away from God. Watching people put themselves at risk of losing their eternal life hurts my heart because I know that God really wants to have them with Him in heaven too. Seeing all this pain makes me homesick: homesick for heaven! Heaven is the home that God has prepared for us where there will be no pain nor sorrow nor sin!

"And God shall wipe away all tears from their eyes; and there shall be no more death, neither sorrow, nor crying, neither shall there be any more pain: for the former things are passed away" (Revelation 21:4 KJV). That wonderful promise cheers me up when things are not going well; it gives me the hope that one day our home will be a safe place where no sadness or pain can ruin a good day.

~ Diane Carvalho

Too Late

Fight the good fight of faith, lay hold on eternal life...
- 1 Timothy 6:12 KJV

When I was younger, my mom often brought my dad to work in the morning, and then in the evening she would drive back and get him. It was always a special treat when we got to leave our routine and go with her.

I remember one particular day when I really wanted to go with her. As she was getting ready to leave, I asked if I could go along. She said no—I was supposed to have set the table for supper, but because I had put it off until the last minute, I would have to stay. Hearing this, I hurried to the kitchen and began to set the table as fast as I could. As soon as I was finished, I ran and threw on some shoes and a coat on my way out the door. Reaching the end of the sidewalk, I realized that I was too late. The van was just disappearing around a bend in the road. Too late, too late—the words pounded into my head as I sat heartbroken on the porch steps, the tears streaming down my cheeks.

As I have grown and matured, I realize that missing the chance to go on a quick road trip with my mom is not the end of the world. But someday soon the world will end, and it is up to you and me whether or not we'll be ready. There is a battle to fight against sin and selfishness, and Satan will try hard to distract us and turn our minds from heavenly things to things of the world. The Bible urges, "Behold, now is the accepted time; behold, now is the day of salvation" (2 Corinthians 6:2 KJV). What about you? Will you procrastinate in your walk with Jesus, or will you choose to fight the battle earnestly and be ready when He comes to take His faithful followers home?

~ Aileen Corrigan

Trusting His Word

The fear of man lays a snare, but whoever trusts in the Lord is safe.
- Proverbs 29:25 ESV

Late one Saturday afternoon, while I was camping in the Stryne Valley with fellow students, we were exploring above the cabin and walking on some fallen logs in the forest. It was fun, but a little tricky, so after a while, some of us decided to go back to the cabin. Our dean, Jonny, gave us specific directions on how to get back; we started walking, and soon the other group was out of sight. And so we walked and walked, and we soon realized that we were lost and it was getting dark in the woods. We were suddenly quiet and afraid. Everything looked unfamiliar. But Jonny had given us directions, and we put our trust in him. A little while later, when we hadn't reached the cabin, we cried out for help. There was no answer. We called again. No answer. Then, to our relief, Jonny came running towards us. He asked, "What's wrong?" I told him that we were lost, and we didn't know where to go. He said, "Hey, just trust me. I wouldn't let you return on your own if I didn't think you could make it." Then he ran back to catch up with his other group.

With a little more confidence we carried on, but we were still a little insecure. We followed his directions, and then I noticed that there was a marker he had talked about; and soon enough we reached the cabin safely just as twilight came. Later that evening, the other group came back, and Jonny then asked me what lesson I had learned.

I had to think about Jonny's question. I realized that we so often worry about all kinds of things, but there is a solution: God offers to remove all our anxieties. "In God I will praise His word, in God I have put my trust; I will not fear..." (Psalm 56:4 KJV). Just like I put my trust in Jonny's word, God wants us to put our trust in His Word. So when your pathway grows dim, and you just can't see Him, remember to trust His Word.

~ Esra Eliasson

Influence

Hear, O sons, a father's instruction, and be attentive, that you may gain insight. - Proverbs 4:1 ESV

Throughout my life there have been many people who have had an influence on me—some for the good and some for the bad. I try to be around people with positive influences, as I can learn so much from them, and that in turn helps me to become a better person.

Someone who has had a positive influence on my life is my Grandma. Ever since I can remember, Grandma has struggled with rheumatoid arthritis. This causes her great pain and makes it difficult for her to do the simplest of things. She is unable to lift her arms up very high as it is too painful, which makes washing or brushing her hair impossible. When she walks, her ankles hurt with every step, and both her knees have been replaced. Yet despite the great pain she is constantly in, she still does things for others. She is always getting up and down to do things even when they don't benefit her. When people come over at meal time, she works away preparing good food for them, even when they don't really need it (that includes me!). Even though she is constantly in pain, and it hurts her to do almost anything, she does it all without complaining. She just goes about it carefully and quietly. Grandma is one of the most self-sacrificing people I have ever met.

I can see Christ shining through my Grandma. Her unselfish and self-sacrificing way is what Jesus was like while He was on this earth. When I look at myself, what do I see? Or, more importantly, what do those around me see? Am I reflecting Christ to those around me and influencing them in a positive way? I know I have a lot of work to do yet to be as selfless as my Grandma, but I know that with the Lord's help, I can be as self-sacrificing as she is, and ultimately be a positive influence for Christ to those around me.

~ Kyle Smith

Blank Paper

The steadfast love of the Lord never ceases; His mercies never come to an end; they are new every morning; great is your faithfulness.
- Lamentations 3:22–23 ESV

Drawing is one of my favorite hobbies. When I was in elementary school, one of my teachers randomly picked me to start training as the school artist. Of course, it was hard for me to learn all the basics at first. However, as I practiced and experienced lots of different techniques, I became more confident in drawing. For the first time, I began to find joy in drawing. I remember after I won a drawing competition, I started to do my best to draw better pictures. Whenever I got a blank paper, I would draw the whole picture in my mind first, and then try my best to draw what I had pictured in my mind. Sometimes, my sketch wouldn't turn out as well as I wanted, or I made mistakes. But my teacher still accepted my pictures, not because I did a good job on them, but because I did my best to draw them.

I think of each new day as a blank white paper. When I wake up in the morning, I think of the outline for my day. I set a goal and push myself hard to draw the best picture by spending time with God, using my time wisely, and working hard. Sometimes, the day doesn't turn out as good as I wanted, but I know that God will still count my day because He knows that, with His help, I did my best.

Blank paper doesn't show the mistakes that I made before. Every new day is like an unmarked piece of drawing paper that God gives us. When the sun rises and opens the day for us, we should thank God for the new day of life and do our best, drawing on the creative strength that He gives us for that day.

~ Hannah Lee

Downfall

*Let your eyes look straight ahead; fix your gaze directly before you.
Give careful thought to the paths for your feet and be steadfast in all
your ways. Do not turn to the right or the left; keep your foot from evil.
- Proverbs 4:25–27 NIV*

A few years ago, I attended a youth conference with thousands of other young people. After each seminar, the endless sea of people simultaneously swarmed towards the door, trying to navigate their way to the next meeting hall. I always seemed to get trapped at the back of the crowd, and I would be one of the last to arrive at the next meeting. After missing the first few minutes of several seminars in a row, I thought of the perfect solution to my dilemma: while everyone else was crowding onto the up escalator, I would simply run up the down escalator. Surprisingly, the first few times I carried out my plan, everything went smoothly, and I beat the throng of people to my next meeting. Then one fateful morning, as I rushed up the wrong escalator, I glimpsed a familiar face.

"Seth!" I hollered, waving excitedly. My distractibility proved to be my downfall—literally. As I turned to greet him, I tripped on the bottom of my skirt and got the heel of my shoe caught in the strap of my purse. The escalator inelegantly carried me down, right back to where I'd started.

In my walk with God, I make the same mistake. As I walk along on the upward trail leading to heaven, I let myself become distracted. Instead of focusing on the straight and narrow path God has called me to walk on, I become sidetracked with my surroundings. Soon, Satan has completely entangled me in his web of sin. And by the time I'm free, I've slid right back down to where I started. But God doesn't leave me there. He picks me up, and sets me back in the right direction. In Psalm 37:5, He's made a promise: "Commit everything you do to the Lord. Trust Him, and He will help you" (NLT).

~ Saraiah Turnbull

Show Me the Way

*Your ears shall hear a word behind you, saying, "This is the way, walk
in it," whenever you turn to the right hand or whenever you turn to the
left. - Isaiah 30:21 NKJV*

One day when I took a hike to the upper intake with my PE class, I
decided to challenge myself; I couldn't catch up with the first group, so
I resolved to walk with the last group. Before coming to Fountainview,
I had not exercised so intensely. My legs were already burning on
the way to the trailhead. About midway, my head started feeling dizzy
and weak. At this point, I realized I needed God to help me. Earlier
that morning, God had impressed me during my devotions to keep
my mind on Jesus. When my thoughts are focused on Jesus, they
are positive and helpful. I cried out to God to help me, *God, give me
something positive to think on. I can't take another step! What do You
want me to do?*

With a strong, reassuring, yet calm voice, God answered the cry in
my mind. "Just do your best, Anna. That's all I expect of you."
But, I want to keep up with the rest and be with them.
"Just do your best."
All right, Lord, I'll obey.

I lagged behind a bit, but eventually caught up with the group.
We went down by a way that was filled with beautiful trees and a
refreshing, rippling creek. It was so revitalizing to see God helping me
through my trial right before my eyes!

Just as God guided me in my trial, so will God guide you in your
trials. He loves us very much and knows our every need. Jesus will
not help us unless we ask for it. It is important to ask for what we want,
because if we don't ask, we will not receive. James 4:2 says, "Yet you
don't have what you want because you don't ask God for it." (NLT). But
Jesus promises, "Ask and it will be given to you" (Luke 11:9 NKJV).

~ Anna Ford

313

Better Than I Thought

Trust in the Lord with all thine heart; and lean not unto thine own understanding. In all thy ways acknowledge Him, and He shall direct thy paths. - Proverbs 3:5–6 KJV

This past weekend, my dad and my brother went to a men's retreat with some other men from our church. That left the four girls in our family home alone for a few days. Although we knew we would miss them, we were also excited about the events we had planned to keep us busy. Then on Thursday evening, we found out that the event we had been so excited about was cancelled, and we had nothing to do Saturday evening. I immediately began praying that God would work out something fun for us to do, but nothing looked promising. To my surprise, after church on Sabbath morning, some friends of ours invited us over for a "girls' evening" at their house! I was so excited!

When five o'clock rolled around, we jumped in the van and drove to our friend's apartment. That evening, we made and ate sushi, had a blast creating 3D paper animal faces, and did a lot of talking and laughing. I really enjoyed myself, and it gave me a chance to get to know another girl who I had not spent much time with before. The Lord had worked things out even better than I could have hoped!

Sometimes we cherish our own plans, and we are very disappointed when things don't happen the way we want them to. Instead of complaining or arguing with God, we can choose to trust Him. Even if He does not see best to give us something exciting to take the place of our plans as He did for me, He always has our interests in mind, and He will do what is best for us no matter what.

~ Aileen Corrigan

By Faith, Not by Sight

*Take heed to yourselves, lest your heart be deceived, and you turn
aside and serve other gods and worship them.*
- Deuteronomy 11:16 NKJV

The German bombers were coming and Jasper Maskelyne didn't
have much time. His mission was to save the vital British port of
Alexandria so that supplies and reinforcements could continue to come
in. If he didn't, the British could lose Cairo to the rapidly advancing
Nazi regime. Before World War II, Jasper had been a world-renowned
illusionist. Now the military had found a use for his skills. His task
was daunting, and he quickly realized that hiding the massive port of
Alexandria was impossible; so he decided to move it.

About three miles away from the port there was a small bay about
the same shape as the one where Alexandria was located. Jasper
constructed a fake city and harbor with everything from city lights to
fake ships and anti-aircraft guns. His trap was set and now he just had
to black out the real city and wait for the bombers to come.

As the German pilots flew toward Alexandria that night, they
were puzzled to see the city a few degrees away from where their
instruments indicated. Believing their eyes more than their compasses,
they changed their courses and peppered the fake city with their
deadly cargo. For eight days they bombarded those empty beaches,
thinking that they were wreaking havoc on the real city.

We have been given a compass that will lead us through the many
battlefields of this war zone called Earth. We must be constantly
vigilant concerning Satan's deceptions and be prepared to trust the
Bible no matter what we think we see. The battle is before us, and our
compass clearly indicates the way. By faith, let us follow our compass
and not be turned aside by illusions that deceive our eyes.

~ Derek Glatts

the
choice

Change

There is no one like the God of Israel. He rides across the heavens to help you, across the skies in majestic splendor.
- Deuteronomy 33:26 NLT

Up until last year, I lived in New Zealand. Down there we drive on the left side of the road instead of the right as they do here in North America. Changing something you have done for years can be tough, making driving in Canada rather challenging for me. Not only do I have to change what side I drive on, but the indicators, the gadget to control the window wipers, and the gear lever are all on a different side than I am used to. After much focus and concentration, I can now manage to drive down the correct side of the road without too much difficulty. Most of the time I am fine on the road, but sometimes I slip back into my old habits. These times usually happen when I am feeling like I have this driving thing all sorted and don't need to worry anymore! The most challenging times are when I have to make a quick decision while driving. If I have to suddenly turn down a road without much warning, I instinctively revert back to the New Zealand way and reach for the indictor on the wrong side. Instead of making the indicators go, I turn the wipers on high! The window wipers are flapping back and forth, I have no indicator going, and I find myself in a spot of bother!

Making changes to our character can be a bit like having to change what side of the road we drive on. It takes focus and determination. There will be times when we will slip up and fall back into our old ways. This can be frustrating. I make most of my mistakes in driving when I think I have mastered it, and don't concentrate. The same is true when I slip up with my character building. It is usually when I think I have solved my problem, that I don't need to ask God for help anymore, that I crash and burn. I can't make these changes alone; I need God's constant help. I know that if God has called me to change, it is only with focus, determination and God's help that I can do it. Let's remember to ask God for His help today.

~ Kyle Smith

316

Abide in Me

Abide in Me, and I in you. As the branch cannot bear fruit of itself, unless it abides in the vine, neither can you, unless you abide in Me. I am the vine, you are the branches. He who abides in Me, and I in him, bears much fruit; for without Me you can do nothing.
- John 15:4–5 NKJV

I love doing things with my hands. That is one reason I love playing cello. I enjoy making little people and animals out of molding clay. Knitting and crocheting are also a couple of my hobbies. These activities would be quite hard to do if I had no hands, wouldn't they? It would be hard to produce music from my cello if I had no hands. I wouldn't be able to shape little people from clay. I wouldn't even be able to hold the needles to knit.

Would my hands be able to do these things by themselves? I don't think so. It would be impossible for them to do anything by themselves because they wouldn't have any life on their own. Only when they are connected to my arms can they do something useful.

Because of my sinful nature, I cannot do anything good without being connected to Jesus. I am spiritually dead without Him in my life; but when I am connected to Christ, He can live through me. When we abide in Christ, we will bear much fruit. In the Bible, fruit is often referred to as the works that we do. If we abide in Christ and bear fruit, we will be bearing good fruit, because this fruit is coming from Him, and His character is perfect. His goodness will be lived out through our actions. This is the only way for sinful humans to bear any good fruit.

I want Christ to live through me. I want to be His hands and touch the world around me for His glory. I want to be alive in Christ, not dead in sins.

~ Kami Rose

We Are All Dwarfs

You armed me with strength for battle; you humbled my adversaries before me. - Psalm 18:39 NIV

In my sophomore year of high school, I received some pictures from juniors and seniors. On the back of these photos, they would write something encouraging to me. One of them wrote, "Live like a giant." I had no clue what that meant until God enlightened me.

Many people can reach the whole white board to erase it, but I need to stand on a chair. A lot of people can do things that I can't, just because they are a little bit taller than I am. God told me to never feel discouraged because of my size, but always be confident and trust in Him, because "I can do all this through him who gives me strength" (Philippians 4:13 NIV).

I remember a story in Numbers 13 when Moses sent twelve spies into the land of Canaan for forty days. When they came back from their journey, they each brought some goodies to show the Israelites just how rich the land was. But after the spies showed the Israelites the fruit of the land, ten of the spies said, "The people living in Canaan are terribly scary! We are the size of grasshoppers compared to those giants!" This report terrified the Israelite camp, and caused them to stop trusting in God's promise.

Only two of those twelve spies still had faith in God. They knew that the Lord would deliver the giants of Canaan into their hands and give them the land. Those two spies believed that God was bigger than the giants that stood in their way. Even though they weren't huge and mighty like the giants, their faith in God was huge. Those two spies were the real giants.

Satan is a mighty enemy, and we are like grasshoppers in comparison. When we trust in God's strength, He gives us the power to be giants and overcome Satan.

~ Bryan Chen

Prodigal Daughter

… there is joy in the presence of the angels of God over one sinner that repenteth. - Luke 15:10 KJV

When I was in the 7th and 8th grade, I was very rebellious. During that time, nothing was more important to me than my friends. I kept away from church, and I had a defiant attitude towards my parents and my teachers. Even though my school had a dress code dictating that skirts must be below the knee, and tops were not to be too tight, I didn't care at all. I did everything that I wanted to, although it was wrong. I ignored my teachers' warnings.

I even began to change my style: shorter skirts, higher heels, excessive makeup. I wanted to look like an adult, and I even began to get into relationships. I knew my parents were upset with me, but I didn't care. My grades dropped sharply, and once my grades almost hit rock bottom. Often I saw my mother crying in her room, and at those moments I would feel so guilty and would try to do better. However, after few weeks, I would catch myself doing the same things again.

At the end of my 8th grade year, I realized that I hadn't lived a very good life for the last two years. I had only one year left of junior high. I started to change my rebellious ways, and began studying hard, being more respectful to my peers. The most important change that I made was that I began to attend church again.

Even though I had pushed God out of my life, He had never stopped loving me. He was still waiting for me at the same place that I had left Him. He had never forgotten about me; and when I came back to my heavenly Father, I felt as if He opened His arms and gave me the warmest hug in the world. Like the prodigal son, I, His prodigal daughter, had come back to Him. I realized that even though I had let go of God, He had never let go of me.

~ Ellen Yoon

The Power's Gone!

And this is the confidence that we have in Him, that, if we ask any thing according to His will, He heareth us. - 1 John 5:14 KJV

"Poof!" Off went the electricity, carrying with it the lights, projector, and PA system. What were we supposed to do? My family was in the Ukraine doing health and evangelistic meetings. Not speaking Russian or Ukrainian fluently, we were stuck using translators. Now my mom and one translator were attempting to control a hundred youngsters in the children's meetings—in the dark. As I groped my way down the stairs to the main meeting, I peered outside and realized the whole city had gone down; it was pitch black everywhere. When I finally found my dad, I found out that it wasn't a short-term outage. What should we do? We were in the middle of a critical meeting that ended calling the audience to make a decision for Christ. I could feel the forces of evil trying to keep the audience from choosing Christ. We realized only Christ could help us. Bowing our heads, we pleaded with God to turn the lights back on and allow us to finish the meeting. As I pled, with my five-year-old faith, we heard a buzzing and then light flooded the hallway. Thanking our Heavenly Father, we raced into the hall to watch the lights slowly all come up! God had answered our prayers! As I turned to run back up to the children's meetings, I saw one of our translators standing by the front door, pointing outside in amazement—the city was still pitch black.

The hall had been full before, but now that the hall was the only building with light, it was packed. God worked wonderfully that night and people made decisions for Christ.

Often I'm tempted to think God only answered prayer in Bible times and only worked miracles in Jesus' day. But, that isn't true, God answered my prayer and worked a miracle. God still works today, and when we are following God, we can pray with faith, knowing God will remove mountains.

~ Katie Sloop

Will You Remember?

For God not call us to uncleanness, but in holiness. herefore but God, who has also given us His Holy Spirit. - 1 Thessalonians 4:7–8 NKJV

I saw her standing in the corner, looking lost and alone. It was footwashing time in the communion service and everyone had a partner except her. I was already done with footwashing by the time I noticed her. I knew that I should offer to wash her feet, but I'm not an outgoing person, so I decided to let someone else ask her. While I was battling with my conscience, she began to look more and more uncomfortable. Finally, I got up the courage to go ask her. As I started to stand up, I noticed two girls heading towards her. Curiously, I watched as they walked over to introduce themselves. I sunk back into my chair as I saw them kneeling down to begin washing her feet. Guilt washed over me like a wave as I realized that I had just ignored the calling of the Holy Spirit and missed a chance to share the love of Jesus with this woman.

Have you ever thought about how many times you have ignored the calling of the Holy Spirit? I can remember a lot of instances where I deliberately ignored His still small voice. Will you forget all of the times that you have had a chance to show the love of God to someone? Or will you remember these times and not let one more chance to show the love of Christ pass by?

Each day you are faced with these decisions, but don't let even one soul who you could teach about the love of Christ be lost because of you.

~ Raina Walker

The Power of Humility

The wicked, through the pride of his countenance, will not seek after God: God is not in all his thoughts. - Psalms 10:4 KJV

The new girl stepped cautiously into the classroom. She flinched as she scanned the people in the room. They were all dressed in the latest fashions, had nice hairstyles, and carried expensive purses and backpacks. She looked down at her own faded blue jeans and sneakers. Her cheeks flushed as she looked up and saw many of the girls and boys looking at her with condescending sneers. She wished she could sink into the floor. Before she could stop them, tears flowed from her eyes, and she turned away in embarrassment. Suddenly, out of nowhere, a voice broke into her thoughts, "Hi, my name is Mary. What's your name?" Cautiously, the girl looked up and saw a smiling, friendly face. Instantly, the world seemed brighter and friendlier to her. It didn't matter that the girls in the corner were snickering at her or that the boys were making faces. All that mattered was that someone had reached out and made her feel welcome.

Lucifer held a very high position in Heaven. He was very proud of his status and his beauty. However, he loved to flaunt his talents in front of everyone around him. His influence could have been much greater if he had used his talents and power in the right way, but he insisted on thinking of himself and gaining all that he could. This eventually severed the bond between himself and God.

We exercise great power in the way that we treat other people. If we think that we are better than others, it will show in our manner, our looks, our words, and our actions. We are called to be humble. Our duty as Christians is to look at all individuals as brothers and sisters, and to reach out to them. When we look down on others, we not only harm our relationship with them, but also with Christ.

~ Ellen Yoon

The Map

Likewise the Spirit also helps in our weaknesses. For we do not know what we should pray for as we ought, but the Spirit Himself makes intercession for us with groanings which cannot be uttered.
- Romans 8:26 NKJV

Navigating the streets of European cities in a rented car can be very difficult, especially at night. My family and I were in Stockholm, Sweden, searching for our hotel at 1:00 A.M. Exhausted from an entire day of driving across Norway and Sweden, we couldn't coax our brains into further study of the streets' complex arrangement. My dad finally stopped the car at a gas station in an attempt to find a map acceptable to our fatigued intelligences. After some time, my mom noticed an armed police officer in the corner. Without hesitation, she strode over to him and asked for directions to the "hidden" hotel. The burly man began to draw a crude map, but quickly realized the futility of such an act. Crumpling the paper, he explained the near impossibility of drawing an atlas portraying the intricate streets of the city.

Walking outside, he offered to escort us to our "fabled" hotel. He knocked on the door of a suspicious-looking, green armoured vehicle. Immediately, ten fully-armed SWAT officers emerged with sub-machine guns at their sides. The leader instructed, "Follow close behind us so you don't get lost. Don't pay attention to road signs." We started the car and embarked on a fast and furious journey down the bewildering streets of the city. Following close behind the SWAT van, we drove busy one-way streets in the wrong direction and negotiated bus-only lanes until we arrived at the hotel. (Aha! It did exist.) Unloading our bags, we thanked them for helping us unearth our "lost" hotel.

When I think of this experience, it reminds me of God's special map that He's provided for us: the Bible. If we accept Him into our lives, He offers to send the "SWAT team" of the Holy Spirit to give us guidance and protection in our walk with Him, especially when we feel tired and consider giving up. Even when His leading doesn't make sense to us, we need to continue on with faith that He knows best and will help us understand the directions that He's given.

~ Christian Welch

Winter is Coming

Now learn the parable from the fig tree: when its branch has already become tender and puts forth its leaves, you know that summer is near; so, you too, when you see all these things, recognize that He is near, right at the door. - Mathew 24:32–33 NASB

Last night was cold, but I did not think anything of it. The weather had been getting colder for a while, so slowly that I hardly noticed it at first. The days have been getting shorter minute by minute. The trees, that had been beautifully green just a month ago, now lay bare, stripped of their leaves. I had watched them day by day changing colors from green to orange and yellow, gold and then to brown, yet the thought hardly crossed my mind that winter was coming soon.

Jesus said that He is coming soon. It has been many hundreds of years since He made this promise, but His promise is still true. I see the signs that the end is near. I notice the pain and suffering around me. I hear stories of war and strife, but I hardly realize that time is running out. I fail to make the connection that He is coming soon.

All of my friends told me that it would be a long time before it would snow. They were older than I and had more experience than I had, so I believed them. I saw the evidence of soon-coming snow, but I chose to ignore it because of what my friends told me. Then last night it came very suddenly with little warning, or so I thought at the time.

While it may not seem like a big deal that I was not expecting the first snow, it reminds me of a much more sobering event that will come in the future. This event is too important, too soon, and too real to be ignored. Jesus told us that He is coming soon, and even though some friends say that His coming is far off, I must look outside, and be prepared on the inside. I must make sure my spiritual boots are ready and that my snow pants fit for this season. I must find both gloves and have my scarf prepared. Winter is coming soon!

~ Derek Glatts

Going Home!

For yet a little while, and He who is coming will come and will not tarry. - Hebrews 10:37 NKJV

The excitement is nearly tangible! Thanksgiving break is only eight days away, and everyone is animated with joy. Even though I saw my family a couple of short weeks ago when they came to one of our concerts, I can hardly wait to see them again. It will be good to talk face to face with my mom. I can't wait to show my dad what I have been learning, not just tell him about it over the phone. I want to talk with my sister, Kristi, about how school is going for her. I'd like to play games with my youngest sister, Kari. However, what I want most is to be able to enjoy the companionship of my parents and younger sisters.

This reminds me of Jesus' second coming. We are going to be going home to our heavenly homes in only a little while. I am so excited about going to heaven! I want to talk with my guardian angel and hear how many times, unbeknownst to me, I was saved from death. I'd like to talk to Joseph and see how it felt to be rejected and sold into slavery by his own brothers. I want to know what he thought when he was given total power over all of Egypt, second only to Pharaoh, and was able to save his brothers' lives. I also want to hear the first-hand accounts of Jesus' miracles from those who were healed. It will be so amazing to be able to ride a giraffe or pet a lion without the fear of harm. It will be so exciting to be taught by the best teacher the world has ever had. But the best thing of all will be to see Jesus, to be able to talk with Him face to face, and to give thanks to Him eternally for the love that He has shown us by dying for you and me.

Just like I can keep in touch with my parents by phone calls or emails, we can stay connected with our heavenly Father by reading His email to us, the Bible, and by our "long distance" chats in prayer. Our lives should show our excitement to be going home; we should live as if we were going home in a little while, because, after all, we are.

~ Kami Rose

Who's Your Source of Strength?

For I can do everything through Christ, who gives me strength.
- Philippians 4:13 NLT

The winter wind howled while the captain of the ship, Peter, slept below. He was awakened by two of the ship's crew, Joe and Howard, who were desperately calling for him to come on deck. There was an emergency: the trolling net was stuck to the bottom of the sea. Peter immediately saw the danger. He could see the tightly stretched line and knew that it needed some slack or it could flip the boat. But before he could even give the order to slacken the line, the whole ship twisted and rolled into the water. As the crew was dumped into the frigid sea, they scrambled to sit on the hull. A second ago they had been safely on board a sturdy ship, but now the ship was upside down, and the three of them were stuck in freezing waters five miles from shore. They would have to swim through the dark, cold water, with only a dim, far-away lighthouse to mark their destination.

The three of them set out for shore. They called periodically to each other throughout the night as they swam, but gradually the voices faded, and Peter knew he was alone. He repeated the Lord's Prayer in his mind, thankful that his grandmother had taught him the comforting words. Finally, Peter was rolled by the waves onto a rocky shore, and staggered three miles over a razor-sharp lava field to his hometown. When he first saw the lights of his village in the distance, it was the most beautiful scene he had ever viewed. He was home!

The trials of life often seem insurmountable, but we must persevere. Peter found his strength through praying to God. By focusing on the lighthouse, he kept his bearings amid the turbulent sea. The same principles apply to us: God gives us strength and direction through His Word, so that we might conquer the trials in our lives. Just like Peter, if we persevere, we will soon arrive at home, and it will be more than worth it.

~ Esra Eliasson

Pride

Pride goes before destruction, and a haughty spirit before a fall.
- Proverbs 16:18 NKJV

After the beginning of second semester, my class seemed to hate me. In time, I found out exactly why.

My friend and I would arrive at class each day, armed. Not with bazookas, bayonets, or bombs, but with an arsenal of words. English and Socials classes were battlefields. We set out to destroy any and every statement we disagreed with. If I countered a comment or claim from a teacher or student, my friend would back me up until the class ended in chaos. It came to the point where I couldn't shut up and respect the opinions of my classmates. To build better relationships with them, I knew something needed to change.

The first thing I realized was that I had a problem with pride. I came across as a "know-it-all," and giving up my status of "knowing" everything would be a major blow. I obviously wasn't building friendships by arguing about everything I disagreed with, but on the other hand, I didn't know how to stop. Then, one evening, a friend in another grade called me into his room and we had a chat.

"Christian… You have a big influence on your class…"

He finished and left me to face my decision. I could either continue quarrelling, ultimately taking the entire class over the cliff, or I could turn around and end the war of words. I chose to change, and with that change I experienced an internal, unnoticed struggle that boiled within me. I realized I couldn't change on my own, so I resolved to seek God's help. In time, my relationships with my classmates, and the atmosphere of the classroom, improved as my pride was replaced with love and humility. I learned to respect their opinions, without forcing my own.

~ Christian Welch

Glorious Home

But as it is written: "Eye has not seen, nor ear heard, nor have entered into the heart of man the things which God has prepared for those who love Him." - 1 Corinthians 2:9 NKJV

It was a sunny Sabbath afternoon. The first substantial snow had fallen on the heights just above our mountain-nestled academy. Our adventurous staff decided that this Sabbath would be best spent in God's creation. So we hopped into pickup trucks and drove out from the Fountainview Academy campus. We wanted to find snow. After being jostled around for about ten minutes, we gladly jumped onto solid ground.

An astounding sight met us. The ground was covered in powdery snowflakes. We started walking on the carpet of crystals glistening in the waning sunlight. The evergreens beside us were elegantly frosted. A peaceful stillness encompassed the wide valley. In front of us stood a grand collage of snowy cliffs and steep white hillsides. My mind filled with thoughts of thanksgiving to God for the beauty surrounding me. I paused for a moment to glance behind me. Immediately I stopped in my tracks, frozen in place. The setting sun was just dropping behind the high peak across the valley. Its last rays were still straining to peek around the massive mountain. The golden sliver of sunshine gave the mountain's edge a celestial glow. Gazing at this picture, I spoke in hushed amazement, "It is a foretaste of Heaven." Later on I repeated similar words to my friend. He replied, "It's because God created it." That was it. The same Almighty God who created Heaven and who will recreate the Earth also created the unearthly scene of beauty spanning before me. He had positioned the mountains and snow and sunshine with me in mind—wanting to give me a special gift. If our Creator is able to give us such beautiful scenery despite the blight of sin, imagine how glorious He will make our new home with Him when He comes to remove all sin.

The best part is that Jesus has promised to take you to this home with Him. Simply invite Jesus into your life. Believe He has freed you from sin by His death. Seek to know Him. Very soon, He will take you to your heavenly home. I can't wait; can you?

~ Andrew Sharley

All Free

*For by grace you have been saved through faith, and that not of
yourselves; it is the gift of God - Ephesians 2:8 NKJV*

About the time that I started to learn how to write and count money,
I really wanted a specific toy. However, one of those toys cost about
$3.00. Of course, I didn't have any money, but I didn't want to ask my
mom for money either. So, I decided to earn the money by being extra
good. The next morning, I woke up early without complaining; I ate all
my beans (I do not like beans); I cleaned my room; and I finished all
my homework before I went out to play. I recorded everything I did on
paper with prices for each action. For example, I charged $0.50 for
waking up early; eating all my beans cost about $0.30; and cleaning
my room was $0.20. The list went on and on; each action that I
thought deserved money was recorded. By the end of the day, I had
about $3.00 listed on my paper, and I excitedly went to show my mom
so that she could pay me.

After she was done reading my list, she smiled at me and then
went over to the drawer where she usually kept her wallet. I thought
my plan had worked, but instead of getting out her wallet, she got a
pen out of the drawer and started to write something on the paper that
I had given her. I was a little annoyed, but I waited calmly because I
was curious to know what she was writing. When my mom gave the
paper back to me, it read, "Protecting you in my stomach for nine
months is free. The pain that I had to bear to show you to the world is
free. All the work that I had to do to feed you and to dress you up is
free. And everything that I'm going to do for you from now on, all free."
I was speechless when I realized how much she gave me without
wanting anything in return.

Before this event, I spent time with God only to get something back
from Him. But God isn't like that. He doesn't love me because of what
that love will get Him. He loves me despite how much I hurt Him. Just
as my mom provided for me and gave me a good life all for free, so
has Christ given me life and an eternal future for free. All He asks of us
is that we accept His gift. Will you accept His gift today?

~ Hannah Lee

His Ways Are Higher

… as the heavens are higher than the earth, so are my ways higher than your ways, and my thoughts than your thoughts.
- Isaiah 55:9 KJV

Life here on Earth is not perfect. Sometimes things happen to us that seem hard, but our amazing God has promised that He will make "all things work together for good to them that love [Him]" (Romans 8:28 KJV).

When my family first moved to Fountainview, we met a young man who didn't have the privilege of being part of a Christian family. He was working in the area, and so my family "adopted" him as a brother. He was the big brother every kid dreams of—he spent hours with us playing Legos, giving "airplane" rides, and taking us exploring outdoors. Eventually, his work took him to live in another country. I was heartsick that we wouldn't be able to see him very often anymore. Then one day, we got startling news: our "brother" was engaged! My parents were very excited for him, but I was crushed. I knew that our relationship with him would never be the same, and I didn't want him to marry some girl we didn't even really know! Worse yet, although he did everything he could, circumstances made it impossible for us to be at his wedding.

As time went on and we got to know his wife, I realized that I had been totally wrong about what their marriage would do to our family. I saw that I had not lost a brother, but had gained a sister—and who wouldn't want such a wonderful sister! She was so much fun, and I began to look forward to their visits even more. Now I am sorry for my bitter feelings, and I am thankful that God provided my "brother" with the perfect wife. Not only is she just right for him, she is a terrific addition to our family!

It doesn't matter what circumstances look like to us. God's ways are higher than our ways, and He always has our best good in mind!

~ Aileen Corrigan

330

Laid Bare

*Purge me with hyssop, and I shall be clean: wash me, and I shall be
whiter than snow. - Psalm 51:7 KJV*

It snowed last night. I woke up and realized that the mud, dirt, dead
leaves, and rotten apples on the ground were covered by a layer of
clean, white snow, as far as my eyes could see. It was amazing; every
trace of the aging summer was gone, and in its place was the simple
yet beautiful blanket of snow. It gave everything a fresh start and new
beginning—a cleansing for the fallen leaves.

Looking out my window, I thought about the snow-covered trees.
They had been preparing themselves for the coming winter. They had
laid themselves bare; stripped themselves of their many leaves and
made themselves ready for the coming cleansing. As I looked closer
though, I noticed that some trees still had leaves on them and their
dead leaves continued to fall and now looked out of place on top of
the clean snow. These trees had not fully prepared themselves for the
snow, and because of that, their cleansing was not complete.

Winter is coming. I will not be able to stand when the storms come
if I am not protected by the cleansing blood of Christ. The Lord is
willing to send me this snow; to give me His blanket of forgiveness.
This is the only protection that I will have against the harsh storms of
winter. However, before I receive Christ's cleansing, I must ask to be
prepared for winter. I, like the trees, must strip myself of all my dead
leaves. I cannot be fully cleansed if I am still holding onto a sin that I
know is wrong.

The good news is that even when I shovel it away, trample it down,
or spread dirt over top the snow—marring God's perfect grace—if I
ask for His cleansing and purity again, He will send snow to cover me
every time.

~ Derek Glatts

Rock Slide

*If I then, your Lord and Teacher, have washed your feet, you also
ought to wash one another's feet. - John 13:14 NKJV*

My legs were burning, my breathing was quick, and my heart
threatened to jump out of my chest. I was climbing near the head
of a hiking group that had decided to scale a large ridge across the
valley from where we were camping. Despite my fatigue, it wasn't long
before I fell into a climbing rhythm, a state where nothing seemed to
slow me down. I scaled obstacle after obstacle, as if unable to stop
making my way upwards. But every so often, in my careless haste, the
rocks on which I placed my weight would give way, bouncing down the
mountain towards the hikers behind me. Gaining speed, the careening
stones would sometimes knock loose more rocks, sending a cluster of
deadly projectiles into the path of whoever happened to be behind me.
But selfishly I would keep climbing, disregarding the safety of others.

Christians sometimes get into a similar climbing rhythm, where
they're so intent upon achieving their goals that they pay little attention
to the people around them. Scrambling upwards, they knock loose
rocks that seem to be of little consequence. But these small stones
gain speed as they hurl down the mountain, knocking loose other
rocks and sometimes triggering a rockslide of pain and insult.

It's amazing how much harm a misspoken word or careless deed
can cause. But even more amazing is how blind we as Christians
sometimes are to the effects of our actions. Despite the fact that
we are called to be a witness for Christ, our selfish climbing often
misrepresents Him and the mission of servitude He entrusted to us. As
you pursue your goals, remember the real goal that Jesus set when
He girded Himself with a towel, and washed His disciples' feet. He told
them "For I have given you an example, that ye should do as I have
done to you" (John 13:15 KJV). Are you treating others the way Jesus
has treated you?

~ Michael Jensen

A Covering

… though your sins be as scarlet, they shall be as white as snow;
though they be red like crimson, they shall be as wool.
- Isaiah 1:18 NKJV

The first real snow of the year fell last night while I slept, covering the landscape in a beautiful layer of glistening white. So today for PE, my teacher decided that we could go sledding on the steep hill behind the boys' dorm. I trudged up the hill and then hurled myself down it, screaming and laughing the whole way. But as I stood at the bottom of the hill, watching my friends fly down, I noticed that the sleds were scraping away the snow. Through the little ruts they had made, I could see streaks of dirty brown. I had forgotten that dirt still lay under the sparkling blanket of snow.

This reminded me of Christ's intercession on my behalf. Jesus is like the snow: pure, clean, and spotless. I'm the ground underneath; by myself, I'm filthy. There is nothing I can do to purify myself. I need to be covered by a layer of clean, white snow: Christ's righteousness. Jesus stands between me and God, so that when God looks at me, He doesn't see my wretchedness. Instead, He sees Jesus' unblemished, perfect character. Like the snow, He covers me and makes me pure. The old hymn, *Cover with His Life*, played through my mind, reminding me of Christ's incredible mercy to me.

Deep are the wounds transgression has made
Red are the stains; my soul is afraid
O to be covered, Jesus, with Thee
Safe from the law that now judgeth me.
Cover with His life, whiter than snow;
Fullness of His life then shall I know
My life of scarlet, my sin and woe
Cover with His life, whiter than snow.

~ Saraiah Turnbull

333

Open Vaulted Hearts

He heals the brokenhearted and binds up their wounds.
- Psalms 147:3 NKJV

I met a girl at the airport whose name was Alonna. Wanting to be a friend and a witness to this stranger, I sat next to her and probed into her life. General questions gave place to intimate details of love and hurt, good and evil. She trusted me more as we talked and told me about things I had never experienced (and experiencing them in the future would be very unlikely).

Alonna's mom was a hard worker and cared for her and her three sisters; however, she was an alcoholic. By default, Alonna acted as mother to her sisters when her mother would sporadically disappear and return weeks later. Alonna was sometimes beaten by her stepfather—it still hurts, she said. Her mother might as well have stayed unmarried because she was with so many men. The reason Alonna was traveling was to see her real father, but she didn't really know him. This girl wanted to be different: she wanted to do well in school, get a job, have a happy life.

My life was unquestionably different. I had a pair of inseparable, God-fearing parents—no alcohol, no drugs. I had a loving home, I did well in school, and I had a trust in the Lord. Trust in the Lord… that sparked the most important question.

"With all that you have been through, do you believe there is a God? Do you believe that He loves you?" I asked.

"Yes, there is a God; but love… I don't think that exists."

Look at this hurting girl! If we know about God's love, shouldn't we be sharing it with other suffering souls like her? She didn't know that He loved her like a Father would, but we do! The knowledge we have from the Bible is our key that perfectly fits the lock to every heart. We need to do our God-given work of opening vaulted hearts to release sin's darkness, anger, pain, and guilt so that His light may shine in.

~ Ashley Wilkens

My Footsteps

All Scripture is given by inspiration of God, and is profitable for
doctrine, for reproof, for correction, for instruction in righteousness.
- 2 Timothy 3:16 NKJV

It was about seven years ago when I first discovered that I couldn't walk straight. At first, it wasn't very noticeable, so it didn't bother me at all. Then one day, it snowed outside and everything was covered by a big, soft, thick blanket. I was amazed by the view, and I started to walk without thinking. Crunch, crunch, crunch; the sound of my steps made me smile. I don't know how long I walked through the snow, but when I stopped, I turned around and looked at my footsteps. Instead of nice, straight footsteps, I saw the ugly, crooked dents in snow where I had walked. I hadn't expected nice, pretty footsteps because I knew that I couldn't walk straight, but still it really made me feel bad. Fortunately, my disappointment motivated me to fix the way that I walked.
Every day, I went outside to walk on the snow. Sometimes the footsteps on the snow made me happy with my progress, but I still tried very hard to make every step prettier and straighter than the one before. Time went by quickly, and when spring came, my footsteps were almost normal. Since there was no snow, I now walked through the muddy ground and sandy soil. With lots of effort, I taught myself how to walk straight.

When I look back at my spiritual walk, I know my footsteps are not straight, but sometimes I don't even realize how incorrect my footsteps are. When I compare my footsteps to the message of the Bible, it shows me what I need to fix, which way to go, and how to fix my footsteps towards Jesus Christ. I have learned that effort and the determination are important in order to fix my footsteps, but I won't be able to correct them if I don't allow Jesus to abide in me. Won't you let Jesus abide in you today, too?

~ Hannah Lee

Shopping

For by grace you have been saved through faith, and that not of yourselves; it is the gift of God, not of works, lest anyone should boast.
- Ephesians 2:8–9 NKJV

I don't go shopping very often. When I do shop, I usually search for items that relate to my technological disposition. This time, however, I found myself walking the seemingly overstocked aisles of a convenience store to acquire some supplies for school. Occasionally pulling an item off the shelf, I collected the articles I was looking for and ambled up to the counter. The cashier greeted me and soon read off the total cost. While fumbling for my wallet, my mind returned to the time in history when I had dropped that hard-earned cash into its confines. As I prepared to empty the contents onto the counter, I came to an embarrassing realization. No cash could be found in my wallet. I had already spent every cent. Looking up to face the impatient cashier, I explained my humiliating predicament…

In the same way, many people go through life with the idea that they need to pay their way to Heaven, but they don't realize that their "righteousness wallets" are empty. This deceptive idea is called "righteousness by works." People feed the hungry, tend to the sick, and perform kind deeds, all in a vain attempt to earn righteousness. Instead of performing good deeds to pay our way to Heaven, we need to follow God and live to serve Him. When we live to serve Him, we will serve others. It's not our works, but the painful work of Jesus on the cross that paid for our sins and gives us His righteousness.

… After explaining my dilemma to the irritated cashier, I found my mom, who was in a grocery store a few blocks away. She came to the convenience store and paid the bill for my supplies, saving me from further humiliation. In a similar way, Jesus paid the bill for our sins and waits longingly for us to accept His payment. In Revelation 3:20 He declares: "Behold, I stand at the door and knock. If anyone hears My voice and opens the door, I will come in to him and dine with him, and he with Me" (NKJV). Don't leave Jesus waiting at the door. Step out in faith and accept His life-changing, unending love and forgiveness.

~ Christian Welch

A Still Small Voice

The way of a fool is right in his own eyes: but he that hearkeneth unto counsel is wise. - Proverbs 12:15 KJV

Have you ever had something that dominated your thoughts? I have. I had an idol that directed all of my thoughts, feelings, and speech away from God. It took over my mind and wormed its way into everything I did. This idol was a girlfriend. All I could talk and think about was her. It drove me to the point where all that seemed important to me was spending time with her. She started to control my life without me even noticing. When I came to Fountainview, it dawned on me that she was in charge of my life. I had begun to read my Bible and spend time with God, and I soon realized that God should be number one in my life, no one else. I felt convicted to give her up, and I turned to my Savior with all my heart.

We sometimes get so caught up in worldly distractions that we forget to look to God. We, as humans, think that "we don't need God's love," and, "I only need another person's love," when Jesus is the one who gives us everything we need. We should stop thinking about ourselves and start thinking heavenly, unselfish thoughts.

My obsession was controlling my life, and it wasn't long before I heard a still, small voice speaking in my heart, convicting me of my mistake. I can't say that I don't struggle with it anymore, but I now have the ability to look back and clearly see what happened. I sometimes listen to my own sinful conscience when really I should take heed and listen to the voice of God.

I challenge you not to listen to your own impulsive lusts and thoughts, but to listen to that still small voice instead.

~ Chris Unfrau

Working on My Heart

I will praise You, O Lord, with my whole heart; I will tell of all Your marvelous works. - Psalm 9:1 NKJV

I struggle with the responses I should give to those who praise me, especially concerning things dedicated to God: playing music for church, singing, and praying aloud. Sometimes I respond to praise by saying, "Thank you." But then I am receiving praise for myself. Or I say, "Praise the Lord!" which is good, but these are often empty words from my mouth. It is just a response I have heard many others say. Other times, I attempt to deny any reason that would outwardly qualify me for praise: "Actually, I made many mistakes during my piano piece." or "No, I am not that great at speaking." or "Others are much better than I am." But that isn't the way either, because it only makes people feel bad that their kind words are not appreciated.

Once, a friend was thankful for a kindness I had shown toward her and said, "You are so sweet!" I denied that I was any sweeter than she, but my friend kept insisting on how kind I was. Unexpectedly, golden words tumbled out of my mouth, "Well, then God is really working on my heart." These words were so true. God was working on my heart, and He talked right through me to make His glory known. The thing that I did out of the goodness of my heart really came from the goodness of His heart.

We should humbly submit to be tools in God's hands, and He will guide us to do good works. Don't worry about how to respond to praise. God will give us the words to reply, and we will know just how to point the praise of others to Him instead of to ourselves.

~ Ashley Wilkens

Simple Prayers

*Then you will call upon me and come and pray to me, and I will hear
you. - Jeremiah 29:12 ESV*

One evening last summer, I was tucking my little sisters into bed,
and as I pulled the covers up to their little chins, both of them begged,
"Pray with us, Beff!" I was surprised, because they had never asked
me to pray with them before. I knelt beside their beds and prayed two
short prayers. When I finished, I looked up to find in their expressions
a mix of wonder and curiosity. They giggled, then immediately
exclaimed, "Again, Beff! Pray your prayers to us again!"

I couldn't help but think as I left their room how such simple prayers
can be so meaningful. When I saw how my prayers caused my sisters
to be so enthusiastic, I realized how much I take God for granted. Too
often, I thank Him for my food out of habit and then carry on with my
day, forgetting the meaning of prayer. Instead of treating Him as the
true and very real best friend that He is, I misuse my Creator. When
you talk to your best friend, you don't say the same thing over and
over again, do you? No, of course not! You constantly have different
conversations, and as you get to know your friend better, you learn
more about him or her. The relationship becomes deeper the more
time you spend with that person. It is the same way with God. He
wants our prayers to be directly from our hearts, and our conversations
to be just like the ones we have with our best friends, only deeper.

"Prayer is the opening of the heart to God as to a friend" (*Steps to
Christ,* pg. 93). Isn't it wonderful to know that our Savior desires us to
talk to Him, just like a friend? Won't you speak to Him today?

~ Elizabeth King

Real Beauty

Charm is deceitful and beauty is passing, but a woman who fears the Lord, she shall be praised. - Proverbs 31:30 NKJV

I have seen many pretty girls in Korea; but since I have come to Canada, I have seen a different level of beauty. From their hair to their toes, North American girls are measurably different from Asians. For example, comparing head sizes is like comparing apples to pineapples. The average young American girl has a face that is petite like a Barbie doll's.

Sometimes, I imagine what it would be like to have been born as an American girl. Instead of having small, slanted eyes, I would have big eyes like a frog's; and instead of having such common-colored black hair, I would be blond. But, because this is not the case, I thought that God didn't give me anything. Since I was thinking this way, when I looked at others, my eyes were clouded with jealousy. I wanted to be prettier, but I also wanted people to like me just the way I am. Like me, many Koreans desire to look like Americans, and many Korean teenagers choose plastic surgery.

Lucifer was once a beautiful angel who served God with all his heart; however, his desire for more beauty and honor ruined his relationship with God. He became jealous of God's Son, who was much more glorious than he. The result of his jealousy caused him to lose all his beauty and be cast out of Heaven's gates.

God has created each of us with unique appearances. Almost all people have some features that they don't like, but we must try to see what beauty God has given us. It may be a beautiful heart, or a beautiful smile. Remember, you will have real beauty as long as you let Christ live in your heart. Just think: to your heavenly Father, you are prettiest the way you are!

~ Ellen Yoon

With Sword in Hand

Put on the whole armor of God, that you may be able to stand against the wiles of the devil. - Ephesians 6:11 NKJV

Quiet. Peace. Security. All was calm, orderly, and normal in the early morning of December 7, 1941. But suddenly, the thick serenity was pierced by the growling of hundreds of airplane engines. Before the startled Americans of Hawaii could react, their peaceful bubble was burst by thousands of bombs, torpedoes, and rounds of ammunition. In a mere one hundred and ten minutes, Pearl Harbor, a prominent military base with more than enough firepower to withstand the Japanese, was nearly demolished by an unforeseen enemy. Despite all its weapons, defenses, and trained soldiers, Pearl Harbor wasn't ready when it was attacked.

When there's an enemy on the loose, it is foolish to be complacently resting in false security—because that's exactly what the enemy wants! The success of the Japanese depended on the unpreparedness of the Americans. Similarly, the Devil's success depends on us being defenseless when he strikes. That's why the Bible warns us to "Be sober-minded; be watchful. Your adversary the devil prowls around like a roaring lion, seeking someone to devour" (1 Peter 5:8 ESV). With such a formidable foe prowling about, sleeping is not only dangerous, but deadly! The devil doesn't kindly wake us up and give us a chance to fight back! If we are not standing on guard with sword in hand, how can we expect to be safe? We must be watchful and vigilant, putting on the whole armor of God. When we are outfitted with the armor of God, we will have all the strength of Heaven to support us; and with Heaven on our side, we cannot lose.

~ Michael Jensen

Night is Coming

… redeeming the time, because the days are evil.
- Ephesians 5:16 KJV

My fingers flew up and down the piano keys as Chopin's *Scherzo No. 2* filled the practice room. All the while my thoughts wandered. *I wonder where I'll be assigned to work today. I wonder what we're playing in orchestra tonight… How will I ever finish learning this piece by classical concert?* The clock glared at me. It was 12:50 PM. *Great,* I sighed. *Now I only have ten more minutes to practice!*

And so my practicing went. By the time I finally did reel in my wandering thoughts, practice time would be over. Only a day or two before my next lesson would I realize how little time I had left to accomplish my goals for the week; pulling myself together, I would furiously practice until I was satisfied with my results. Thus, progress came very slowly, frustrating me terribly.

Soon, I realized how wasteful I was with my time, and that I really needed more self-control. Then the Holy Spirit inspired me with something: "Practice as if your lesson is tomorrow." The gentle voice continued to whisper, "Practice like there is no tomorrow." When I took this to heart, and applied it to not only my practice, but also to the menial everyday tasks, my perspective on time changed. No longer did every passing minute seem to slip through my fingers like fine sand; instead, I started to enjoy whatever I was doing much more!

Soon it will be night—spiritual night. Soon spreading the gospel will be met with the greatest challenges yet. Soon Jesus will come. Time is short. Am I doing everything I can *today*? Are you?

~ Esther Ferraz

Gospel Cookies

… Freely you have received; freely give. - Matthew 10:8 NIV

This past week, my father came out to surprise my sister for her 18th birthday. Before he left home, my mom made a bunch of fresh cookies for him to bring out for us to eat and share with our friends. The cookies were really good; they were soft and chewy with small oatmeal bits, colorful berries, and white chocolate chunks evenly dispersed throughout. When he brought the bag of cookies into my sister Loralee's room, she exclaimed, "This is so exciting! These cookies are just too good to share; I know a ton of girls who will love them!" The cookies did not last long; she gave some away and then brought the rest to class with her, where they were instantly devoured.

You know, I have another Father who makes cookies for me to share. My Father in Heaven made me a batch a gospel cookies. If I were to keep them all for myself, I would end up getting sick from all the richness found in them. But by sharing them, everyone will gain more than just a good taste in their mouth; they will find salvation through them. When God began the church, His purpose was for its members to spread the gospel throughout the world. First, God grants us salvation; then He desires for us to share what we know with others. When something really wonderful happens to me, or if I hear of something exciting that is going to happen very soon, my first reaction is to go find someone to share it with. This is what we are supposed to do with the gospel—share it with others, because the good news of a God who loves us and desires the best for us is just too good to keep to ourselves.

Have you experienced the joy of sharing the gospel? Just like Loralee found joy in sharing her cookies, so you will find joy in sharing the goodness of the Lord with those around you. Why don't you ask God to show you someone who needs His "gospel cookies" today.

~ Sarah Miller

Stains

*I will give you a new heart and put a new spirit within you; I will take
the heart of stone out of your flesh and give you a heart of flesh.
- Ezekiel 36:26 NKJV*

It was Christmas Eve, and my family and I were enjoying a quiet
evening filled with Christmas music, stories, and scrumptious food.
Being that it was Christmas time, our decorations were up; little white
lights were all over our house bringing a feeling of coziness to our
home.

As we ventured further into our evening, we made blueberry
smoothies as an evening treat. For the special occasion we brought
out our red, velvety, flower-patterned glasses. As my dad brought the
smoothies into the living room, the most unexpected thing happened:
the bottom of one of the glasses shattered, causing pieces of glass
and blueberry smoothie to fly everywhere. There was a huge stain
right in the middle of our off-white carpet, and unless we cleaned it up
fast we knew that it would be stained permanently.

Since it was Christmas Eve, we felt awful calling our friend Len, the
carpet guy, but we did in order to save our floor. The very next day—
Christmas morning—he came and took all the stains out with his fancy
hoses and cleaners. Even though it was a holiday, he went out of his
way to remove our blueberry stain.

Sometimes it may seem like your life has just exploded all over the
place. Maybe you have a huge stain on your heart that you cannot
get out by yourself. I have a Friend who is willing to come, anytime,
anywhere, to take your stains away. Don't worry if you have stained
your life with your broken heart; Jesus wants to give you a brand new
one! Nothing can keep His love and grace from you. If you allow Him
to come in, He will transform you, and your life will be spotless.

~ Elizabeth King

Example is Power

Let your light so shine before men, that they may see your good works and glorify your Father in heaven. - Matthew 5:16 NKJV

I entered the airplane praying to be useful to God—a tool in His hand to reveal His love. I imagined talking about Him to some stranger that would sit next to me, explaining important Bible truths. But I didn't know how to defend my faith from scripture without studying a certain topic beforehand. In what way would I further God's work?

Two men sat down beside me. The man closest to my left spoke with a delightful English accent, and we began discussing ordinary things like the weather and destinations. All the while, blue eyes from the aisle seat watched intently. Our discourse progressed to my life in the country versus their city lives. "In the past, I wanted to live in the city; now I wouldn't trade the country for anything. I love the beautiful nature that surrounds me," I commented. The man in the aisle seat stared at me more intently, shocked and impressed that a teenager would say such a thing.

We fell silent soon after, the Englishman to a novel, the aisle man to a movie. I wondered when the opportunity to witness would come. I decided to do what I had never done in an airplane before: read my Bible for morning devotions. As I read and contemplated, I thought for sure that one of my two seat partners would comment or question my action. Instead both were silent, and I kept praying to be a witness.

Though the Englishman sitting next to me was engrossed in his novel, I knew he noticed my Bible. But who really noticed was the fellow in the aisle seat. Though I couldn't see him, I felt his eyes on me—staring. Then the sensation of being watched went away, and I glanced in his direction. The movie hadn't finished, no words had been spoken, yet he had taken out his own Bible to read!

~ Ashley Wilkens

Today or Tomorrow?

But seek first the kingdom of God and His righteousness, and all these things shall be added to you. Therefore do not worry about tomorrow, for tomorrow will worry about its own things. Sufficient for the day is its own trouble. - Matthew 6:33–34 NKJV

Ratatatatatatat! I ducked behind a tree just before a wave of small plastic pellets flew past me from my younger brother's airsoft gun. My brothers, a few friends, and I were enjoying the hot summer temperatures of Minnesota and playing a game of airsoft.

During those escapades, many memories were made. I often thought of what it was like for the Americans fighting for freedom in 1776. I got an idea of the courage required of the French, defending their homeland in World War II from the oncoming forces of Germany and Italy. I began to understand the fear that the practically defenseless Native Americans had when the British raided their lands. For my friends and me, however, we knew deep down that our battles were only in fun, and, in the end, everything would be all right. We were in no real danger. But I sometimes think about what it would be like if we were. What if the next step I take will be my last? What if I never make it back home? If such things were to happen, what legacy would I leave behind? Would people think of me as a loser who made some stupid mistake and got blown up by a grenade, or as a brave and courageous soldier who loved and served God and died for a worthy cause?

Too often we are living for some "heroic" tomorrow, for the adventure of next week, or for the excitement of next year. We live for the things that are coming up in the future, and not for the present. But we need to live in the present, not the future. What if that neglected tension between you and God is not rectified? What if your next breath is your last? Will you be satisfied with the way you lived your life today?

~ Ben Dietel

Fateful Forgetfulness

Assuredly, I say to you, inasmuch as you did it to one of the least of these My brethren, you did it to Me. - Matthew 25:40b NKJV

When I was younger, I had a pet budgie. He was mostly white with a little bit of mauve on the tips of his wings—he was beautiful. He reminded me of a white fluffy cloud. He lived in a cage in my room, and during the day I would set the cage outside on our porch in the fresh air. I would always make sure that I brought the cage in at night so that nothing would happen to him.

However, one night I forgot to bring him inside. That fateful night, we believe a wild cat jumped on the cage and knocked it off the ledge. The bang of the cage falling to the ground must have scared the cat away. However, when the cage hit the ground, the door came open, and because of his clipped wings, he couldn't fly away. He got himself out of the cage and hopped off the porch onto the lawn. The next morning, not knowing what had happened, my dad let our Rottweiler out for her run. The dog had seen the bird on the lawn, and she went straight for it. She grabbed the bird in her mouth and mauled it. Dad did manage to get the bird from the dog, but it died in his hands.

I felt terrible that because I neglected to bring the cage in that night; I was the cause of my bird's death. This innocent little creature suffered and died because I failed to do my part.

Sometimes we think that it is just the commission of sins that is bad. But the omission of what we know is right is equally bad. If we pass by a situation where we could help someone, this is just as surely a sin as committing a sin. Jesus says in Matthew 25:40, "Assuredly, I say to you, inasmuch as you did it to one of the least of these My brethren, you did it to Me" (NKJV). I didn't try to kill my bird, but because I neglected to bring him in, he died. If we neglect to help others, we are neglecting Christ.

~ Kyle Smith

347

Running on Reserve

… In six days the Lord made the heavens and the earth, and on the seventh day He rested and was refreshed. - Exodus 31:17 NIV

I was writing a paper for English class one day when suddenly, about a half an hour into writing, my computer gave me a notification that it was running on reserve power. I had forgotten to charge it the night before, and I barely had enough power to save my files. I had also forgotten to bring my power cord down to the school building; so before long I had to borrow a power cord from one of my friends so I could finish up my project. Since then I have been much more careful to remember to charge my computer before class. A fully charged battery is very important. It seems that I am surrounded by items that need batteries: the annoying bird clock on the wall, my iPod, my brother's tin can robot, my watch, the camera next to me, the pacemaker controlling a grandfather's heart, and the car starting next door. I am often reminded of how dependent we are on energy stored in the form of batteries.

How ironic it seems that our world remembers to charge cell phones and computers but neglects spiritual renewal. God has given us a special day, called the Sabbath, to recharge our spiritual batteries. In the garden of Eden He rested with Adam and Eve and communed with them, equipping them with divine power for the week ahead. How much more do I need the power of the Sabbath? So often, I have just gone through the motions of the Sabbath, waiting for the sun to go down so that I can have some fun. We have been given an incredible gift, so don't just go through the motions; truly get charged!

~ Derek Glatts

Baking with God

… Choose for yourselves this day whom you will serve… But as for me and my household, we will serve the Lord. - Joshua 24:15 KJV

"Boom! Bang! Clash!" I angrily crashed the pots together as I pulled them out of the cupboard. My mom and I were making an apple pie together for a baking contest at our church. Although I loved to cook, I did not like anyone else telling me how to do so. As I began measuring out the ingredients for the crust, Mom poked her head over my shoulder. "Hey, Sarah, why don't you use about half that much sugar and put in some quick oats instead of using just flour. That'll make the crumble top different than the other pies." Rolling my eyes, I grudgingly complied and cut the sugar in half. Everything I did she seemed to contradict with her own ideas of how to "make it better." When the pie was finally in the oven, I was fuming at my mom and sure the pie would be a flop. But that night, my pie won third place amidst the thirty other pies that were entered in the contest. I was very humbled because I knew that if my mother had allowed me to do things my way, my pie would not have turned out as well as it did.

Lucifer had the same attitude towards God and His laws as I had toward my mom and her pie-baking abilities. He thought that God's laws were unfair and unreasonable, and that his own ideas were much better. Time and time again God tried to correct Lucifer's wrong ideas about His law, but Lucifer was not willing in the least to reconsider. So, to show the world how his recipe of sin would really turn out, God allowed him to make it himself. Sure enough, when left alone, Satan's "pie" didn't turn out at all like he had thought it would.

God allows you to choose which recipe you will follow: yours or His. Lucifer's experience shows us how they will each turn out. I don't know about you, but I am going to follow God's recipe. He has had lots of experience and knows how to make it better than I do. Won't you accept His help? The choice is yours.

~ Sarah Miller

A New House

Create in me a clean heart, O God; and renew a right spirit within me.
- Psalm 51:10 KJV

Closing the door, I stepped into the dark and into another world. A world away from boxes, packing, bare walls, empty shelves, and the frustration of moving. I see a world full of twinkling red, green, and blue lights hanging gently from eaves, and lighted presents, reindeer, and sleighs, awaiting the promise of white fluff. Turning onto the street, I ambled along, enjoying the magical Christmas feel. Then, white icicle lights catch my attention, reminding me of my family's own lights packed already. Turning, I headed back up the street, past candles shining in windows and over-sized candy canes. I glared at our peaceful little tree and the big *For Sale* sign, as my own house came into view. We had tried to make our house look Christmasy, but hadn't really succeeded. Climbing my front steps a couple minutes later, I again stared at our peaceful looking fir wrapped in sparkling lights and thought of what it looked like inside. Moving the key holder and opening the door, I stared at the boxes and empty shelves.

I am like my house. I put up a Christmas tree and wind lights around it; I try to make the outside festive, but you can still see the real estate sign in the front yard, the light-less eaves, and key holder on the front door. I try to hide the pain of moving; I try to make the outside look bright and cheerful, but my emotions still show through. Only as inside settles down and boxes are unpacked at a new house, can the outside be landscaped and decorated. Similarly, only as I surrender my emotions and frustrations to Christ and allow Him to fill me with His love; only as I allow Him to create within me a new dwelling place—a new heart—can I truly be loving and cheerful.

~ Katie Sloop

Sanding Is Rough

… You have been grieved by various trials, that the genuineness of your faith, being much more precious than gold that perishes, though it is tested by fire, may be found to praise, honor, and glory at the revelation of Jesus Christ… - 1 Peter 1:6b–7 NKJV

Having gulped down a few mouthfuls of toast, I scurried across campus to the auto shop. My work supervisor at Fountainview Academy had instructed me to meet him there. After joining him, we had prayer for God's guidance, then I went to work taking apart wooden benches for sanding. Another student began running the wooden pieces along a massive belt sander. Once I finished taking the benches apart, I went over to take a turn at the sander. I held one of the pieces against the rapidly moving sandpaper. Its surface was quickly smoothed and became obviously more beautiful, but a rough area down the middle of the wood called for another rub by the rough sandpaper. I held it tightly against the coarse paper again, until the wood was velvety smooth. The deteriorated, discolored wood had become ready to be part of an elegant seat.

God's work of recreating us is much the same as my sanding job. Our Creator wants to take our sin-stained, dilapidated lives and make us into beautiful, new creations, free of all rough spots. When the weathered layer had been removed, the wood was restored to its original color. God will restore us to His likeness—as He originally created humanity. But the sandpaper is not soft. Its coarse surface is what scraped on the old wood to restore its beauty. We too have old, discolored material to be scraped away. God has to allow coarse circumstances to sand away our sinfulness. He allows us to rub up against painful difficulties, yet each rough trial is used by our Creator to bring us into His image. He will make us into beautiful, smoothed masterpieces, ready to work for Him.

With this in mind, isn't it be possible to thank God the next time we are rubbed up against a difficult trial? We can choose to praise Him for making us into brand-new creations for His honor. Won't you choose to praise Him for allowing you to be reshaped into His image?

~ Andrew Sharley

Shooting Star

I delight to Thy will, O my God: yea, Thy law is within my heart.
- Psalms 40:8 KJV

Shelly Pennefather was once a legendary, all-American basketball player. In 1987, she was named the best college-aged player in the United States. She seemed to be living the ultimate athlete's life. But even though Shelly had the sweet life that many athletes covet, she felt impressed that she had a different calling.

In 1991, Shelly decided to enter the monastery of the Poor Clare Sisters as a cloistered nun. For Shelly, this would be a big change. The life of a cloistered nun is one of absolute abstinence and asceticism. The sisters eat only one full meal a day, sleep a maximum of four hours at night, and spend hours each day in prayer and meditation. Only twice a year may they see their family, and then they may only visit with them from behind a screen. On June 8, 1991, Shelly stepped into the monastery of the Poor Clare Sisters. She left her career, her family, and even her name behind as she began a life that follows the timeless rhythms of the Middle Ages. Although I do not believe God wants any of us to be nuns, she believed that God had called her to give her life completely to Him in this way, even if it meant giving up everything she loved.

In the Bible, there was another man who gave up a normal life for the glory of God. He dressed himself in camel's hair and ate locusts and wild honey. His name was John the Baptist: a man who had dedicated his life to prepare the way for Jesus' appearing on Earth. John the Baptist accepted the silence and humility of his calling with joy, so that all the eyes of his audience would be turned to Christ. If we are to be messengers for God, we should not seek any glory for ourselves. To think of living a life of humility and self denial may seem unpleasant to us, but when we are filled with the love of Christ, nothing will make us happier than to be swallowed up in the act of serving and giving our all to Him.

~ Sierra Buhler

What Do They See?

… be thou an example of the believers, in word, in conversation, in charity, in spirit, in faith, in purity. - 1 Timothy 4:12 KJV

Tonight would be the long-awaited Christmas banquet. The girls' dorm had turned into a whirlwind of dresses, shoes, curling irons, and a million different perfume scents that threatened to choke out the warm thoughts that had been bouncing around in my head for the last few days. Sure, tonight would be the banquet, but that was not what I was so excited about. I had been away from home, and finally, tonight, my parents and younger sister would be joining me here at Bogenhofen, the Austrian boarding academy I had called "home" for the past three-and-a-half months.

While there, I made friends with some very sweet twin girls. We had a lot in common, but there was one blatant difference. These sisters did almost *everything* together! They sang and worked together, laughed and cried together, prayed together, and were the best of friends. This Christ-like example burned an inerasable mark in my conscience, and I realized that what I saw in them, I wanted with my sister, Jessica. We weren't enemies, but we didn't have the same loving bond between us that I had observed. So I had made up my mind that I would change the way I treated my sister and that our relationship would be making a U-turn for the better.

Finally my family arrived, and, spotting them, I made Jessica my first hug-target. That evening, I made sure to sit right next to her, and from then on, I strove, with God's help, to treat Jessica more lovingly, to stick up for her at school, and to be a friend to her, not just a sister. Our hearts were softened, and as we grew closer, I couldn't help but think back to the example of the two sisters who had made me want something better. I had seen Jesus in them, and as a result, part of my life was changed. It makes me wonder what people see when they look at me. Do they see Jesus? Who do they see in you?

~ Esther Ferraz

A Change of Plans

And we know that all things work together for good to them that love God... - Romans 8:28 KJV

A few weeks before the Christmas of 2003, my family decided to go sledding. We usually go sledding behind our house, but that day we were going to a larger hill about half an hour away. Before we left, Dad called us for family worship. As He led out, I tried to listen and concentrate, but it was difficult. Dad's last question was: "What if God chooses to change our plans today? Will you be content with that?" I didn't really like the idea of our plans changing, but I chose to give my feelings to God and let Him take care of it.

As we wound our way up the road, we could see that more and more snow was piling up on the ground. This didn't concern me, but Dad asked Mom to pray that God would be with us. Mom prayed, and just as she said "Amen," Dad yelled, "We're going over!"

"What?" I asked myself—it happened so fast! We rolled and rolled and rolled down a sixty-foot embankment and landed on our roof. Our van was finished. As we crawled out through the broken windows, I could see that God had kept us safe. Dad had minor cuts on his head, but the rest of us were fine.

This doesn't really seem good, does it? I didn't think it was either! Who wants to roll over an edge, ruin their new van, and then have to go to the hospital? But God had a plan. His plan was different than mine, but it all worked out for our good in the end. We were able to see many miracles, and we also got to meet new people who didn't know about God. Now, because we know them we can share the knowledge of God with them.

Are you willing to let God change your plans today? Will you choose to let Him be in control? If so, He will make everything work out for your best.

~ Bethany Corrigan

Prepared?

… Therefore if you will not watch, I will come upon you as a thief, and you will not know what hour I will come upon you.
- Revelation 3:3 NKJV

I love sleep! Sometimes that can be a good thing, but at other times it can have me scrambling around at the last minute trying to get everything together. It seems to happen to me more than I'd like. Instead of putting all my efforts into getting up at the right time, I simply make excuses to try to get around the problem. Just like I do with many other things in my life, I don't exactly want to face it head on. I either make excuses or divert the attention to someone else's faults.

Sometimes we look at the life of the disciples and scoff at their misunderstandings of what Jesus said. For example, when Jesus explained to them about His death and resurrection, His disciples didn't understand because they were too caught up in their own preconceived ideas about what Jesus should do as the Messiah. They were looking for an earthly king, one who could free them from the Romans and set up a powerful kingdom here on earth. Thinking that the One they believed in would die a horrible death on a cross was far beyond their comprehension. So instead of trying to grasp it, they simply banished the thought from their minds. "…and when the time of trial came, it found them unprepared" (*The Great Controversy,* pg. 594).

There is a great event soon coming that we do not want to be unprepared for: the coming of our Lord Jesus Christ. The Bible tells us plainly of all the signs and events that will occur before the time of His return. Satan is trying everything in his power to distract us from the truth. Many people will listen to the deceiver, and when the time comes, they will find themselves unprepared. If Jesus was to come today, would you be prepared?

~ Julie Kelly

Waiting Friends

Search the scriptures… - John 5:39a KJV

I happily bounded down the stairs—it was so good to be home again! I didn't mind being away at school, but this Christmas break was very welcome. A good night's rest in my own loft-bed, waking up to the sound of Jessica's piano playing, the warm terracotta painted walls in the living room, the soft couches, the familiar smells, and Mummy's good German cooking—it all was so nice! One particular thing—or maybe I should say family member—was especially pleasant to be around again: my woolly black miniature poodle, Lisa. I got to the bottom of the stairs and almost tripped over this hyper bundle of wiggles and whimpers. I tried to make my way to the kitchen, but with Lisa jumping up at me to lovingly nip my fingers, I just had to bend over and give her the good-morning scratch and attention she was begging for. As I looked into those button eyes and tried to hold "Ms. Wiggles" close, I realized I had almost forgotten how it felt to be so warmly greeted every morning. It was as if Lisa tried to make me believe that she had been waiting all night to see me, and that she couldn't wait for me to take a few moments to play with her.

It reminds me of another friend who waits for me every morning and makes me feel very special as well! However, this Friend doesn't want to play with me, He wants to teach me life-changing truths from His Word. I like to spend time with this Friend, but sometimes other things seem more important than greeting Him, and I neglect to spend those important moments in His Word.

In the past, it was that Satan kept the Word from people. During the era of the Reformation, anyone who owned the Scriptures was considered a heretic. But now Satan still keeps people from the Word. No longer chained to Papal desks, it sits in our rooms, its pages containing the power to change our lives, while we let ourselves be distracted. Jesus is waiting to spend that special time with you! Will you let Satan distract you, too?

~ Esther Ferraz

Priceless Gift

For unto you is born this day in the city of David a Saviour, which is Christ the Lord. - Luke 2:11 KJV

I never really connected Jesus with Christmas while I was growing up. Sure, He was in the mini-nativity scene at Grandma's house, but so was the little drummer boy, and I found him much more intriguing. Although I never believed in Santa Claus, I tried to pretend that he was real; I loved the idea of a big jolly man in red giving me toys and candy.

What I didn't realize was that there's Someone far better. Santa is only a cheap copy of the real thing. Jesus Christ came down to the world, but He didn't come on a shiny red sleigh. He came as a baby to a little town that no one knew about. Instead of bringing toys and candy, He brought a gift that cannot be equalled: the gift of salvation. He lived with us and taught us. While Santa only comes once a year, Jesus is always with us! We can talk to Him whenever we need to, unlike Santa, where you're only allowed to send him a letter once a year with all your selfish requests.

Legend has it that Santa lives in the North Pole with little elves to make all the toys. Jesus lived on earth with us—healing the sick, helping the poor, and working hard for our salvation. Santa requires milk and cookies, but Christ doesn't expect anything in return for His gift; it's a free gift—all we have to do is accept it. But the most compelling argument in Christ's favor is this: Jesus is real! He's not merely an old legend created in an attempt to make children good, like Santa is. He is the real reason we celebrate. Christmas isn't about the lights or the food or the traditions. It's a celebration of the birth of Christ. But this celebration shouldn't take place on just one day. This celebration can occur in our hearts daily as the result of God's gift for us. His son, whom He sent to earth to die for us, is truly the ultimate gift—one that money could never buy.

~ Moriah Mays

We Wish You a Merry Christmas

*The Savior—yes, the Messiah, the Lord—has been born today in
Bethlehem, the city of David! - Luke 2:11 NLT*

"We wish you a merry Christmas, we wish you a merry
Christmas..." I heard it on the radio as I was in the house having a
hot drink. There was a scent of cinnamon and pine trees in the air as
I watched the snow slowly cascade to the ground, piling a little higher
every minute. The house was decorated: the kitchen with boughs, the
living room with a nativity scene, and a tall tree surrounded by gifts for
loved ones. On top of the piano was one of the gingerbread houses we
make every year. It was Christmas Eve and our family was all together.
My mom, my sisters, and I were all getting Christmas preparations
ready while my dad was outside working on the ice skating rink in our
front yard.

To me, this seems like a perfect way to spend Christmas. But when
I think about Christmas, I realize how different the first Christmas must
have been from how my family celebrates it today. I can only imagine
being in a barn with a newborn baby and a bunch of animals. Every
time I think about that, it just seems so imperfect. Yet the imperfections
to us are the perfections of God. God had a plan in it all. Every little
thing, down to the animals that were in the barn that night, was placed
there for a purpose.

So often it is easy to forget what the first Christmas was like. We
get so wrapped up in buying presents, cooking, and making Christmas
cards that we almost forget the real reason behind Christmas. God
sent His only Son to earth to seek and save the lost. He gave us the
best Gift we could ever imagine. That is why we celebrate Christmas
today. I encourage you today to go and read the Christmas story in
Matthew 1:18-25 and Luke 2:1-20 and remember what the very first
Christmas was like.

~ Rebecca Hall

Christmas Dreams

*And the angel said unto them, Fear not: for, behold, I bring you good
tidings of great joy, which shall be to all people. - Luke 2:10 KJV*

Samuel stirred on his mat. The open sky shone with the stars
beaming down on the hill where he laid. There seemed to be an
abstract ambiance glowing all around. The older shepherds talked
nearby, speaking with hushed excitement. He watched them for awhile
as they pointed excitedly to the scrolls in their hands. Samuel already
had enough going through his mind, and all this talk of prophecies
and a coming Messiah confused him. He believed in the arrival of a
Savior, but could it truly be happening this soon? His eyelids grew
heavier and heavier, telling his body he needed to sleep. The fight for
consciousness was in vain, and he succumbed to the peaceful bliss.

Suddenly, a great light burst forth. Samuel opened his eyes, letting
in the scene before him. In the sky was a great choir of angels, singing
harmonies more beautiful than he could have ever imagined. By now
the rest of the shepherds were awake and watching the phenomenon
unfolding before them. He had never seen such happy beings, literally
glowing with joy. From the middle of the multitude emerged one angel,
coming closer and closer. The others quieted down in anticipation
of what this angel would say. The angel burst forth in a loud, clear
voice, saying: "Don't be afraid! I have good news. The Savior whom
you have been waiting for is born this day in Bethlehem. You will find
him in swaddling clothes, lying in a manger." With that, the angel went
back into the multitude as they sang with renewed enthusiasm. Now
Samuel and the other shepherds had only one thing on their mind:
they must find this newborn king.

Many years have passed since the first Christmas; however,
the excitement of a newborn King has not died out. I'm sure the
shepherds were full of excitement when they received the tidings of a
newborn Savior. Let us praise His name with renewed enthusiasm this
Christmas season.

~ Mason Neil

Glory?

For you know the grace of our Lord Jesus Christ: Though He was rich, for your sake He became poor, so that by His poverty you might become rich. - 2 Corinthians 8:9 HCSB

It was completely unexpected: not the event, but the circumstances. Almost everyone knew that the Messiah was about to come, but almost no one knew how. The Jews of Christ's time were expecting a forceful and glorious ruler. They reasoned that they were going to be visited by God: the God who created the entire universe. They assumed He must be powerful and glorious, just like the glorious earthly kings who dress in gold and have control over everyone. Consequently, they figured, the Messiah must come as a powerful, forceful, splendorous king. However, this logic failed to take into account exactly what glory is. The Jews erred in applying their concept of earthly glory to a Heavenly king. It's not that Jesus wasn't glorious; we know that He was. It's just that His life forces us to reconsider what true glory is.

Could it be that God's glory is not His splendor, but rather His unselfish character? Could it be that God's glory is not His gold, but His love? Could it be that it was Jesus' glory that compelled Him to a life of servitude rather than life in a palace? As Christians, when we try to emulate Christ, are we truly trying to imitate His unselfish glory? Or is our idea of glory the same that the Pharisees, Sadducees, and other Jews had? Do we really understand the concept of glorious humility? If so, are we willing to apply it?

~ Michael Jensen

Lego

And He said: "Truly I tell you, unless you change and become like little children, you will never enter the kingdom of heaven."
- Matthew 18:3 NIV

It was Christmas morning; I woke up early and rushed to the Christmas tree. Tearing the wrapping off the first package in sight, I gazed in delight at what was in the box. There before me was a set of Legos—my favorite! I sat down on the floor and started at once, assembling the pieces together, cube after cube. Then when I was about halfway through, I could not figure out how to assemble the next piece. After much effort, I bowed my head and asked my Best Friend— my Heavenly Father—to help me figure out how I could move on in building my Lego set. I opened my eyes and looked at the instructions once more. Suddenly, it all became clear. I rapidly finished up the masterpiece, anxious to play with it.

When I was little, the faith and trust that I had in God was so simple, yet unbreakable. If I asked for God's help with something, I knew without any doubt that He would help me. I know that this kind of relationship and faith in God has dwindled as I have reached my teenage years. Sometimes I wish I could just go back to being a child, having that simple faith.

Jesus said that we should become like children. Was this meant literally? Should we become like silly little kids? Or is it talking about how we should adopt the simple faith of a child? What God really wants is for us to hold onto His hand as tightly as a small child would grasp his parent's hand.

~ Esra Eliasson

Strength to Resist

All Scripture is given by inspiration of God, and is profitable for doctrine, for reproof, for correction, for instruction in righteousness...
- 2 Timothy 3:16 NKJV

"I've done it again." These were the words that haunted me over the summer. I thought I was over it. I had a problem: movies. During the first week of summer I resisted them like a dog resists a bath. But as the weeks went on, I found myself watching them more and more. When this started to happen, I decided to read anything that pertained to the subject of entertainment for my devotions. I read from the Bible and *Messages to Young People*, and they provided me with answers. What I read convicted me to stop. So I made a decision right there that I was going to cease watching movies and rid my life of that idol.

I thought that was it. I would never struggle with movies ever again. But instead, I struggled with it even more. Every time I faced the television, I faced a battle. A voice inside me would say, "It's all right. You've done it for years. A little show isn't going to hurt you." Then my conscience would say, "Don't you remember what you read? I thought you were going to stop watching." But that was the problem: the things I read went out of my head as fast as they came in. I didn't have a quote or verse that I kept in my mind to help me stay strong. I couldn't resist temptation because I didn't have God's word as my aid.

When Jesus was on earth, God's word was His partner in the fight against evil. He had the Scriptures written in His heart, and they enabled Him to resist Satan's temptations in the desert. Every time Satan tempted Him, He simply said, "It is written..." and with those three simple words, Satan couldn't get a hold on Jesus. We also can conquer the temptations we struggle with in this way. I know that I was able to refrain from watching television immediately after returning from Fountainview, because the warnings given there from the Bible and Ellen White's books were still fresh in my mind. I encourage you to read God's word and store it in your mind. Pray that He will give you strength. The combination of prayer and the Bible is the key that will unlock the door to freedom from sin.

~ Shenel Cruz

"Work-k"

… There is nothing better than that a man should rejoice in his work, for that is his lot… - Ecclesiastes 3:22 ESV

I love working on my farm. Early on winter mornings, I go outside into the biting cold to feed the calves. As soon as the crisp cold air hits me, my hands plunge into the deep pockets of my hand-me-down, heirloom winter jacket. Jogging to keep warm, I run through the dim light towards the milking parlor to pick up the fresh, frothy milk for the hungry calves. As I near the calf barn, I can hear them mooing lustily for their breakfast. I carefully pour each their portion, and grin as they wag their thin little tails with happiness. Although some mornings are longer and colder than others, I can honestly say that working on my farm in the early morning is one of my favorite things to do.

My whole family enjoys working, too. Every morning between 4:00 and 4:30 AM, three little pinpricks of light come on across the rolling hills of our farm. I have often wondered how my dad, uncle, and grandfather have been able to work there for so long and still enjoy it. They say that there is something about being alone on a vast field of waving grass and watching the sun slowly make its way up and over the land, houses, and barns that you have built by your own hands. There is a satisfaction that comes with working the soil with your hands to provide for the people that you love. There is something about living your life in complete service to others.

God desires for you to partake of and delight in the duties He has called you to today. Regardless of how hard and unrewarding they might seem at the moment, He has a bigger picture of all the lives that will be blessed by your selfless service. Why don't you try looking for joy in your work today?

~ Sarah Miller

Alchemy

And he shall sit as a refiner and purifier of silver: and he shall purify the sons of Levi, and purge them as gold and silver, that they may offer unto the Lord an offering in righteousness. - Malachi 3:6 KJV

Huddling over the bubbling cauldron, he wondered how much longer this laborious task would last. He had been slaving away at this experiment for as long as he could remember, dedicating much of his life to something he was sure would make him rich. He was an alchemist, one of many who were convinced that lead could be turned into gold. But after year upon year of experimenting, he was no closer to fulfilling his objective. Why? Because lead is not gold, and it cannot become gold no matter how much it's heated, pounded, or otherwise chemically attacked. The only way to change lead into gold is to actually change the element's atomic number, an operation that must take place at the very heart of the atom.

Unfortunately, the only thing any of us are capable of producing is great quantities of worthless, cumbersome lead. However, God requires us to have golden characters; so we face the same problem that confronted the alchemists: lead is not gold! No degree of external manipulation can change that. Only through a transformation of the heart is such a miracle possible.

Thankfully, we serve a Master Heart Surgeon. Even though we're absolutely incapable of producing spiritual gold in our characters, we're not out of luck. God can change our hearts, transforming our filthy lead of righteousness into the pure gold of Ophir. The process is not always easy and painless—it involves a catastrophic redefinition of our hearts. But if we ask God, He will perform the surgery. Our worthless lead will become gold by the tender touch of the Master Surgeon!

~ Michael Jensen

We Will Be Like Him!

But we all, with open face beholding as in a glass the glory of the
Lord, are changed into the same image… - 2 Corinthians 3:18 KJV

A few weeks ago, my family and I went on a five day camping trip with some of our friends who used to live near us. Since we moved away, we have been separated by many miles, and I anxiously wondered how our time together would work out. "Will they be okay with our simple, quiet lifestyle?" Even though we considered ourselves friends, as we had been pen pals through the years, we didn't really know each other. Five days would be a long time to spend with another family if we didn't get along.

After the first day, I knew that we were going to enjoy ourselves. They liked the same kinds of things we did. The way they talked, ate, played, and worshiped complemented our own. We had so many similarities that it almost felt like they were part of our family. The time we spent with them was so refreshing that it was hard to go home to our regular routine.

As I thought about this experience, it reminded me of our relationship with God. At the beginning of this world, we humans were perfect. We had never sinned. God was our friend, and He came to visit every evening in the cool of the day. Then man sinned, and we could no longer see God. Thankfully, God made a way for us to be able to see Him again. He sent Jesus to this world so that we could see what God is like. John 14:9 says that if you have seen Jesus, you have seen the Father. We can talk to God through Jesus. As we talk to God, and read His letter, the Bible, we learn about Him. He becomes our friend! When He comes back, we are going to be able to go and live with Him. Even though we haven't seen each other for a long time, we will be like Him. And this vacation will last for ever!

~ Bethany Corrigan

The Gift

"Who shall be able to stand?"
Is the challenge made.

Clean heart? Clean hands?
"Not me, I am too weak," say I.

"My strength is made perfect in weakness,"
Comes the quick reply.

So I go on with my day, strengthened
For a time.
But before long, I've fallen again.
"Did you see how far I slid?"

"Even in height and depth you cannot lose My love."

"Can you see how far I've gone?"

"You might fall, but keep getting back up."

"Why do You follow me, strengthen me, and pick me up?"

"Because you are Mine, bought with a price."

"But can't You see my stubborn, dirty heart?"

There is a long pause before He answers.
"Can't you see how far *I've* gone?"
Comes the gentle reply.

"I love you with a love stronger than death;
I've fallen for you, put Myself in your place,
Born your guilt, and suffered your shame.
Won't you take My gift?
It's free –
I bought it just for you."

Now it's my turn to pause.
Will I take this gift?
Can I really trust Him with my grime?
I look at His bruised hands, and see His arms open wide.
"You did that,
For me?
You really do mean it, don't You?"

He smiles, and says,
"I *do* love you.
Won't you let Me?"

~ Sarah Miller

Freedom from Surrender

One day as I began my task,
I heard a voice—my Savior—ask:
"My child will you depend on Me?
I'll give you peace and make you free!"

"Without Your help I'll be just fine.
I won't my sinful self resign."
With this I feigned a happy smile,
"I'll keep to pleasure for a while."

But though I looked and tried to find,
The pleasure that I had in mind,
I failed in all I sought to do—
"At last I see my need of You."

"Lord, help me for the right to stand,
To live beneath Your guiding hand.
Give me grace to heed Your call,
To give myself; surrender all."

He came into my heart that day,
And took my sinful self away.
"My child, now depend on Me
I've giv'n you peace and made you free."

~ Aileen Corrigan

About the Authors

Sierra Buhler, 18
British Columbia, Canada
Interests/Goals: God, family, friends, music, photography, travel, poutine; If God wills, become a medical doctor, get a hat-trick in hockey, rock climb El Capitan, learn another language, reflect Jesus.

Diane Carvalho, 16
Iceland
Interests/Goals: Laughing, sports, hiking, climbing trees, being out in nature, playing violin, studying the Bible; Travel around the world as a missionary, go wherever God wants me to go.

Bryan Chen, 18
Canton, China
Interests/Goals: Making people laugh, deep quotes, biking, photography, rice, Ecclesiastes, pianoforte; Become a luthier, follow after Jesus.

Aileen Corrigan, 16
British Columbia, Canada
Interests/Goals: Making cards, playing my cello, family, friends, orchestra; Become a wife, mother, and homemaker, follow God's plans for my life.

Bethany Corrigan, 18
British Columbia, Canada
Interests/Goals: Crocheting, animal care, cake decorating, hair styling; Have a family, follow God's leading.

Shenel Cruz, 17
Northwest Territories, Canada
Interests/Goals: Reading, listening to music, singing, playing tennis, babysitting, hanging out with my family and friends, tickling people; Be a witness for Christ, visit each continent, follow God's will.

Benjamin Dietel, 15
Minnesota, USA
Interests/Goals: Jesus, oboe/piano, parkour, football, frisbee, calculus, physics, liquid nitrogen, computer graphics, rock climbing, caving, hiking/bushwhacking, composing; Do an Ironman, save souls, learn ten languages.

Chris Donatelli, 17
British Columbia, Canada
Interests/Goals: Sports, mechanics, music, art, getting buff, and health; To be a man of God and follow where He leads.

Nateesha Dorrington, 17
Queensland, Australia
Interests/Goals: Cooking, swimming, piano, scrapbooking, friends, family; Become a dental assistant/hygienist, grow closer to God

Esra Eliasson, 17
Þorlákshöfn, Iceland
Interests/Goals: Singing, cello and piano, listening to classical music, basketball, biking, downhill skiing. traveling, becoming more like Christ, red, Mediterranean food; Work in medicine/business.

Esther Ferraz, 17
Michigan, USA
Interests/Goals: Music, health, learning new things, encouraging people, gardening, cooking, anatomy, red, smiling; be Naturopathic doctor and a music major.

Anna Ford, 17
Oregon, USA
Interests/Goals: My family, flowers, the Bible;
Be a nurse practitioner or whatever else God
has in mind, have perfect character, see
Jesus!

Derek Glatts, 18
British Columbia, Canada
Interests/Goals: History, public speaking,
politics, backpacking; Become a pastor,
get married, travel the world, get a Canon,
become a student missionary, continue to get
closer to the Lord.

Agnes Grétarsdóttir, 17
Copenhagen, Denmark
Interests/Goals: God, family, friends,
photography; Learn ten languages, visit
every continent, get a doctorate, start an
orphanage, learn to snowboard/wakeboard/
guitar, climb a mountain, backpack Europe.

Rebecca Hall, 16
British Columbia, Canada
Interests/Goals: Cello, singing, the colour
yellow, horses, reading books, occupational
therapy using horses, spending time with
family and friends, crocheting, laughing,
math; Growing closer to God every day.

Julie Kelly, 16
Missouri, USA
Interests/Goals: Family, friends, swimming,
guitar, volleyball, baseball, country and Celtic
music, search and rescue, modern design;
Own a monster truck, travel the world, learn
another language, follow God's will.

Elizabeth King, 17
Oregon, USA
Interests/Goals: Jesus, family, friends,
reading, singing, photography, travel; Work
at an orphanage, speak Danish/Spanish
fluently, become a teacher, physical therapist,
if God's will wife and mother.

Nolan Knuppel, 17
Missouri, USA
Interests/Goals: Farming, mechanics,
things that go fast; Have a family, outreach,
following God's leading anywhere.

Hannah Lee, 17
South Korea
Interests/Goals: Family, friends, music,
playing violin and guitar, reading, cooking,
photography; Be an international translator,
make my family smile, and be what God
wants me to be.

Moriah Mays, 17
Albania
Interests/Goals: Archeology, reading, music,
NASCAR, traveling, horseback riding, eating;
Play banjo, become a missionary/teacher
and run an orphanage.

Morgan Metcalf, 17
North Carolina, USA
Interests/Goals: Photography, drawing,
reading, pulling teeth, cooking, outdoor
sports, horseback riding, architecture,
learning; Be a mission pilot, have a perfected
character, and be who God wants me to be.

Sarah Miller, 17
Vermont, USA
Interests/Goals: Baking, gardening, raising
puppies, farming, time with my family; For
Jesus to be my closest Friend, to help others
see themselves through God's eyes.

Kami Rose, 16
Oregon, USA
Interests/Goals: Playing cello, knitting,
sewing, the color red, reading, occupational
therapy, spending time with friends and
family, singing, laughing, smiling; Going
where God leads me.

Andrew Sharley, 18
Washington, USA
Interests/Goals: Cooking, interaction with family, singing, talking with the elderly, hiking; Help others to develop optimal brain function and live as enthusiastic Christians.

Katie Sloop, 17
California, USA
Interests/Goals: Spending time with my family, hiking, camping, running, music, cooking, gardening; B.S. in Nursing, A.R.N.P., missionary, most of all following God.

Kyle Smith, 17
Waikato, New Zealand
Interests/Goals: Serving God, singing, playing violin, riding motor bikes, helicopter pilot, farming, filming and video editing,audio recording, technology.

Daniel Tentea, 16
Michigan, USA
Interests/Goals: Family, anything that flies and is remote controlled, fishing; Be a pilot, be where Christ wants me, be a mechanic for all vehicles, get every license possible.

Chris Unfrau, 17
British Columbia, CA
Interests/Goals: Snowboarding, mountain biking, traveling, hanging out with friends, God, family; Become a dentist, backpack Europe and the United States with friends, live a Godly life.

Sarah Wahlman, 16
Colorado, USA
Interests/Goals: Photography, reading, music, being flexible, seeing things in new ways, interior decorating; Be an encouragement to others, learn to always be cheerful, share God's love with others.

Raina Walker, 17
British Columbia, Canada
Interests/Goals: Running, snowboarding, driving, travelling; Work in the medical field, and run a marathon.

Christian Welch, 17
Washington, USA
Interests/Goals: Ham radio (NA7CW), swimming, sailing, skiing, biking, outdoors, electronics, travel, family, friends, "running numbers;" become electrical engineer/ mathematician, follow God's leading.

Ashley Wilkens, 17
Tennesee, USA
Interests/Goals: Wakeboarding, running, listening to wisdom, gardening, family, oatmeal, play in rain, mission stories, piano/singing alone, learning; Missionary doctor, triathlon, KNOW my Bible, cook and sew.

Ellen Yoon, 17
South Korea
Interests/Goals: God, playing piano, spending time with friends and family, snowboarding; Being Christ-like, use my talents to spread the gospel, be a missionary and go to heaven with all my family!

MIchael Jensen, Junior Student Editor, 16
Florida, USA
Interests/Goals: Viola, hiking, experimenting, learning about almost everything, nuclear physics; Improve my mind, transcend my influence, travel the world, skydive, learn to snow ski well, follow God's plan for me.

Mason Neil, Junior Student Editor, 16
Maine, USA
Interests/Goals: Books, tea, writing, animals, family, nature, blogging, art, trees; Become a librarian, write a book, live on an organic farm, fulfill God's purpose in my life.

Saraiah Turnbull, Junior Student Editor, 16
North Carolina, USA
Interests/Goals: Family and friends, guitar,
double bass, laughing, cookie dough, the
color yellow; Work with kids, backpack
Europe, busk, learn to surf, become a trauma
surgeon, reflect Christ's character.

Morgan Barrow, Senior Student Editor, 17
Tennesee, USA
Interests/Goals: God, family, friends, English/
writing, exercise, my horses, swimming;
Skydive, write a book, drive my light-blue
pickup, run a marathon, serve God overseas,
follow Christ/reflect Him more every day.

Matthew West, Senior Student Editor, 18
Washington, USA
Interests/Goals: Snowskiing, frisbee, soccer,
music, backcountry hiking, reading, climbing
trees, debate; Learn throughout my life, own
a wilderness cabin, have my own property,
follow God's plan for my life.

Mike Lemon, English Teacher
British Columbia, Canada
Interests: Jesus, my wife & children,
teaching, preaching, reading, writing,
horseback riding, gardening, learning new
things, and getting lost in the mountains.